40 Days of Discipleship
A Self-Paced Doctrinal Education Plan
Volume 3: The Third 40 Days

By Joseph Tkach, Gary W. Deddo,
Michael D. Morrison, J. Michael Feazell, and others

Published by Grace Communion International

3120 Whitehall Park Dr.

Charlotte, NC 28273

www.gci.org

All Scripture quotations, unless otherwise indicated, are taken from the Holy Bible, New International Version®, NIV®. Copyright ©1973, 1978, 1984, 2011 by Biblica, Inc.™ Used by permission of Zondervan. All rights reserved worldwide. www.zondervan.com. The "NIV" and "New International Version" are trademarks registered in the United States Patent and Trademark Office by Biblica, Inc.™

First edition

Copyright © 2016 Grace Communion International

Minor edits 2018

All rights reserved.

ISBN-13: 978-1537665610

ISBN-10: 1537665618

Contents

Introduction iii

Theology in general

1. What's So Special About Trinitarian Theology? by Joseph Tkach 1
   Beware Theological Labels, by Joseph Tkach 2
   Questions & Answers About Trinitarian Theology 4
2. Questions & Answers About Trinitarian Theology, part 2 6
3. Theology as a Framework for Life and Ministry, by Joseph Tkach 12
   Foundations of Theology of Grace Communion International 13
4. Foundations of Theology of Grace Communion International, part 2 16

The Triune God

5. The Trinity: Just a Doctrine? By J. Michael Feazell 20
6. Perichoresis – What's That? By C. Baxter Kruger 23
   Is the Doctrine of the Trinity in the Bible? By Paul Kroll 25
7. Predestination: Does God Choose Your Fate? By J. Michael Feazell, part 1 27
8. Predestination: Does God Choose Your Fate? By J. Michael Feazell, part 2 32

Jesus Christ

9. Jesus – The Complete Salvation Package, by Joseph Tkach 36
   Christ's Resurrection – Our Hope of Salvation, by Neil Earle 38
10. The Incarnation: The Greatest Miracle, by Don Mears 41
    The Birth of Jesus – A Story of Shame, by Joseph Tkach 42
11. Appreciating Christ's Sacrifice, by Joseph Tkach 45
    It Isn't Just About How He Died, by John Halford 47
12. Don't Cry for Jesus, by Gary Deddo 49

The Holy Spirit

13. A Theology of the Holy Spirit, by Gary Deddo, part 3 52
14. A Theology of the Holy Spirit, by Gary Deddo, part 4A 57
15. A Theology of the Holy Spirit, by Gary Deddo, part 4B 60
16. A Theology of the Holy Spirit, by Gary Deddo, part 5 63

The Scriptures

17. Scripture, God's Gift, by Gary Deddo, part 5 67
18. Scripture, God's Gift, by Gary Deddo, part 6 72
19. Be Devoted to Scripture, by Joseph Tkach 78
20. Timeless Truths in Cultural Clothes, by Michael Morrison 82

The gospel

21. What Jesus Said About Himself, by Michael Morrison 87

22. Good News in an Alabaster Jar, by Michael Morrison 90
23. Marketing the Gospel? By Joseph Tkach 95
24. A Theological Look at Evangelism, by Michael Morrison 98

Grace and salvation

25. Do We Teach Universalism? By Joseph Tkach 103
    Why Would Anyone Want to Be a Christian? By Michael Morrison 105
26. Grace and Obedience, by Gary Deddo 108
27. Relationship With Christ, by Michael Morrison 112
28. A New Look at the Good Samarian, by Joseph Tkach 115
    Grace From First to Last, by Joseph Tkach 117

The church

29. Responding to the Church With Teamwork, by Joseph Tkach 119
    The Three-Fold Meaning of the Lord's Supper, by Joseph Tkach 121
30. Lay Members' Role in the Early Church, by Donald Jackson 124
31. Upward, Inward and Outward in Words and Deeds, by Joseph Tkach 128
32. Leadership in the Church, by Joseph Tkach 132
    The Pastor's Calling, by Joseph Tkach 134

Christian life

33. Sanctification, by Michael Morrison 136
    Tell Peter, by Eugene Guzon 139
34. Our Relationship With Jesus Christ, by Joseph Tkach 141
35. Trusting God With the Problem of Sin, by J. Michael Feazell, part 1 144
36. Trusting God With the Problem of Sin, by J. Michael Feazell, part 2 147

The future

37. The Resurrection of the Body and Why It Matters, by Joseph Tkach 150
    Hell, by Joseph Tkach 152
38. Revelation: Book of Cosmic Symbols, by Paul Kroll 154
39. The Rewards of Following Christ, Joseph Tkach 158
40. What About the Millennium? By Paul Kroll 161
    A Balanced Approach to the Millennium, by Michael Morrison 163

Appendix

A Theology of the Holy Spirit, by Gary Deddo, part 6 166
A Theology of the Holy Spirit, by Gary Deddo, part 7 172

About the authors 179
About the publisher 180
Grace Communion Seminary 181
Ambassador College of Christian Ministry 182

Introduction

A self-paced doctrinal education plan

This is the third volume in our series for church leaders who want to continue their theological education with free resources from the GCI website. Some articles are long, and some are short, but the average is still 2500 words per day, which can be read in about 20 minutes.

On each of the major topics, much more could be said, and we often have additional resources on our website. For example, we have more than 100 articles about different chapters in the Bible, numerous articles on church history, prayer, missions, and other topics.

Many of the website resources have been compiled into books, and are available as free PDF files, or as printed books on Amazon.com. We list the titles below. For links to the PDF and other files, see the online version of this volume, at https://www.gci.org/articles/40-days-of-discipleship-the-third-40-days/ .

A Guided Tour of the Bible, Its Inspiration, Authority, and Purpose
Christians and Old Testament Laws
Exploring the Word of God, volume 1: The Old Testament
Exploring the Word of God, volume 2: The Gospels
Exploring the Word of God, volume 3: The Book of Acts
Exploring the Word of God, volume 4: The Letters of Paul
Introductory Theology, volume 1: The Trinity, the Bible, and the Holy Spirit
Introductory Theology, volume 2: Jesus the Savior
Introductory Theology, volume 3: The Church and Its Functions
Ten Biblical Teachings and How They Make a Difference in Our Lives (=Discipleship 101)
The Gospel: From the Bible to the World Today
Trinitarian Conversations, Volume 1: Interviews With Twelve Theologians (transcripts of *You're Included*)
Trinitarian Conversations, Volume 2: Interviews With More Theologians (all other YI transcripts)
What Does the Bible Say About the Kingdom of God?
What the Bible Says About Women in Church Leadership

Michael Morrison
Dean of Faculty
Grace Communion Seminary

What's So Special About Trinitarian Theology?

Learning more about the nature of God has dominated my Bible study for the last decade. I find it to be more and more fascinating. Having the correct perspective of who God is cannot be overestimated. Viewing his sovereignty over eternity and the nature of his being orders all of our doctrinal understandings.

I love the following quote from Charles Haddon Spurgeon, England's best-known preacher for most of the second half of the 19th century:

> The highest science, the loftiest speculation, the mightiest philosophy, which can ever engage the attention of a child of God, is the name, the nature, the person, the work, the doings, and the existence of the great God whom he calls his Father. There is something exceedingly improving to the mind in a contemplation of the Divinity. It is a subject so vast, that all our thoughts are lost in its immensity; so deep, that our pride is drowned in its infinity.

I am sometimes asked, "What's so special about Trinitarian theology—don't most orthodox churches believe in the Trinity?" Yes, they do. Belief in the Trinity is considered the hallmark of authentic Christian doctrine. It was our acceptance of the Trinity that brought our denomination "in out of the cold," allowing us to break free from being considered a cult.

As I studied what various churches believe about the Trinity, I observed that while most consent to the doctrine, it does not have a central role in their faith. Many consider the Trinity to be an abstract idea, of interest to theologians but not of much use to the rest of us. This is sad because when the Trinity is not at the center, shaping all other doctrines, strange ideas and distortions arise. For example, those who proclaim a health/wealth/prosperity gospel tend to view God as a divine "vending machine." Others tend to view God as a mechanistic version of fate who has determined everything from before creation—including who will be saved and who will be damned. I find it hard to accept a God who creates billions of people just for the purpose of condemning and damning them for eternity!

Trinitarian theology puts the Trinity at the center of all doctrinal understanding, influencing everything we believe and understand about God. As theologian Catherine LaCugna wrote in her book *God for Us:*

> The doctrine of the Trinity is, ultimately…a teaching not about the abstract nature of God, nor about God in isolation from everything other than God, but a teaching about God's life with us and our life with each other. Trinitarian theology could be described as par excellence a theology of relationship, which explores the mysteries of love, relationship, personhood and communion within the framework of God's self-revelation in the person of Christ and the activity of the Spirit. [Note: While I appreciate much of what is in this book, I don't agree with all of it.]

We know of this triune life of God from Jesus, who is God's self-revelation in person. It should be our rule that anything we say about the Trinity must come from Jesus' life, teaching, death, resurrection, ascension and promised return.

I have seen many diagrams that attempt to explain the Trinity. The best of them fall short and some are confusing. It is impossible to explain the nature of God in a diagram. However, a good one can help us grasp some aspects of the doctrine. You may find helpful the diagram shown at right. It summarizes early church teaching, pointing out that correct biblical understanding concerning the nature of God upholds three essential beliefs about God. It also indicates that we end up denying that God is Triune when even one of these beliefs is rejected.

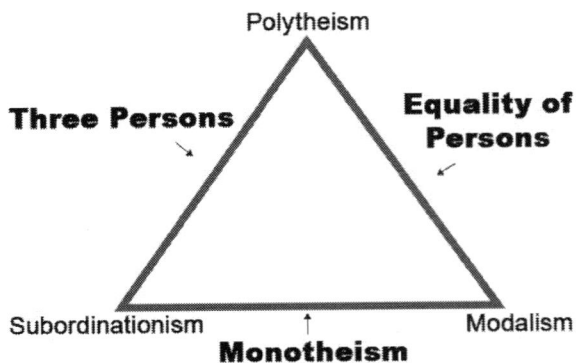

The three sides of the triangle in the diagram represent these three essential beliefs, and the point of the triangle across from each side represents the corresponding error when that particular belief is denied:

- Denial of the Three Persons results in Modalism (sometimes referred to as the Oneness teaching), the erroneous belief that God appears to us in three ways or modes, wears three hats, acts in three different roles or just has three different names.
- Denial of the Equality of Persons results in Subordinationism, the erroneous belief that one of the divine Persons is less than fully and truly God.
- Denial of Monotheism (the idea of the Unity of God) results in Polytheism, the erroneous belief in two or more separate gods (including the error of tri-theism—a belief in three gods).

When we are careful to uphold all three of these essential beliefs about God, we avoid the corresponding false teachings and thus bear faithful witness to the glorious mystery of the Trinity.

I thank God daily for answering our many prayers to reveal to us greater truth. His revealing himself to each of us as the Triune God was a miraculous moment for each one of us.

Joseph Tkach

Beware Theological Labels

As our understanding of who God is (our theology) developed, we began using the term "Incarnational Trinitarian theology" to identify and summarize our understanding. However, use of that term (and others like it) might cause some problems. First, it might confuse some who are not trained in theology. Second, it might be used by some who do not understand it well. Third, it might be overused and thus become cliché. Last, it might become a denominational label that could lead some to misunderstand what we actually believe and teach.

It is helpful to think of Incarnational Trinitarian theology as describing *how* we believe rather than merely what we believe. All orthodox Christians accept the doctrines of the Trinity and the Incarnation. But for us, they are more than two doctrines on a list of many—they are the heart of our faith and worship.

Why is that not so for all Christians? Partly because these truths are deep mysteries beyond our fallen human imaginations. Also, these doctrines are sometimes poorly taught or not taught at all. Thus it is easy to drift away from this defining core and begin to emphasize secondary (even tertiary) issues. When that happens, everything becomes distorted.

This was seen clearly in the way Jewish religious leaders resisted Jesus. Those leaders looked to Scripture as a source of truth, but disagreed about its details. Nevertheless, they were united against Jesus. So Jesus told them,

> You have your heads in your Bibles constantly because you think you'll find eternal life there. But you miss the forest for

the trees. These Scriptures are all about me! And here I am, standing right before you, and you aren't willing to receive from me the life you say you want. (John 5:39-40, *The Message*)

Note how Jesus placed himself at the center as the living key to interpreting Scripture. He himself was the source of their life. If they would accept and understand that, they would put their petty disagreements in perspective and come together in acknowledging him as Messiah. Instead, they saw him as a heretic and plotted to kill him.

As Christians today, we can make the same mistake. Even if we accept Jesus as Lord and Savior, we can sideline the fundamental truths that define who he is. The result is the fragmenting of Christianity into competing "schools" of thought with their own doctrinal distinctives. This leads to a "my Christianity is better than yours" mentality. Though the distinctives may be accurate, they emphasize peripheral matters. The result is that the reality of who God is and what he has done for us in his Son is diminished, if not lost. Division within the Body of Christ results.

That is why we need to avoid using labels in ways that imply that we are setting ourselves apart as having a Christianity that is superior in comparison to others. The reason we use a label is to remind ourselves (and others, if they are interested) of the focus of our renewal—the reality of what is revealed in Jesus Christ according to Scripture.

Also, in using a label, we must avoid implying that we are slavishly beholden to some systematic theology or to certain theologians—even those identified as Incarnational or Trinitarian. There are approximately 50 systematic theologies in existence today. However, there is no single concrete, uniform, particular school of thought called "Trinitarian theology."

For example, Barth, the Torrance brothers and Thomas Oden drew on many other theologians throughout the ages and on the writings of the early church councils. Rather than seeking to establish a new theology, they were seeking to serve Jesus Christ and to build up his church through their teaching and research. They might be described as "Incarnational Trinitarian theologians" because they saw that these elements of Christian faith were being neglected or even forgotten. They discerned that the church needed to get back on the central path of Christian faith.

When we use the term "Incarnational Trinitarian theology," we are referring to the fact that Jesus is the lens through which we read and interpret the Bible and how we have come to know God. Consequently, any other doctrinal points should flow from and fit with the Trinitarian nature of God. Our role in the administration of our denomination is to pass on the best formulations of Christian theology that we can find—especially on the major issues. We are blessed to incorporate the ideas of the great theologians of Christian history, and we can learn from those alive today. But we do not do so slavishly, and biblical revelation always has the controlling authority.

So, when we say that we believe and teach Incarnational Trinitarian theology, we are describing how we understand and believe Scripture based on Jesus as the centerpiece of God's plan for humanity. It is perhaps more like your computer's operating system rather than one of the many programs you load into it. Individual doctrines are like the software applications, which must be able to interface with the operating system if they are to work properly. But it's the operating system that orders, organizes, prioritizes and produces all other useful results.

The focus of our renewal as a denomination has been the very theological issues that have been central to historical, orthodox Christianity. We are not the only branch of the church that neglected or even misunderstood the doctrines of the Trinity and the Incarnation. We hope that we might benefit other parts of the Body of Christ with what we have learned. It is in this spirit that we offer our *Speaking of Life* and *You're Included* videos. If you have not viewed them, I urge you to do so. They will help us all keep the Center in the center, feed our continuing renewal in the Spirit, and enable us to join with all Christians down through the ages in giving witness to the glory of our triune God: Father, Son and Holy Spirit.

Joseph Tkach

Questions and Answers About Trinitarian Theology

Let's address several questions and objections.

Are you saying there is no difference between a Christian and a non-Christian?

No. We are saying that because of who Jesus is and what he has done, all humans—believers and non-believers—are joined to God in and through Jesus, through his human nature. As a result, God is reconciled to all people. All have been adopted as his dearly loved children. All, in and through Jesus, are included in the Triune love and life of God: Father, Son and Spirit.

However, not all people acknowledge who Christ is and therefore the truth of who they are in Christ. Those who have not yet repented and put their trust exclusively in Christ are not believers. They are not living in relationship with him and receiving the abundant life he gives.

One way to speak of the distinction between believers and non-believers is to say that all people are included in Christ (objectively) but only believers are actively participating in that inclusion.

We see these distinctions throughout the New Testament, and they are important. However, we must not take these distinctions too far, creating some kind of separation or opposition, and think of non-believers as not accepted by and not loved by God. To see them in this way would be to overlook the great truth of who Jesus Christ is and what he has already done for all humanity. It would be to turn the "good news" into "bad news."

When we see all humanity joined to Christ, some of the categories we might have held in our thinking fall away. We no longer see non-believers as "outsiders" but as children of God in need of personally acknowledging how much their Father loves them, likes them, and wants them. We approach them as brothers and sisters. Do they know who they are in Christ? Do they live in personal communion with Christ, No—and it is our privilege to tell them of God's love for them that they might do so.

If all are reconciled already to God in Christ, why does Scripture say so much about repentance and faith?

In the New Testament, the Greek word translated "repentance" is *metanoia*, which means "change of mind." All humanity is invited and enabled by the Spirit to experience a radical change of mind away from sinful egoistic self-centeredness and toward God and his love experienced in union with Jesus Christ through the Holy Spirit.

Notice Peter's invitation to this change of mind in Acts 2:38-39:

> Repent and be baptized, every one of you, in the name of Jesus Christ for the forgiveness of your sins. And you will receive the gift of the Holy Spirit. The promise is for you and your children and for all who are far off—for all whom the Lord our God will call.

God does not forgive people in exchange for their repentance and belief. As Scripture proclaims, forgiveness is an unconditional free gift that is entirely of grace. It is a reality that exists for us even before we enter into it in our experience.

We repent because we are forgiven.

The gospel truth—the truth about Jesus and about all humanity joined with God in Jesus—is that God has already forgiven all humanity with a forgiveness that is unconditional and free: "Therefore," invites Peter, "repent and believe this truth—and be baptized by the Spirit with the mind of Jesus—which involves supernatural assurance that we truly are the children of God."

Repentance is a change of mind and heart; it involves coming to acknowledge who Jesus is for us and who we are in him, apart from anything we have done or will yet do. Through repentance, which is God's gift to us through the Spirit, our minds are renewed in Jesus and we turn to him and begin to trust him.

The Spirit moves us to repent because our forgiveness has already been accomplished in Christ, not in order to be forgiven. We repent because we know that, in Jesus, our sins have already been forgiven, and that, in Jesus, we are already a new creation. In this repentance, we turn away from the alienation within us as the Spirit baptizes our minds in Jesus' acceptance and in the assurance that comes with it.

Why does Paul say that if you don't have the Spirit, you don't belong to Christ?

Romans 8:9 says, "You, however, are not in the realm of the flesh but are in the realm of the Spirit, if indeed the Spirit of God lives in you. And if anyone does not have the Spirit of Christ, they do not belong to Christ."

The sentence "And if anyone does not have the Spirit of Christ, they do not belong to Christ" is not meant to be lifted out of context and turned into a proof that some people do not belong to God. In the context of this passage, Paul is addressing believers; he is not making a statement here about non-believers. He is warning disobedient believers who are refusing to submit to the Holy Spirit in their lives. In effect, he is saying, "You say that the Spirit of God is in you, and you are right. However, your life should be reflecting the presence of the Spirit of Christ. Your actions do not demonstrate that you really do belong to Christ as you claim to. I don't dispute that you belong to Christ. But if you do, then on that very basis act in accordance with that reality."

As Paul says to believers in verse 12, "We have an obligation—but it is not to the flesh…" We have an obligation to live in the light of who Christ has made us be.

Questions and Answers About Trinitarian Theology
continued

If the world is reconciled, why would Jesus say that he doesn't pray for the world?

In John 17:9, Jesus says: "I pray for them [his disciples]. I am not praying for the world, but for those you have given me, for they are yours."

Just because Jesus said in one instance that he was not praying for the world, but instead for his disciples, does not imply that he never prayed for the world. It is just that right then, his emphasis was on his disciples. He is praying in particular for them, focusing on them.

It is important to understand how John uses the word "world" (*kosmos* in Greek) in the flow of his Gospel. At times the word can refer to all people (who are all loved by God; see John 3:16) while at other times it can refer to the worldly "system" that is fallen and hostile toward God.

It is apparently this system that Jesus has in mind in John 17. Since this fallen system or world resists God, Jesus' prayer does not include it. He is not praying for the world in its current fallen form, rather, he is praying for a group of people whom he can use to declare his love in this fallen world.

Later on in his prayer, Jesus turns his attention to those who are not yet his disciples. He prays "also for those who will believe in me through their message." He prays for them that they, along with those who are already believing, "may be one, Father...so that the world may believe that you have sent me" (John 17:21). This aligns with the Gospel of John's message (3:16): God loves the whole world and wants to save everyone.

If all are reconciled already to God, why does Scripture speak of hell?

Scripture speaks of hell because it is the natural consequence of rebellion against God. When we cut ourselves off from God and refuse his mercy, grace and forgiveness, we are rejecting communion with him and cutting ourselves off from the very source of our life. Christ came to prevent that from happening. Grace enters in and disrupts the natural course of a fallen creation. Being created for personal communion with God means we must be receptive to what he has done for us in Christ. All are included in what Christ intends for everyone, but we can refuse our inclusion. We are reconciled to the Father, but we can refuse to receive that reconciliation and live as if God had not reconciled us to himself.

However, such refusal does not negate what God has done for all humanity in Christ.

In *The Great Divorce*, C.S. Lewis wrote:

> There are only two kinds of people in the end; those who say to God, "Thy will be done," and those to whom God says, in the end, "Thy will be done." All that are in hell, choose it. Without that self-choice there could be no hell. No soul that seriously and constantly desires joy will ever miss it. Those who seek find. To those who knock it is opened.

Why does the Bible talk about people whose names are not in the book of life?

Revelation 13:8 says, "All inhabitants of the earth will worship the beast—all whose names have not been written in the Lamb's book of life, the Lamb who was slain from the creation of the world."

Revelation 17:8 says, "The inhabitants of the earth whose names have not been written in the book of life from the creation of the world will be astonished when they see the beast."

We need to consider the literary context of these statements in Revelation. John writes using a literary genre (style) known as apocalyptic. This genre, which was commonly used by Jewish writers in John's day, is highly symbolic. There is not a literal "book of life." The "book of life" is a figure of speech, a symbolic way of referring to those who are in allegiance with the Lamb. These verses in Revelation refer to people who reject the new life that Christ has already secured for them.

Why does Peter say it is hard to be saved?

First Peter 4:17-18 says: "It is time for judgment to begin with God's household; and if it begins with us, what will the outcome be for those who do not obey the gospel of God? And, 'If it is hard for the righteous to be saved, what will become of the ungodly and the sinner?'"

The point of verses 17-18 is found in verse 19: "So then, those who suffer according to God's will should commit themselves to their faithful Creator and continue to do good."

Peter has been encouraging persecuted believers to live in accord with their identity as children of God and not like those who live in debauchery and idolatry (verses 1-5). The difficulty is not in Jesus' power to save but for those believing to live faithfully through times of the suffering of persecution. The difficulties involved in being saved call for perseverance. Peter does not say that salvation is impossible for anyone. (See also Mark 10:25-27, where Jesus replies to his disciples' query as to how anyone could be saved if it was difficult for the wealthy. Jesus answered, "For mortals it is impossible, but not for God; for God all things are possible," NRSV).

As part of his argument, he points out that persecution is participation in the suffering of Christ, and therefore if believers are to suffer, they should suffer for their faith and godly behavior instead of suffering for sinful and ungodly behavior (verses 12-16). His point is that believers, who know that Jesus, the Savior, is the merciful Judge of all, should not be living in the same base and evil ways as those who oppose Christ even under the threat of persecution.

It is actually impossible for anyone to be saved—were it not for Christ. Christ has done what is impossible for humans to do for themselves. But those who reject Christ are not participating in Christ's suffering; they participate in their own suffering as they reap what they sow. That experience is a far more difficult path to be on than the narrow one of those who know Christ and can have fellowship with him even in their sufferings.

What is everlasting contempt and destruction?

Daniel 12:2 reads, "Multitudes who sleep in the dust of the earth will awake: some to everlasting life, others to shame and everlasting contempt."

2 Thessalonians 1:6-9 says,

> God is just: He will pay back trouble to those who trouble you and give relief to you who are troubled, and to us as well. This will happen when the Lord Jesus is revealed from heaven in blazing fire with his powerful angels. He will punish those who do not know God and do not obey the gospel of our Lord Jesus. They will be punished with everlasting destruction and shut out from the presence of the Lord and from the glory of his might.

Both of these passages refer to the time of the final judgment when Jesus is "revealed" (sometimes referred to as the Second Coming or Jesus' "return in glory"). All humans will then see clearly who Jesus is and thus who they are because of who he is and what he has done. This "revealing" presents to them a choice—will they say "yes" to their belonging to Christ, or will they say "no"?

Their decision neither creates nor destroys their inclusion, but it does determine their attitude toward it—whether they will accept God's love for them and enter the joy of the Lord, or continue in alienation and frustration (and thus in shame and everlasting contempt and destruction). The destruction is a self-destruction as they refuse the purpose for which they have been made, and the redemption that has already been given to them. They refuse to submit to God's righteousness through repentance and so refuse to receive his life, effectively cutting themselves off from it.

In the Judgment, everyone will face Jesus, the Judge who died for all, and they will have to decide whether they will trust him and count on his being judged in their place. Those who trust their Savior agree with the judgment of God as to what is evil and must be done away with. They humbly receive the joy of the life God has given them in Christ. Those who reject him continue in their hostility and the hell that goes with denying the truth and reality of their sin and Christ's salvation for them.

What about the "narrow gate"?

Jesus says in Matthew 7:13-14: "Enter through the narrow gate. For wide is the gate and broad is the road that leads to destruction, and many enter through it. But small is the gate and narrow the road that leads to life, and only a few find it."

Jesus describing what is happing in the present. A clearer translation is: "many are entering" and "only a few are finding it." In his day, at that time, most were living on the "broad road" of destruction. What Jesus offers here is descriptive, not prescriptive. It does not say what Jesus wants nor what God intends. This is a warning, and warnings are given to prevent the negative outcome from occurring. No parent says to their child, "Watch out, a car is coming!" because they hope the child gets run over! Jesus gives the reason for the need to be warned: under fallen conditions the way to destruction is wide, inviting and easy to follow, or we can simply be swept along into it. The narrow way to life can be easy to miss, may seem difficult to follow and takes our being deliberate and intentional. There were only a "few" who had at that time embraced the truth that is in Jesus—and it is he who is "the narrow gate." But Jesus wants to turn that around so that there are many, not a few, who enter into the life that Jesus has for them. So he gives this warning out of his love for them.

Jesus addresses a similar issue in Matthew 7:21-23:

> Not everyone who says to me, "Lord, Lord," will enter the kingdom of heaven, but only the one who does the will of my Father who is in heaven. Many will say to me on that day, "Lord, Lord, did we not prophesy in your name, and in your name drive out demons and in your name perform many miracles?" Then I will tell them plainly, "I never knew you. Away from me, you evildoers!"

These people have done miracles, and in doing so have deceived many. They claim to know Jesus. Although Jesus knows them (he is omniscient), he does not see himself in them with regard to their actual faith or behavior, and so he proclaims, "I never knew you." That is, I don't recognize you as a follower of mine. We haven't been in relationship, in communion with one another despite what you were doing.

Don't we become God's children only at the point of belief?

John 1:12-13 says, "Yet to all who did receive him, to those who believed in his name, he gave the right to become children of God—children born neither of natural descent, nor of human decision or a husband's will, but born of God."

We have seen in Scripture that God has provided for everyone in the vicarious humanity of Jesus. When he died, we all died; when he rose, we rose. Our human natures have been regenerated in him. Therefore all humans are, from God's perspective, already adopted into his family. In Jesus, God gives people that "right" long before they accept it and live in it. They have an inheritance, as Paul puts it.

If we say that we don't have a right to become the children of God until after and unless we believe, then we end up denying what John goes on to say: that it doesn't come from natural descent or from human decision. Such an understanding would make our having the right depend on our decision!

Those who believe in and accept Jesus as their Lord and elder brother enter into and begin to experience the new life as children of God. But that place in God's family has been theirs all along. It is the new life that has been "hidden with Christ in God" (Colossians 3:3). In other words, what has been objectively true for them all along in Jesus, becomes subjectively and personally experienced by them when they become believers. They begin taking up their right and living as the children of God.

Is this universalism?

No, not in the sense that every person ultimately will be saved (or enter into or receive their salvation) regardless of whether they ever trust in Christ. There is no salvation outside of Jesus Christ (Acts 4:12). Those who absolutely refuse to enter into their salvation, or to receive it by repentance and faith in what Christ their Savior has done for them, have refused the benefits of their salvation, refused their inheritance, and repudiated the "hope laid up for [them] in heaven" (Colossians 1:5).

Jesus' atonement has universal intent (Romans 5:18). He died for all and he was raised for all because God so loved the world. He is the "Lamb of God, who takes away the sin of the world" (John 1:29). Scripture shows that God, in Christ, has reconciled all humans to himself (Colossians 1:20; 2 Corinthians 5:19), but he will never force any person to embrace that reconciliation. Love cannot be coerced.

A relationship of love as the children of God could never be the result of a cause-effect mechanism. God wants sons and daughters who love him out of a joyful response to his love, not people who have no mind or choice of their own.

As has been revealed in Jesus Christ, God is love in his innermost being, and in God the Persons of the Trinity relate to one another in the truth and freedom of love. That same love is extended to us in Christ that we might share in it, and in nothing less.

To hope that all people will finally come to Christ is not universalism—it is simply Christian and reflects the heart of God (1 Timothy 2:3-6; 2 Peter 3:9). If God calls us to love our enemies, does God himself do less? If God desires that all turn and be saved, can we do anything less?

This does not mean we can proclaim that every person will finally come to faith and receive their salvation. However, it means that, given who God is and what he has done for us in Christ, we ought to be more surprised that some may somehow come to reject the truth and reality of their salvation than to find many in the end turning to Christ to receive his forgiveness and eternal life as his beloved children.

If we are reconciled already, why struggle to live the Christian life?

Some people do not like the idea that others who do not work as hard as they do will end up with the same reward as they (see parable of the laborers in the vineyard, Matthew 20:12-15). But this concern overlooks the truth that no one, no matter how hard they work, deserves salvation. That is why it is, for everyone, a free gift.

However, in Scripture we learn that is why God doesn't want us to live that way. Consider the following passages:

> No one can lay any foundation other than the one already laid, which is Jesus Christ. If anyone builds on this foundation using gold, silver, costly stones, wood, hay or straw, their work will be shown for what it is, because the Day will bring it to light. It will be revealed with fire, and the fire will test the quality of each person's work. If what has been built survives, the builder will receive a reward. If it is burned up, the builder will suffer loss but yet will be saved—even

though only as one escaping through the flames. (1 Corinthians 3:11-15)

Do not be deceived: God cannot be mocked. People reap what they sow. Whoever sows to please their flesh, from the flesh will reap destruction; whoever sows to please the Spirit, from the Spirit will reap eternal life. (Galatians 6:7-8)

We are joined to Christ in order to live in fellowship with Christ. We are united to Christ in order to participate with him in all he does. It makes no more sense to say that since we belong to Christ there is no point in living the Christian life, than to say, since a man and woman are married, there is no point to them living together. No. They are married in order to live together. We are joined to Christ in order to live with him. Similarly, it makes no sense to say that we want to experience the life of Christ in eternity if we refuse to experience it now.

How do we explain John 6:44?

John 6:44 says, "No one can come to me unless the Father who sent me draws them."

The Jewish religious leaders were seeking to deflect Jesus' seemingly outrageous claim: "I am the bread of life that came down from heaven" (John 6:41). This statement was practically the same thing as claiming divine status.

Jesus' reply to the Jewish leaders' complaint concerning this claim was that they "stop grumbling" (verse 43) and realize that "no one can come to me [the bread of heaven] unless the Father who sent me draws them..." (verse 44). Jesus' point is that the people would not be responding to him, except that God was making it possible for them to do so. If they really knew God, they should recognize that people were coming to the Son according to the will and purpose of the Father. What they see happening in Jesus' ministry is not evidence that Jesus is a blasphemer, disobeying the will of God, but rather that God the Father is accomplishing his will through Jesus, his faithful Son.

In this passage, Jesus is not limiting the number of people who are drawn to him; he is showing that he is doing the Father's work. Elsewhere he says: "When I am lifted up, I will draw all people to myself" (John 12:32). Since Jesus does only what his Father wants, John 12:32 shows that the Father indeed draws all people to Jesus.

How does this theology compare to Calvinism and Arminianism?

In comparing and contrasting Christian theologies, we are talking about different approaches or understandings among Christian brothers and sisters who seek to serve the same Lord and thus share the same faith. Thus, our discussion should reflect respect and gentleness, not arrogance or hostility.

Calvinism is a theology that developed from the teachings of the Protestant reformer John Calvin (1509-1564). Calvinism emphasizes the sovereignty of God's will in election and salvation. Most Calvinists define God's "elect" as a subset of the human race; Christ died for only some people ("limited" or "particular" atonement"). Those elect for whom he did die were truly and effectively saved in the finished work of Christ, long before they became aware of it and accepted it. According to Calvinist doctrine, it is inevitable that those Christ died for will come to faith in him at some point. This is called "irresistible grace."

Trinitarian theology's main disagreement with Calvinism is over the scope of reconciliation. Its objection is based on the fundamental fact of who Jesus is and that he is one in will, purpose, mind, authority and act with the Father in the Spirit. The whole God is Savior, and Jesus is the new Adam who died for all. The Bible asserts that Christ made atonement "not only for our sins, but for the sins of the whole world" (1 John 2:2). While Trinitarian theology rejects the restrictive extent of "limited atonement" and the determinism of "irresistible grace," it agrees with Calvinism that forgiveness, reconciliation, redemption, justification, etc. were all accomplished effectively by what Christ did, and these gospel truths have been secured for us irrespective of our response to them.

Arminianism derives from the teachings of another Protestant reformer, Jacob Arminius (1560-1609). Arminius insisted that Jesus died for all humanity, and that all people can be saved if they take personal action, which is enabled by the Spirit. This theology, while not ignoring God's sovereignty, gives a more central or key role to human decision and free will. Its premise is that salvation, forgiveness, reconciliation, redemption, justification, etc., are not actually effective unless a person has faith. Only if God foresees a person using their free choice to receive Christ, does he then elect them. Those whom he foresees rejecting his salvation, he condemns. So like the Calvinist, in the end God wills the salvation of some and the condemnation of others.

Trinitarian theology differs from Arminianism over the effectiveness of the reconciliation. Atonement, or at-one-ment between God and humanity, is only a hypothetical possibility for Arminians; it does not become an actuality unless God foresees someone's decision of faith. In this view, God, on the basis of his foreknowledge of an individual's acceptance or rejection, then accepts or rejects that person. Trinitarian theology, however, teaches that the atonement and reconciliation represents the heart and mind of God towards all and is objectively true in Christ, even before it has been subjectively accepted and experienced. It remains true even if some deny it. God has one ultimate will or purpose for all, realized from the Father, through the Son and in the Spirit.

While Calvinism and Arminianism emphasize different aspects of salvation theology, Trinitarian theology has attempted, as did early church leaders Irenaeus, Athanasius, and Gregory, to maintain in harmony the wideness of God's love emphasized by Arminians with the unconditioned faithfulness of God emphasized by Calvinists. The Incarnational and Trinitarian theology of GCI aligns neither with traditional Calvinism nor Arminianism. It emphasizes the sovereignty of God's Triune holy love that calls for our response. His sovereign will is expressed in accord with God being a fellowship of holy love. Its center is the heart, mind, character and nature of God revealed in the person and work of Jesus Christ, the Incarnate Savior and Redeemer. God's sovereignty is most clearly and profoundly shown in Jesus Christ. The place and importance of human response to God's grace is also shown in Jesus Christ, who makes a perfect and free response to God in our place and on our behalf as our Great High Priest. Our response then is a gift given by the Holy Spirit by which we share in Christ's perfect response for us in our place and on our behalf.

What is perichoresis?

The eternal communion of love that Father, Son and Spirit share as the Trinity involves a mystery of inter-relationship and interpenetration of the divine Persons, a mutual indwelling without loss of personal identity. As Jesus said, "the Father is in me, and I in the Father" (John 10:38). Early Greek-speaking Christian theologians described this relationship with the word *perichoresis,* which is derived from root words meaning "around" and "contain." Each person of the Trinity is contained within the others; they dwell in one another, they envelop one another.

Theology as a Framework for Life and Ministry

Theology is important to us because it offers a framework for our belief in God. But there is a lot of theology out there, even within the Christian faith. One thing that is foundational for GCI as a denomination is our commitment to what's known as "Trinitarian theology." Although the doctrine of the Trinity has been widely embraced in the church down through the ages, some have called it the "forgotten doctrine," because it is often overlooked.

However, at GCI, we believe that the reality of the Trinity changes everything. The Bible teaches that our salvation depends on the Trinity. It shows us how each person of the Godhead plays a vital role in our lives as believers. God the Father has adopted us (Ephesians 1:5) as his "dearly loved children" (Ephesians 5:1). This is because God the Son, Jesus Christ, has completed his work, and he is enough for our salvation (Ephesians 1:3-7). We can be confident in our salvation because God the Holy Spirit dwells in us, as a seal of our inheritance (Ephesians 1:13-14). Each member of the Trinity plays a unique role in welcoming us into God's family.

Even though we worship God in three divine persons, the doctrine of the Trinity can sometimes feel like it is difficult to live it out in a practical way. But when our understanding and practice conforms to this central doctrine, it has the potential to transform our daily lives. I see it like this: The doctrine of the Trinity reminds us that we cannot do anything to earn our place at the table – God has already invited us and accomplished the work necessary to get us there. Thanks to salvation through Jesus and the indwelling of the Holy Spirit, we can come before the Father, caught up in the love of the Triune God. This love is available to all who believe because of the eternal, unchanging relationship of the Trinity – at no cost to us.

However, this doesn't mean that we don't have a chance to participate. Living in Christ means that God's love enables us to care for those around us. The love of the Trinity overflows to include us, and through us, it reaches others. God doesn't need us to complete his work, but he does invite us, as his family, to join with him. We are empowered to love because of his Spirit inside of us. When I recall that his Spirit dwells in me, I feel my own spirit grow lighter. The Trinitarian, relational God wants to free us to have richer relationships with him and with others.

Let me give you an example from my own life. As a minister, I can get caught up in "what I do" for God. Recently, I was meeting with a group of people. I was focusing so much on my own agenda that I forgot to pay attention to who else was in the room with us. When I realized my worry about accomplishing things on God's behalf, I took a moment to laugh at myself – and to celebrate that God was there with us, guiding us. We don't have to be afraid of making mistakes when we know that God oversees it all. We can serve him joyfully. It transforms our daily interactions when we recall that there is nothing God can't redeem. Our Christian calling is not a heavy burden, but a wonderful gift. Because the Spirit of God indwells us, we are liberated to participate in his work without worry.

You may know that one of GCI's mottos is "You're included." But do you know what that means to me? It means that we seek to love one another the way the Trinity loves – to care for one another in a way that celebrates our created difference while still coming together. The Trinity is a perfect model of love. Father, Son, and Holy Spirit enjoy perfect unity, while remaining distinct divine persons. As Athanasius put it, "Unity in Trinity, Trinity in unity." The love expressed within the Trinity teaches us the significance of loving relationships within God's kingdom.

Trinitarian theology defines the life of our denomination. It motivates how we care for one another. We want to love those around us, not because we need to achieve something, but because our God is a God of community and love. God's Spirit of love guides us to love others, even when it isn't easy. We know that his Spirit is not only in us, but in the lives of our brothers and sisters as well. This is why we don't just meet together to worship every week – it's why we also eat meals together, why we eagerly anticipate what God might do in each other's lives. It's the reason we offer help to those in need in our own neighborhoods and around the world, why we pray for the sick and those who are struggling. It's because of our belief in the Trinity.

When we grieve or celebrate together, we seek to love each other as the Triune God loves. When we live out Trinitarian theology in everyday life, we embrace our call to be "the fullness of him who fills everything" (Ephesians 1:22-23). We are showered with the Father's love through the salvation of his Son and the presence of his Spirit – and through the care of his body, the church. From a meal made for a sick friend, to rejoicing with a family member's accomplishment, to a donation that supports the work of the church, we are able to live out the good news of the gospel.

Joseph Tkach

Foundations of Theology for Grace Communion International

Transcript of a video presentation

Joseph Tkach: Acts 17:11 tells us that the Bereans "examined the Scriptures every day" to see if what Paul said about Jesus was true. The Bereans were engaged in theology — studying to know God. The English word "theology" comes from two Greek words, *theos* and *logia* — meaning "God" and "knowledge." Theology is what we as Christian believers do — we involve ourselves in "God knowledge" or "God study" seeking to know God as fully as we can. Theology is simply the study of God. What we believe, and what a Christological, or Trinitarian, theology is all about, is that theology itself needs to emerge from God's witness to himself in Scripture.

Michael Morrison: The idea of studying theology, or even thinking about theology, can be frightening to many people. But everyone has a theology, whether they know it or not. Even atheists have a theology. A college student once admitted to the college chaplain that she did not believe in God. The chaplain was curious, so he asked: "What sort of god is it that you don't believe in?" She described an old man in the sky, someone who is just looking for people to do something wrong so he can zap them. The chaplain replied, "If that's what you mean by the word *god*, then I'd be an atheist, too. I don't believe in that kind of god, either."

JT: A person's theology is just their beliefs about God. Some people think that God is an angry judge; others believe that he is like a grandfather who means well but can't do much. Others see him as a cosmic concierge who exists to grant us our every desire. Some people think of God as far off and unknowable; others think of him as near and accessible. Some people think God never changes his mind; others think that he is always changing in response to the prayers of his people. How people view God affects how they read and interpret the Bible.

MM: When Paul tells us that Adam brought condemnation on everyone, and that Jesus brought justification for everyone, then we have to think about what that means about humanity and about Jesus and about salvation. When Paul says that we were baptized into Christ's death, or when Jesus says, "If you have seen me you have seen the Father," we need to think about what that means — and that's theology.

A study of theology helps us learn to put all our various doctrines or beliefs or teachings together, to see if they are consistent with one another, or if they seem to contradict one another. But we don't do theology just according to what sounds good to us. We are not the authority — God is. If he didn't reveal himself to us, then we wouldn't know anything for sure about him. But he has revealed himself to us, and in two ways — in Scripture, and in Jesus — and we know Jesus through Scripture as well. So Scripture should provide our foundation for theological thought.

J. Michael Feazell: At the heart of all our doctrines and beliefs in our denomination is the Bible. Yet, as is clear from our own history (not to mention the history of the Christian church in general), people do not agree on how the Bible should be interpreted. A person's theology, or their perspective on who God is and how he relates to humanity and how humanity relates to him, is like a lens though which people interpret what they read in the Bible. What we believe, and what a Christological, or Trinitarian, theology is all about, is that theology needs to emerge from God's own witness to himself in Scripture. God's own witness to himself in Scripture is Jesus Christ. "If you have seen me," Jesus said, "You have seen the Father."

Dan Rogers: In Jesus, God fully revealed himself to humanity. Karl Barth once said you really can't do theology. If theology is the study of God, the knowledge of God, how can the human mind ever study God? Well, there is a way — as he then pointed out. God fully revealed himself in Jesus Christ.

JT: In our denomination, our theology is what gives cohesion and structure to our beliefs and establishes priority for our doctrines. It has developed over the years as we have worked through various doctrinal issues, all the while being careful to maintain a Bible-based understanding of who God is and how he relates to humanity.

JMF: God is known by faith, and by that we mean that we know God not merely as we hear about him through the Scriptures, but as we actually put our trust in him. In that obedient life, the Spirit engages us to think about and reflect on what God reveals about himself. That is why a Christological, or Christ-centered, theology is important, so that we have the right starting place for our journey of growing in the grace and knowledge of God.

JT: As our theology developed, we found the writings of Thomas and James Torrance and Karl Barth to be especially helpful because of their intense focus on the biblical revelation of God through Jesus Christ.

MM: We have a Christ-centered, or Trinitarian, theology. That means not only that we accept the doctrine of the Trinity, but that this doctrine lies at the heart of all other doctrines. The central Bible truth that Jesus Christ is God in the flesh, that he and the Father with the Spirit are one God, forms the basis for how we understand everything we read in Scripture.

In John 14, the apostle Philip asked Jesus, "Lord, show us the Father." Jesus replied, "If you have seen me, you have seen the Father. I am in the Father, and the Father is in me." In other words, Jesus reveals to us what the Father is like. Jesus shows us a God who is love, is compassion, patience, kindness, faithfulness, and goodness. God is like that all the time.

Some people imagine that the Father is angry at humanity and really wants to punish everyone, but that the Son intervened for us and paid the price to save us from his Father's wrath. That's quite confused, because the Bible says that the Father is just like Jesus. The Father loved the world so much that he sent his Son to save the world. It's not like Jesus was working behind his Father's back — no, it's just the opposite: the Father was working in and through Jesus. The Father is just as eager to save humanity as Jesus is.

When Jesus was born, he was Immanuel, which means "God with us." When the Word became a human being, he showed us that God is present with humanity, and he is working for humanity. We are his creations, and he doesn't want to let us go to ruin. When God came in human flesh, he, as a representative of humanity, was able to do what other humans had not been able to do. As the perfect human, Jesus offered God perfect worship, and a perfect sacrifice, and God accepted this worship that was offered on behalf of the human race. Just as in Adam we are all condemned, so also in Christ we are all acquitted, and accepted, and welcomed into the love and fellowship of the Trinity.

DR: As we study Jesus, we begin to see God and his relationship with us as his creation — with humanity. So we began to view the Scriptures through that lens, and we noticed that many others had done likewise; men such as Athanasius and in our modern times theologians like Karl Barth had looked through this same lens, and we began to interact, to participate in a dialectical discussion with the writings and the thoughts of these great Christians from ages past. As we did, we began to focus more and more on a certain theology, the theology of adoption, the theology of God's love for humanity. How God wanted to take us into himself and share his life with us because he is a God of love — a God who gives, and a God who shares.

Foundations of Theology for Grace Communion International
continued

JT: Thomas Torrance is widely considered to be one of the premier Christian theologians of the 20th century. He was awarded the Templeton Foundation Prize for Progress in Religion in 1978, and his book, *Theological Science*, received the first "Collins Award" in Britain for the best work in theology, ethics, and sociology relevant to Christianity for 1967-69. Torrance founded the *Scottish Journal of Theology* and served as moderator of the General Assembly of the Church of Scotland in 1976-77. He served for more than 25 years as chair of Christian Dogmatics at the University of Edinburgh, and is author of more than 30 books and hundreds of articles.

Torrance, following in the theological tradition of Athanasius and Gregory of Nazianzus, is a leading proponent of what is called Trinitarian theology: theology rooted in God's own revelation of himself through the Scriptures in the person of Jesus Christ. In the Scriptures, human life and human death find their meaning only in the life and death and resurrection of Jesus Christ, the Son of God, who in becoming human for our sakes has brought humanity into the eternal joyous fellowship of the Father, Son and Spirit. Because Christ has done in our place and on our behalf everything needed for our salvation, all that remains for us is to repent and believe in him as our Lord and Savior.

JMF: When we take seriously passages about the width and breadth of God's gracious and powerful reconciling work in Jesus Christ, such as Colossian 1:19-20, some people respond with "You're just teaching universalism." Colossians 1:19-20 says: "God was pleased to have all his fullness dwell in him, and through him to reconcile to himself all things, whether things on earth or things in heaven, by making peace through his blood, shed on the cross." Paul wrote the passage, not us, not Karl Barth, not Thomas Torrance.

Barth, responding to accusations that he was teaching universalism, said, "There is no theological justification for setting any limits on our side to the friendliness of God towards humanity which appeared in Jesus Christ." We have no reason to make apologies for the wideness of God's grace. Paul also wrote, in 1 Timothy 2:4, that God "wants all men to be saved and to come to a knowledge of the truth." Still, as Barth pointed out, God declares an eternal "No" to sin, and God's "No" is the power of God by which evil is overthrown and negated, and its power and future denied. God rejects and opposes all opposition to himself, and yet in Jesus Christ, God's elect, all humanity is indeed elect and reconciled, as Colossians says.

But kingdom life is none other than a life of faith in Jesus, not a life of unbelief. That means that even though all humanity is elect in Christ, unbelieving elect aren't living a kingdom life; they aren't living in the joy of fellowship with the Father and the Son and the Spirit. So if it were to be that everyone would ultimately enter into the life of the kingdom (and that is not something we are given to know), but if it were to be, it would only be after repentance, which is turning to God, and faith in Jesus Christ. "Now this is eternal life," Jesus said in a prayer to the Father, "that they may know you, the only true God, and Jesus Christ whom you have sent." There is no salvation outside of a life of faith in Jesus Christ.

That's what hell is all about—life outside the fellowship of the Father, Son and Spirit—life, if you can call it that, in the dark, outside the king's banquet, being left to the miserable fruit of one's own self-centeredness. Call it fiery, call it outer darkness, call it weeping and gnashing of teeth — the Bible uses all those metaphors in describing the existence of those who refuse to embrace his grace and love, that amazing grace and love God has even for his enemies.

JT: The Bible confronts us with a wonderful, amazing, reconciliation in Christ that is so broad as to encompass not only all things on earth, but even all things in heaven, Colossians tells us in no uncertain terms. Yet God calls on humanity to receive, to accept, that grace he so powerfully bestows on all humanity in Jesus Christ. But for those who refuse it, who persist in their rebellion, and in their rejection of God's grace for them, hell is what remains for them. As Robert Capon puts it, God will not allow them to spoil the party for everyone else.

MM: Ancient Greek philosophers reasoned that since God is perfect, that must mean that he never changes, and that he never has any feelings, because if he would ever change, then that would mean that he wasn't perfect before the change. So they thought of God as static, the so-called "unmoved mover" who made everything happen, but who could not ever change course, because to do so would call his perfection and his power into question. This kind of God would never dirty himself by getting involved with people and their problems. He was far off, watching, but not directly and personally involved. This concept of God has often affected even how Christians think about God.

But the Bible reveals a different sort of God — one who is not constrained by the limits of a philosopher's logic. God is completely sovereign — he can do whatever he wants to do — and he is not limited by any external rules or ideas or human logic. If he wants the eternal Word to become a human being, then he does it, even though it constitutes a change. The God of the Bible is free to be whoever he wants to be — free to become what he was not before: the Creator; and free to create human beings who would be free, who could go astray, and God is even free to become one of those human beings in order to rescue humanity from its rebellion and alienation.

In this theological thinking, it is not our logic that is in charge — God is the one in charge, and our task, our desire, is to try to understand God not the way that we might reason him out to be by our finite forms of logic, but rather to seek to understand God the way that he has revealed himself through the Bible in the person of Jesus Christ.

Throughout church history, people have defined theology as "faith seeking understanding." We believe, and now we want to understand as much as we can about what we believe. It's like we've fallen in love with someone, and we want to find out as much as we can about that person. Theology is faith, trying to understand more about the God who loves us. We must seek that understanding in the context of God's own revelation of himself as Father, Son and Spirit revealed to us perfectly in Jesus, the Son of God made flesh for our sakes.

JT: When it comes to theologies, it is not so much a matter of a particular theological perspective being totally "right" or totally "wrong." It is more a case of how adequate a particular theology is in fully addressing believers' biblical understanding of God and how God relates to humanity. We have found that of all approaches to Christian theology, Christo-centric, or Trinitarian, theology reflects and adheres most faithfully and carefully to what God reveals about himself and humanity in the Bible.

We should keep in mind that theology is a journey, not a destination. We will always be seeking as clear and adequate a theological vision as we can, in order to soundly convey the biblical vision and understanding God has given us over

15-plus years of doctrinal reformation. Theology includes the task of seeking adequate thought-forms to convey doctrinal truths in a rapidly changing world.

JMF: Many people today, even believers, are afraid: They're afraid of their standing with God, worried that they're not measuring up, that they're not doing enough, worried that their sins and failures have cut them off from God's love. That's what theologies that start from ideas of, say, holiness, or of judgment, cause. Instead of taking confidence in Jesus, and knowing that Jesus has already done for them everything God requires of them, instead of knowing that Jesus is their perfection, their obedience, their faithfulness, they suffer under a burden of guilt and anxiety.

When we know that it isn't our righteousness but Jesus' righteousness that has already put us in good standing with God, then we are freed from ourselves and our sinfulness to trust in Jesus and to take up our cross and follow Jesus as we could never be free to do when we're afraid that God is mad at us. A sound, biblically rooted theology will always start with and be centered in Christology, because in Scripture we are confronted with a God who chooses to be God in Jesus, with Jesus and for Jesus. If we let the Bible forge our theology, we cannot look outside of Jesus to understand who God is, or to define God.

MM: In Jesus we meet God as God really is, the way God has revealed himself to be, as the God who is for us, because he is for Jesus. We find that the Father loves us unconditionally, that he sent Jesus not out of anger and a need to punish someone, but out of his immeasurable love and his unbending commitment to our redemption. The love we see in Jesus is none other than the love of the Father, because the Father is in the Son and the Son in the Father and they are one. That means that when we know Jesus Christ, we know God the Father.

JMF: In Jesus, God reveals himself as our Creator and our Judge, and also as our Reconciler and Redeemer. In other words, the God who made us and whom we stand under as our Judge is also the one who reconciles and redeems us. That means we can believe him and trust him instead of being afraid of him and hiding from him. In Jesus, we are free for obedience and faith because we aren't relying on our own obedience and faith, but on his. That takes our minds off ourselves and rests them in Jesus.

JT: In Trinitarian theology, which is centered on Jesus as God's perfect revelation of himself, we see that 1) God is free in the fullness of his divine love and power to be with us and for us and 2) that humanity, secure in God's grace manifest in Jesus, is free to be with God and for God. That is because Jesus is both the fullness of God and the fullness of humanity, exactly as God reveals himself in the Bible.

MM: The Christian life is a response to God's grace. It is letting God's grace work in us, change us, and shine through us. Paul said, "It is not I who live, but Christ lives in me." His grace works in us, and as we are united to Christ, we have a new life, and we walk in newness of life, in a new way — a way that is being transformed by Christ in us.

We are not working our way into salvation, or trying to obey Jesus in order to be a child of God. No, by grace God has already said that we are his children. That is who we are, and that does not change. God says to us, "You belong to me. Now, I invite you to live a new way, a better way, a way that gives meaning and purpose to life. I invite you — I urge you — to join and enjoy the life of love — the way that has worked for all eternity. I invite you to the banquet, to the party, to the never-ending fellowship of the Father, Son, and Holy Spirit."

DR: As we began to look at certain doctrines, every doctrine was viewed through the lens of Jesus Christ. As time has gone by, we have seen that our statement of beliefs has held up very well and we are coming more and more into a fuller and fuller understanding of the implications of this theology of adoption, of God as Trinity and as God fully revealed in the person of Jesus Christ.

JT: The articles and Statement of Beliefs posted on our website express the official doctrines of our fellowship and discuss our theological vision. We are adding high-quality biblical studies, Christian living and theological material to our website continually. It is important that our preaching and teaching reflect sound theology, and that it remain rooted in the good news, the biblical revelation of Jesus Christ as the incarnate Son of God in whom we live and move and have our being.

Christo-centric, or Trinitarian, theology originates as far back as the early Church Fathers with Irenaeus, Athanasius and the Cappadocian Fathers. Some of the greatest theologians in modern history have devoted their life's work to explaining the relationship between God's triune nature and his redemptive work on behalf of humanity. Theologians whose work has been of special help to us in understanding and articulating a sound, Bible-based theology include Karl Barth, Thomas and James Torrance, Michael Jinkins [now president of Louisville Seminary], Ray Anderson, [recently deceased] professor of theology and ministry at Fuller Theological Seminary, Colin Gunton, Robert Capon, Gary Deddo, C. Baxter Kruger, Donald Bloesch, Michael Green and others. We have also found the writings of C.S. Lewis of particular value, although Lewis was not a theologian, per se.

Although it is not likely that you or I would necessarily agree with every single statement in any particular book, we are able to recommend a number of books on theology that we believe provide a sound and faithful reflection of biblical doctrine. These would include such books as:

Invitation to Theology, by Michael Jinkins
The Mediation of Christ, by Thomas Torrance
Dogmatics in Outline, by Karl Barth
Worship, Community and The Triune God of Grace, by James Torrance
The Christian Doctrine of God: One Being Three Persons, by T.F. Torrance
The Trinitarian Faith, by Thomas Torrance
Theology, Death and Dying, by Ray Anderson
Judas and Jesus: Amazing Grace for the Wounded Soul, by Ray Anderson
On the Incarnation, by St. Athanasius
The Christian Foundations Series by Donald Bloesch
The Parables of Judgment, The Parables of Grace, and The Parables of the Kingdom, by Robert Capon
The One, the Three, and the Many, by Colin Gunton
Across All Worlds, by Baxter Kruger
The Great Dance, by Baxter Kruger
The Promise of Trinitarian Theology, by Elmer Colyer
How to Read Thomas F. Torrance, by Elmer Colyer
The Humanity of God, by Karl Barth
Mere Christianity, by C.S. Lewis
The Great Divorce, by C.S. Lewis

This is not a complete list, but it's a good start. Most pastors will find Michael Jinkins' *Invitation to Theology* especially helpful as a one-volume, easy-to-read, basic theology text.

I want to take this and every possible occasion to thank all of you who labor in the gospel for your faithful work and to let you know how much all of us here in Glendora appreciate your service in Christ to his people. May God bless and keep you always in his faithful embrace.

Joseph Tkach, J. Michael Feazell,
Dan Rogers, and Michael Morrison

The Trinity: Just a Doctrine?

Ask ten average Christians in ten average churches to explain the doctrine of the Trinity, and you'll probably get ten different explanations. Most Christians "accept" the Trinity as orthodox Christian doctrine. But they would be at a loss to explain why the doctrine matters, or how it affects their Christian lives.

As Catherine Mowry LaCugna explains in her introduction to *God for Us,* the Trinity is a doctrine that most people "consent to in theory but have little need for in the practice of Christian faith" (Catherine Mowry LaCugna, *God for Us,* page ix). She continues,

> On the one hand, the doctrine of the Trinity is supposed to be the center of faith. On the other hand, as Karl Rahner [one of the most influential theologians of the 20th century] once remarked, one could dispense with the doctrine of the Trinity as false and the major part of religious literature could well remain virtually unchanged. (ibid., 6)

Does it make any difference?

And no wonder. The doctrine is hard to understand, and most discussions about it are boring. For the average Christian, the kind of people who have families to feed, jobs to get to, and lives to live, what difference does an ancient doctrine make? God is God, isn't he? Isn't that enough? If he happens to be Father, Son and Spirit instead of just Father, fine, but that doesn't change anything from our end, does it?

Actually, it does matter. It matters a lot — which is what you'd expect us to say since, why else would we be writing an article about an ancient, boring doctrine?

First, let's dispense with going through the biblical proof that the doctrine is correct. You can find that other articles. Instead, let's spend some time talking about why the doctrine of the Trinity matters, and especially, why it matters to you. Let's start by looking at the common idea that God is a single, solitary being "out there" somewhere, looking down on Earth, watching us, judging us. Bette Midler put it to music in the chorus to her tune "From a Distance" with the lyrics, "And God is watching us, God is watching us, God is watching us from a distance."

This God comes in three main flavors: first, vanilla, the one who just kind of wound up the universe and then stretched out in the heavenly gazebo for a few-billion-year nap. (Who knows, maybe he wakes up once in a while and does something nice, like the kind of God George Burns portrayed in the film *Oh God*.) Second, red hot cinnamon, the one who keeps careful tabs on everything everybody does, and since everybody blows it now and then, he gets madder and madder. His worshippers say he takes joy in watching people who offend him slowly roast but never quite get done. Third is apricot, the one who might or might not like you, depending on many things, none of which are all that clear to anybody. He's the one that Oakland Raiders fans pray to for touchdowns.

Sometimes this God comes in an alternate flavor, water balloon. You might think water balloon isn't a flavor, but it is. It's chewy, and the variety of colors is endless, but it always tastes watery. This God is more of an abstract principle than a supreme being, kind of a "spirit of everything" that you can try to get in touch with if you empty your head of all thoughts and sit still long enough without going to sleep.

A God who wants to share

The God of the Bible is not like that. The God of

the Bible is Father, Son and Holy Spirit—three Persons. (The Father, Son, and Spirit are not "persons" in the same way we humans are. They are not three Gods, but one. Each "Person" of the Godhead is distinct, but not separate from the others.) These three divine Persons share perfect love, joy, unity, peace, and fellowship.

Why is it important to know that? Because, when the Bible talks about us being "in Christ," it means that we get to take part in that divine kind of life. Just like Christ is the beloved of the Father, so we too, because we are "in him," are also the beloved of the Father. That means that you are included in the household of God. You're not an outsider or a stranger. You're not even a respected guest. You're one of the kids, beloved of the Father, with free run of the house, the grounds, and the fridge.

The trouble is, you probably have a hard time believing that. You know what you're really like deep down inside, so you think God doesn't like you. How could he, you think. You don't even like yourself. So, based on your assessment of your "goodness/badness" ratio, you determine that God is more than likely mad at you, and far more than likely mad at all those other types you meet in traffic every day.

But the whole point of God letting us know through the Scriptures that he is Father, Son and Spirit, and not just "God out there somewhere," is so that we'd know he really does love us and we really are on the ins with him. How do we know? Because Jesus, "God with us," "God in the flesh," the one the Father sent not to condemn the world but to save it (John 3:17), is the Father's Son, and that means that the Son of God is now one of us. As one of us, but still God, now God in the flesh, he dragged the whole bunch of us home to the Father right through the front door.

No, we didn't deserve it and no, we didn't earn it. We didn't even ask for it. But he did it anyway, because that's the reason he made us in the first place—so he could share with us the life he has shared eternally with the Father and the Spirit. That's why he tells us that he made us in his image (Genesis 1:26).

Showing us the Father

Salvation isn't about a change of location, floating off to some set of coordinates in the Delta Quadrant called heaven, as if that would solve all our problems. And it's not about a new super government patrolled by angelic cops who never miss an infraction of the divine penal code.

Salvation is about getting adopted into God's family—and learning how to live in it. The Trinity is at the heart of it: The Father (the First Person of the Godhead) loves us so much, in spite of our screw-ups, that he sent the Son (the Second Person of the Godhead) to do everything it took to bring us home (John 1:1, 14), and the Father and the Son sent the Spirit (the Third Person of the Godhead) to live in us, teach us and strengthen us in how to live in God's family so we can enjoy it like we were created to do, instead of being screw-ups forever.

In other words, the God of the Bible is not three separate Gods, where one, the temper-challenged, unpredictable Father, is so furious at humans that he just has to kill somebody in order to calm down, so the sweet, loving Son, seeing Dad about to lose it, steps up and says, "If you've got to kill someone, then kill me, but spare these people." The doctrine of the Trinity is important precisely because it keeps us from seeing God in such a ridiculous way, and yet, that is how a lot of people do see God.

If you want to know what the Father is like, just look at Jesus, because Jesus is the perfect revelation of the Father. Jesus told Philip, "Anyone who has seen me has seen the Father" (John 14:9). He told the crowd, "I and the Father are one." We know how the Father feels about us because we know how Jesus feels about us.

To summarize, God is not some cosmic bean counter "out there" keeping tabs on us in preparation for Judgment Day, nor is he three Gods with very different ideas about how to deal with humanity. The God of the Bible is one God who is three divine Persons, in perfect unity and accord, who love each other in perfect love and dwell in indescribable joy, and who created us for the express purpose of sharing that life with them through our adoption into Christ, who is eternally the beloved of his Father.

That's why the doctrine of the Trinity matters. If we don't understand God the way he reveals himself in the Bible, then we wind up with all kinds of messed up and scary ideas about who God is and what he might be planning to do to us some day.

Reconciliation for everyone

You're still not convinced? Try reading this one again: "…while we were yet sinners Christ died for us" (Romans 5:8). God did not wait for you to get good enough to bring you into his household. You can't get good enough, which is the reason he went after you to bring you home in the first place. When Paul says God saves sinners, he's talking about everybody, since that's what everybody is—a sinner. (If you're worried that God might find out how rotten you are and send a lightning bolt your way, take heart, he's known all along and loves you anyway.)

Paul makes the point stronger in verse 10: "If, when we were God's enemies, we were reconciled to him through the death of his Son, how much more, having been reconciled, shall we be saved through his life!" Did you notice how Paul puts reconciliation with God in the past tense? Jesus died for our sins—past tense. God does not count our sins against us—period. They've already been paid for. Jesus has already put us in good standing with God. All that remains for us now is to turn to God (repent), believe the good news (have faith), and follow Jesus (let the Holy Spirit teach us how to enjoy life in the new creation).

Jesus said, "If anyone would come after me, he must deny himself and take up his cross and follow me." When we think of God in any way other than the way he revealed himself in the Bible—as the Father, Son, and Spirit who created us and redeemed us and have made us to share their joy though union with Jesus Christ—we're going to find these words of Jesus daunting and discouraging.

But when we know God the way he reveals himself, we can say with all assurance of joy, "There is no condemnation for those who are in Christ Jesus…" (Romans 8:1). Paul wrote to the Colossian church, "God was pleased to have all his fullness dwell in him [Jesus], and through him to reconcile to himself all things, whether things on earth or things in heaven, by making peace through his blood, shed on the cross" (Colossians 1:19-20).

All humanity is included in that reconciliation, according to Paul. In the doctrine of the Trinity, God has shown himself to be the God who loves the world and who beckons every person to come to Christ and take part in the joy of life in the household of God. There is no person whom God does not want, whom God does not include, whom God does not love. In Christ, following the Spirit's lead, we are all freed from the chains of sin to come to the Father, whose arms are open wide to receive us, if only we will come.

That's why the doctrine of the Trinity matters. Without it, we might as well join the Canaanites wondering whether Baal will flood out the crops with storms this year or burn them out with lightning. In Jesus Christ, God has taken up our cause as his own. God has, through the atoning work of Jesus, healed us from head to toe, mind and heart, and made us the Father's Son's best friends – no, much more than that – he made us adopted children of the Father, brothers and sisters of our older Brother and full members of the household of God.

With Paul, we can only say, "Thanks be to God for his indescribable gift!"

Key points

- God created all humans in his image, and he wants all people to share in the love shared by the Father, the Son and the Holy Spirit.
- The Son became a human, the man Jesus Christ, to reconcile all humanity to God through his birth, life, death, resurrection and ascension. In Christ, humanity is loved and accepted by the Father.
- Jesus Christ has already paid for our sins, and there is no longer any debt to pay. The Father has already forgiven us, and he eagerly desires that we turn to him.
- We cannot enjoy the blessing of his love if we don't believe he loves us. We cannot enjoy his forgiveness unless we believe he has forgiven us.
- When we respond to the Spirit by turning to God, believing the good news, and picking up our cross and following Jesus, the Spirit leads us into the transformed life of the kingdom of God.

J. Michael Feazell

Perichoresis – What's That?

A discussion with C. Baxter Kruger, PhD, founder of Perichoresis, Inc.

Question: Most of us can't even pronounce perichoresis, much less spell it. What does it mean?

Baxter Kruger: Some years ago a woman walked into my office around Christmastime with a stack of newsletters in her hand. She was crying, and she slammed the newsletters down on my desk and said, "I just feel like a pile of junk!"

I said, "What is wrong?"

She said, "I've been reading these newsletters from these people from all over the world, and they and their children are all doing all these great things for God, and it just hit me what a worthless life I have. For Pete's sake, I'm married and I've got three kids. When I'm not grocery shopping, I'm cooking the groceries, and when I'm not cooking the groceries I'm cleaning up, and when I'm not doing that I'm trying to find clothes for my children and keep this mess of a house presentable. Sometime in there I'm trying to find time for my husband. I don't even have time to read my Bible. What do I have that I can do for God?"

I said, "Wait a minute, hang on here a minute. Yesterday you spent two hours driving around Jackson searching for a coat for your daughter. A winter coat, and not just any winter coat, but one she would like, one that would be large enough to put away for next year but not look like it was bought this year. One that was on sale. You did it, you found it, and she's thrilled."

The woman said, "What's that got to do with this?"

I said, "Where did that concern for your daughter come from? Did you wake up yesterday morning and decide you were going to be a good momma?"

She said she had been thinking about the coat for a week.

I said, "Isn't Jesus the good Shepherd who cares about all his sheep? He put his concern for this sheep (your daughter) in your heart. You are participating in nothing less than Jesus' life and burden. He was tending to his sheep through you. What is greater than that?"

In the light of the fact that Jesus Christ has laid hold of the whole human race, cleansed us in his death, lifted us up in his resurrection and has given us a place in his relationship with his Father and Spirit in his Ascension, we've got to rethink everything we thought we knew about ourselves and others and our ordinary human life.

There is nothing ordinary about us and the life we live. Caring for others, from orphans to our friends and the poor, our love for our husbands and wives and children, our passion for music and beauty, for coaching, gardening and fishing; these things do not have their origin in us. They are not something that we invented. It is all coming from the Father, Son and Spirit. When this dreadful secular/sacred divide is exploded, we can see and honor life as it truly is—the gift of participating in the life and relationship of the Father, Son and Spirit.

Question: So we're talking about God meeting us in our day-to-day lives?

BK: Exactly. Through the work of Jesus, we have been adopted into the Trinitarian life. The concept of perichoresis helps us understand what our adoption means for us. We could define perichoresis as "mutual indwelling without loss of personal identity." In other words, we exist in union with the Triune God, but we do not lose our distinct personhood in the process. We matter. We are real to the Triune God.

Only the Trinity could have union without loss of personal distinction. If you have union without distinction, you tumble into pantheism, and we would be united to God in such a way as to be completely absorbed into him. There would no longer be a distinct "us" to feel and taste and experience the Trinitarian life. If you have distinction without union, you end up with deism, where God is up there watching us from a distance, and we never see our humanity as included in the Trinitarian life. Motherhood and fatherhood, work and play and music then appear to be merely secular, non-divine aspects of our human experience. Deism leaves us with a Christ-less humanity, and forces us to search beyond our humanity for connection with God.

In Trinitarian theology we say "no" to both pantheism and deism. We have union but no loss of personal distinction, which means that we matter and that our humanity, our motherhood and fatherhood, our work and play and music form the arena for our participation in the Trinitarian life of God. The Triune God meets us not in the sky or in our self-generated religions, but in our "ordinary" human existence.

Question: So the gospel is about God knowing us and us knowing God?

BK: Exactly. Let me give you a quick story. I like stories better than long and convoluted theological explanations. Many years ago when my son was six (he's 18 now), I was sitting on the couch in the den sorting through junk mail on a Saturday afternoon. He and his buddy came in and they were decked out in their camouflage, face paint, plastic guns and knives, the whole nine yards. My son peers around the corner of the door and looks at me, and the next thing I know, he comes flying through the air and jumps on me. We start wrestling and horsing around and we end up on the floor. Then his buddy flies into us and all three of us are just like a wad of laughter.

Right in the middle of that event the Lord spoke to me and said to pay attention. I'm thinking, it's Saturday afternoon, your son comes in and you're horsing around on the floor, it happens every day all over the world, so what's the big deal? Then it started to dawn on me that I didn't know who this other kid was. I had never met him. He had never met me. So I re-wound the story and thought about what would have happened if this little boy would have walked into my den alone. Remember, he didn't know me and I didn't know him, and he didn't know my name and I didn't know his name. So he looks over and sees me, a complete stranger, sitting on the couch. Would he fly through the air and engage me in play? Would we end up in a pile of laughter on the floor? Of course not. That is the last thing that would have happened.

Within himself, that little boy had no freedom to have a relationship with me. We were strangers. He had no right to that kind of familiarity and fellowship. But my son knows me. My son knows that I love him and that I accept him and that he's the apple of my eye. So in the knowledge of my love and affection, he did the most natural thing in the world. He dove into my lap. The miracle that happened was that my son's knowledge of my acceptance and delight, and my son's freedom for fellowship with me, rubbed off onto that other little boy. He got to experience it. That other little boy got to taste and feel and know my son's relationship with me. He participated in my son's life and communion with me.

Then it dawned on me that that's what perichoresis and our adoption in Christ mean. Jesus is the one who knows the Father. He knows the Father's love and acceptance. He sees the Father's face. Jesus has freedom for fellowship with his Father, and Jesus shares his heart with us. He puts his own freedom for relationship with his Father in us through the Spirit, and like that little boy we get to taste and feel and experience the relationship Jesus has with his Father. He shares it all with us. He unites himself with us, and we get to experience his divine life with him. He shares with us his own knowledge of his Father's heart, his own knowledge of the Father's acceptance, his own assurance of his Father's love, his own freedom in knowing the Father's passionate heart.

He reaches into his own soul, as it were, and pulls out his own emotions, and then puts them inside of the whole human race. We're all included in the Son's relationship with the Father in the fellowship of the Holy Spirit.

Question: Then we never have to worry about whether God accepts us and loves us?

BK: Never. What does the understanding that we are accepted into the mutual indwelling and communion with God remove from our hearts? Fear and hiding. Because of Jesus' knowledge of the Father's acceptance, which he shares with us, we now are free to let go of our racial and personal prejudices, and to love and accept one another, which leads to the freedom to know and be known, which leads to fellowship and mutual indwelling.

This is what the kingdom of the Triune God is all about. The kingdom is simply the life and love, the communion, the fellowship, the camaraderie and joy of the Father, Son and Spirit, being shared with us and coming to full and abiding and personal expression in us, in our relationships with one another and in our relationships with the whole creation, so that the whole earth is full of the Son's knowledge of his Father in the Spirit.

Is the Doctrine of the Trinity in the Bible?

Some people who reject the Trinity doctrine claim that the word "Trinity" is not found in Scripture. Of course, there is no verse that says "God is three Persons" or "God is a Trinity." This is evident and true, but it proves nothing. There are many words and phrases that Christians use but are nevertheless not found in the Bible. For example, the word "Bible" is not found in the Bible.

Opponents of the Trinity doctrine claim that a Trinitarian view of God's nature and being can't be proven from the Bible. Since the books of the Bible are not written as theological tracts, this may seem on the surface to be true. There is no statement in Scripture that says, "God is three Persons in one being, and here is the proof..."

However, the New Testament does bring God (Father), the Son (Jesus Christ) and the Holy Spirit together in such a way as to strongly imply the Trinitarian nature of God. Three Scriptures are quoted below as a summary of the various other biblical passages that bring together the three Persons of the Godhead. One Scripture is from the Gospels, another is from the apostle Paul and a third is from Peter. The words in each passage referring to each of the three Persons are italicized to emphasize their Trinitarian implication:

> All authority in heaven and on earth has been given to me. Therefore go and make disciples of all nations, baptizing them in the name [singular] *of the Father and of the Son and of the Holy Spirit* (Matthew 28:19).
>
> May the grace of *the Lord Jesus Christ,* and the love of *God,* and the fellowship of *the Holy Spirit* be with you all (2 Corinthians 13:14).
>
> To God's elect…who have been chosen according to the foreknowledge of *God the Father,* through the sanctifying work of *the Spirit,* for obedience to *Jesus Christ* and sprinkling by his blood (1 Peter 1:1-2).

These three passages, one on the lips of Jesus, and the other two from leading apostles, each bringing together the three Persons of the Godhead in an unmistakable way. But these are only a sampling of other similar passages. See also Romans 14:17-18; 15:16; 1 Corinthians 2:2-5; 6:11; 12:4-6; 2 Corinthians 1:21-22; Galatians 4:6; Ephesians 2:18-22; 3:14-19; Ephesians 4:4-6; Colossians 1:6-8; 1Thessalonians 1:3-5; 2 Thessalonians 2:13-14; and Titus 3:4-6. Read each of these passages and note how God (Father), Son (Jesus Christ) and the

Holy Spirit are brought together as instruments of our salvation.

Such passages show that the New Testament faith is implicitly Trinitarian. None of these passages say directly that "God is a Trinity…" or "This is the Trinitarian doctrine…," but they don't need to. The books of the New Testament are not formal, point-by-point treatises of doctrine. Nonetheless, these and other Scriptures speak easily and without any self-consciousness of God (Father), Son (Jesus) and Holy Spirit working together as one. The writers show no feeling of strangeness in joining these divine Persons together as a unity in their salvific work. Systematic theologian Alister E. McGrath makes this point in his book *Christian Theology:*

> The foundations of the doctrine of the Trinity are to be found in the pervasive pattern of divine activity to which the New Testament bears witness.… There is the closest of connections between the Father, Son, and Spirit in the New Testament writings. Time after time, New Testament passages link together these three elements as part of a greater whole. The totality of God's saving presence and power can only, it would seem, be expressed by involving all three elements. (page 248)

Such New Testament Scriptures answer the charge that the Trinity doctrine was developed only after several centuries and that it reflects "pagan" ideas, and not biblical ones. If we look at Scripture with an open mind regarding what it says about the being we call God, it's clear that he is shown to be Triune in nature. The Bible reveals that the Father is God, Jesus the Son is God, and the Holy Spirit is God, and yet the Bible also insists that this is only one God. These biblical teachings led the early church to formulate the doctrine of the Trinity.

We can confidently say that the Trinity, as a truth regarding God's essential being, has always been a reality. It was not completely clear in the Old Testament. But the Incarnation of the Son of God and the coming of the Holy Spirit revealed that God was Triune. This revelation was made in concrete fact, in that the Son and the Holy Spirit broke into our world at definite points in history. The Triune revelation of God in historical time was later described in the word of God we call the New Testament.

James R. White, a Christian apologist, says in his book *The Forgotten Trinity:* "The Trinity is a doctrine not revealed merely in words but instead in the very action of the Triune God in redemption itself! We know who God is by what He has done in bringing us to himself!" (page 167).

Paul Kroll

Predestination: Does God Choose Your Fate?

"I am wondering about predestination. Are some people predestined to be saved and the rest predestined not to be saved?"

The doctrine of predestination is sometimes referred to as "election," in the sense that God chooses people for his own purposes. For example, Abraham was chosen, or elected, by God, as were his son and grandson, Isaac and Jacob. Other chosen ones included Moses, Joshua, David, the prophets, and the Israelites were the "chosen people."

The apostle Paul wrote about predestination, or election, in several passages. In Romans 8:28-30 and Ephesians 1:3-6, he emphasized that election is "in Christ," and that it is a matter of God's own choice for God's own purposes. In Romans 9-11, Paul takes the topic of election further by exploring Israel's rejection of her Messiah. In the course of his argument in Romans 9-11, Paul asks the question,

> What if God, desiring to show his wrath and to make known his power, has endured with much patience the objects of wrath that are made for destruction; and what if he has done so in order to make known the riches of his glory for the objects of mercy, which he has prepared beforehand for glory — including us whom he has called, not from the Jews only but also from the Gentiles? (Romans 9:22-24)

This passage has been much debated over the centuries. Taken out of context, it might sound as though some people are predestined to be saved and the rest are predestined for destruction. But that is not what the passage says, nor is it the argument Paul is making. Paul argues in Romans 9 and 10 that Israel has failed to be found righteous before God because they sought after righteousness their own way instead of putting their trust in Christ (9:31-32; 10:3). This does not mean that God's covenant promises have failed, however, because God is free to have mercy on whomever he chooses (9:15) and is using Israel's unfaithfulness to draw the Gentiles to himself though faith (9:16, 22-26, 30; 10:11-13).

Next, Paul asks, "Have they stumbled so as to fall? By no means! But through their stumbling salvation has come to the Gentiles, so as to make Israel jealous. Now if their stumbling means riches for the world, and if their defeat means riches for Gentiles, how much more will their full inclusion mean!" (11:11-12). Yes, Paul argues, Israel has rejected Christ and therefore, except for a believing remnant, falls under the covenant judgments.

But that is not the end of the story, even for those who rejected Christ. Paul declares in verse 23, "And even those of Israel, if they do not persist in unbelief, will be grafted in, for God has the power to graft them in again." These people rejected Christ, yet God does not abandon them. The God who is forever faithful to his covenant love is so powerful that he can and does provide opportunity for unbelievers to become believers, even dead unbelievers (many of the unbelieving Israelites were dead, but God's work of mercy involves all of them, see 11:32). We aren't told how or when God does it, only that it is so.

Paul continues:

> So that you may not claim to be wiser than you are, brothers and sisters, I want you to understand this mystery: a hardening has

come upon part of Israel, until the full number of the Gentiles has come in. And so all Israel will be saved; as it is written, "Out of Zion will come the Deliverer; he will banish ungodliness from Jacob. And this is my covenant with them, when I take away their sins." (verses 25-27)

God works in his own ways and in his own times, but his work is aimed toward one final outcome, his desire for all people to be saved:

> God has imprisoned all in disobedience so that he may be merciful to all. O the depth of the riches and wisdom and knowledge of God! How unsearchable are his judgments and how inscrutable are his ways! (verses 32-33)

Even if God were to predestine some to destruction and some to salvation, it would be his right; pots don't tell the potter how to make them. But the good news, the gospel truth, is that even though God has every right to destroy us all, he instead takes our sins on himself in Christ and forgives us and saves us. The "objects of God's wrath" who were "prepared for destruction" in Romans 9:22 are unbelieving Israel, the same unbelieving Israel who will be "grafted back in" if they don't persist in unbelief (11:23). In other words, Romans 9:22 is not a proof that some people are predestined by God for damnation. We need to read the context to see Paul's full teaching on it.

Common ideas

Probably the best-known view on predestination is the one called "Calvinism." This view of predestination is named after the Reformation theologian, John Calvin. It was constructed in this form by some of his followers at the Synod of Dort in 1618, and is found in most Reformed churches, which includes many Presbyterians, Congregationalists and Dutch and German Reformed Churches. (However, many of the members of these churches are unaware of the doctrines that were so crucial in the formation of these denominations.)

Though there are variations, the Calvinist view is usually defined using the acronym TULIP. It looks like this:

> Total depravity
> Unconditional election
> Limited atonement
> Irresistible grace
> Perseverance or preservation of the saints

Because TULIP has five points, its adherents are often called "five-point Calvinists." Let's look at each point of the TULIP.

"Total depravity" refers to the sinful condition of human beings. It means that there is no part of the human condition that has not been touched and tainted by sin. Therefore, all humans are unfit for the kingdom of God apart from Christ.

"Unconditional election" means that through his free sovereignty God chose some people before the world was made to be saved by grace without any conditions being required or met for that choice.

"Limited atonement" means that Jesus' sacrifice is not effective for all humans. It is effective only for those who were predestined to be saved, not for those who are predestined to be damned.

"Irresistible grace" means that the grace God gives to the elect cannot be resisted. God's grace has saved them no matter how hard they might resist it. The idea is that if a human could ultimately refuse God's grace, then it would mean that God's will could be thwarted by humans, which would undermine the Calvinist view of God's sovereignty.

"Perseverance of the saints" means that those predestined to be saved will not only become believers, but they will remain under the grace of God and cannot ever permanently fall away, no matter what they do.

Practical terms

Let's look at how TULIP plays out in practical terms: First, it is based on a certain concept of the sovereignty, or ruling power, of God. In this concept, nothing can ever happen that God did not, before all time and creation, decide and design to happen. God knew all along who would be saved and who would be damned because he is the one who decided it. This is sometimes called "double predestination."

However, some theologians who teach predestination of the saved do not take a stance on predestination of the damned. They explain it along these lines: Since all humans are sinners and lost without God's grace, those who are not elected to be saved simply receive the just results of their rebellion. It is not that God specifically predestined, or elected, them to be damned, it is just that since God didn't elect them to receive grace and be saved, they simply wind up getting what they deserve. This view is sometimes called "single predestination." Whether single or double, it boils down to this: God made lots of people; they are all sinners and can do nothing about that themselves; God extends grace and mercy to a select few and all the others are condemned.

In practical terms, it works like this: If you're saved, you're saved, but if you're damned, you're damned, and there is nothing you can do about it either way. Further, there is no way of knowing for sure whether you are saved or damned. However, you can have some evidence that you might be saved—good works. So, it is a good idea to do lots of good works. The more you do, the more likely you might be saved. If you don't have any good works, it is good evidence that you are probably damned (but even that is not certain). So what this doctrine gives with one hand (assurance of salvation for the elect), it takes away with the other (the only evidence you have that you are saved is your changed life in terms of good works, and you can't even be sure that proves anything).

This doctrine is bad news for most of humanity (the damned, the non-elect), and it is hard to call it good news even for the elect (they never know for certain in this life whether they are elect or damned). The real gospel, on the other hand, is good news.

Aristotelian influence

The TULIP viewpoint on predestination is based on a Ptolemaic/Aristotelian concept of the way in which God is sovereign. That is, it rests on a marriage of Christianity with the earth-centered concept of the cosmos formulated by Ptolemy, a Greek astronomer, and on a concept of God that was formulated by the Greek philosopher Aristotle. It does not rest on the concept of God we can read about in the Hebrew Bible. To put it another way, it is rooted in Greek philosophy and not in God's revelation of himself in the Bible.[1]

Aristotle taught that God is "the unmoved mover." God is not only the original source or fount of all things, he is static, unmoved and unmovable, because, Aristotle reasoned, in order to be the original source and fount of all things, God cannot be capable of being acted upon, or moved by anything else. Further, God cannot change, since any change on his part would render him not God, because, after all, God causes change, not is changed. (In Aristotle's view, God was an impersonal force.)

With this "unmoved mover" idea of God lying behind our reasoning, how are we to understand the way in which the Christian God is sovereign, that is, the way in which God controls the universe? The TULIP idea is that if God is sovereign, he must be in complete control. If something happened that was not ultimately caused by God, then God would not be in complete control. Since God is in complete control, then everything must ultimately be caused by God.

Further, God is not only omnipotent, or all-powerful (sovereign), he is also omniscient – all-knowing. Nothing can ever happen that God has not always known would happen.

What do we have so far? First, since God is sovereign, that is, completely in control of everything, nothing happens that God is not ultimately the cause of. Second, since God knows everything that is going to happen, nothing can ever happen that 1) God doesn't already know about, and 2) that God hasn't caused to happen.

This means that God is "immutable" – he cannot change. In this view, if God could change, it would mean he was not already perfect to begin with.

Dilemmas

TULIP presents a picture of a God who is omnipotent, omniscient and immutable. It appears to have safeguarded God's sovereignty with an airtight formulation of what it means for God to be completely in charge of the universe. But several dilemmas appear. First, if the creation is not eternal, then God has not always been a creator – he had to become a creator. And if God the Word became a human being, part of the creation, then there was a change within God.

A third dilemma is that there is evil in the world. How did that happen? In this world in which God 1) is the cause of everything that happens, 2) knows everything that will happen from the beginning because he is the cause of it, and 3) cannot change because any change would mean he is not perfect, how did sin get in?

Did God want evil in his universe? If he did, then he would be the ultimate cause of the evil. On the other hand, if God did not want evil in his universe, but it is there anyway, then God must not be in complete control. And the dilemma gets bigger. If nothing happens that God has not caused to happen (including catastrophes of nature, birth defects and acts of terror), then somehow God is also the cause of human sin. Even more disturbing, if people are sinners because God made them that way, then on what basis can we say that God is righteous when he condemns them for doing what he caused them to do? The idea of free will among humans becomes a matter of special definitions.

TULIP plays out in some startlingly non-biblical ways. The Bible says God hates sin, yet this construct says he made some folks damned sinners on purpose. The Bible says "for God so loved the world" (John 3:16) and that God wants "all to come to repentance" (2 Peter 3:9) and Christ says "I will draw all people to myself" (John 12:32), yet the TULIP construct suggests a God who "loves" some (most, as it turns out) by damning them before they ever drew breath. This does not fit our normal definitions of "love."

The Bible, in contrast, presents God as interacting with humans in meaningful ways and even records some conversations with people in which God is said to learn something or change his mind. The concept of prayer suggests that God is sometimes willing to change what he does based on what we ask.

Where does five-point Calvinism leave us? It leaves most of us predestined human wretches in hell, where God supposedly created us to go, and, according to this construct, he enjoys our eternal torment as a tribute to his supreme justice and righteousness.

The Bible draws the picture rather differently, thank God. It might be a good idea for us to draw our picture from the Bible, instead of reading the Bible with our assumptions about God being colored by philosophies alien to the biblical world. Let's see what we can learn about how the Bible unpacks God's sovereignty.

Sovereign

Three questions arise. Can God be sovereign and perfect, and also be able to change? Can God be in control of the universe, and also give humans freedom? Can God create a universe in which he is an active partner with humanity, without determining every choice humans must make?

The answer to all three questions, from a biblical perspective, is Yes, God can.

God is God; he can do what he, of his own free will, decides to do in accord with who he is. The Holy Spirit inspired biblical writers to record occasions in which God changed. The Bible shows us that God created a world for himself in which he can and does abide, work, enjoy himself and rest. The universe depends on God for every moment of its existence, the Bible tells us, yet God takes pleasure in what he has made and is actively involved in its life and journey.

Consider the biblical picture of God. He loves a cool breeze (Genesis 3:8). He walks and talks with people (Exodus 33:11). He finds out things about them (Genesis 22:12). He makes friends (James 2:23) and gets betrayed by them (2 Samuel 12:7-9). This God, the God of the Bible, is sovereign, yet not so "otherly" that he cannot enjoy the world he made. When he finished making it, he proceeded to rest in it. He even calls on us to join him in his rest. He is a God who freely makes things and then sets out to use and enjoy what he has made.

Is such a God, who doesn't seem to mind "getting his hands dirty," truly in control? It seems to me, and you may disagree, that such a God is in far more control, and has far more power than the sort of God described by the TULIP. The "God of the TULIP" has to create what amounts to a grand DVD recording of entirely predetermined outcomes and characters who can't wrestle with him, can't talk back to him, challenge him, or, conversely, can't truly love him, except as he has written it all into the script. He is in control, but of what? Of what amounts to an enormous cosmic screenplay. He has set up the universe and is now letting it play itself out in the way that he determined, and it goes like clockwork.

But the God of the Bible—who in his divine freedom has created a universe that is free, with truly free people—exercises his awesome creativity and genius continually, because, in spite of sinning and rebellious humans, he brings about his purpose for them. He allows choices because he is able to handle all the possible outcomes.

God is neither threatened by, nor overcome by, human free will and the time and chance he built into his universe. Rather, he works within them to bring about a human redemption that is purified in the midst of authentic relationships. He is constantly bringing good out of evil and light out of darkness through his indescribable grace freely demonstrated most supremely in Jesus Christ.

The God of the Bible does not force anyone to trust him. He doesn't remove anyone's freedom to refuse him. Yet, he is infinitely creative in his means of knocking on the doors of our human castles, inviting, even urging, us to invite him in. This is the God who became one of us in Jesus Christ. This is the God who is united with us and in communion with us through Christ. This is the God who loves us and who calls on us to love one another as he loves us.

Important endnote

[1] Please do not take anything I have written here to mean that I think people who hold the TULIP position are in any way "lesser" Christians than those who don't. That would be a great mistake. Christians are people who put their faith in Jesus Christ, pure and simple. We are not measured by our theologies, but by God's grace freely given to us in Jesus Christ. Our faith is in him, not in theology books. Theology is important, but it is not the root of our salvation. Jesus is.

Devoted and faithful Christian theologians have struggled throughout the centuries to find adequate words and concepts to inform our faith about how God exercises his sovereignty in the world. They do not always agree. Even so, the Christian struggle to understand and talk about God theologically is a worthy pursuit. It reflects our desire as Christians to use the reasoning power God has given us to seek greater understanding of our biblically grounded and personally experienced faith.

Though we may disagree with one another on certain points (none of us has perfect understanding), as believers we are all God's children, washed in the blood of our Savior, and he calls on us to love one another. In Christ, we can respect one another's views, hear the issues that we each raise, in humility form our own conclusions, and still love one another as fellow partakers of the mercies of God.

Predestination:
Does God Choose Your Fate?
continued

Divine freedom

God is free to be who he is. "I Am Who I Am," or "I Will Be Who I Will Be," is who this God says he is (Exodus 3:14). He is free to create the universe and humanity and interact with them in whatever way pleases him, and what pleases him is to be faithful to and with his creations.

God is *able* to create a windup, predetermined universe, but that does not mean that he had to. The Ptolemaic-Aristotelian concept of God, reflected in TULIP, demands that God had to. It demands that a proper, logical, totally sovereign God could have done things no other way. That concept, in its effort to safeguard God's sovereignty, winds up tying God's hands by limiting him to one particular and nonbiblical way of being sovereign with his creation.

On the other hand, if we are to take the biblical record of God's self-disclosure seriously, we must conclude that God is free both to create and to interact with his creation in any way he pleases, because he is free to be and do as he pleases in accord with who he is (and he is "I Am Who I Am").

Our freedom to be who we are in Christ is not a freedom that we have simply by virtue of existing. It is a freedom given to us by God, entrusted to us, and dependent on God's own freedom to give it to us. We are free to accept or reject God's grace only because God holds us in the palm of his hand, not because we have personal sovereignty in and of ourselves. People can reject God, but in rejecting God they are also rejecting themselves, because their freedom is upheld only by the God they are rejecting.

Immutable and impassible

In our efforts to discuss and describe God, we have no choice but to use analogies and comparisons to created things we know about. But we must keep in mind that in all our analogies and comparisons, God is not even on the same plane as any of the created things (objects, roles or passions) we might use in describing him. Even the pronoun "he" is only an analogy; we should not get the idea that God is actually male or female. (The term "Father" refers to the relationship between the Father and the Son [John 1:14, 18, 34] and the Father and creation [Ephesians 3:14-15]; the Father is infinitely greater than any human concept of "father.")

God—Father, Son and Spirit—is the source and cause of all being and existence. He brings everything into being without anything bringing him into being. He is pure Being, that "Is-ness" from which all other being flows. All things depend on him for their existence, and he depends on nothing for his existence.

When we say God is "immutable" or "unchangeable," we do not mean that God cannot change as he, in his eternal, uncreated freedom, chooses to change. We mean that God cannot be changed by anything outside himself, as though he were a created being.

But what about Malachi 3:6: "For I the Lord do not change"? This and other passages about God's unchangeableness are declarations of God's faithfulness to his covenant promise. ("Therefore you, O children of Jacob, have not perished," he continues.) Within that unchanging faithfulness to his beloved people, there are many ups and downs, twists in the tale, disappointments and surprises. God declares that despite all your trials of faith and doubt, he will not change his mind about loving you and saving you. God's covenant faithfulness is the theme throughout the Bible. God made promises to Abraham, and those promises included the salvation of the whole world through the seed of Abraham (Galatians 3:16, 29). The Bible is the record of God's faithfulness to those promises.

When we say that God is "impassible" (incapable of feeling), we do not mean that God cannot feel. We mean, rather, that God cannot be hurt against his will by anything outside himself. In his divine freedom, God can, and does, of himself, change and feel. God cannot be acted on against his will, but in his divine freedom, he acts. When God created the universe, he freely in grace and love became something new—Creator—and he did so in the freedom of his grace and love. Likewise, when the Son became flesh in the Incarnation, God became something new—human like us and for our sakes. God did not have to create, nor did he have to become flesh, but he did so in his divine freedom out of the abundance of his grace and love.

In control

In his eternal serenity and tranquility, God is not depressed, confused, worried, or bowled over by human sin, tragedy and disaster. He knows his power and purpose and what he is bringing out of it all. As Michael Jinkins put it,

> God the Creator is intimately, passionately involved in creation continuously from beginning to end and at every nanosecond in between…. All things spring continuously from the God who loves them into existence, loves them redemptively throughout their existence and loves them toward God's final and full purpose. (*Invitation to Theology*, InterVarsity Press, 2001, p. 90)

The universe is not "on its own." "Cause and effect" is not all there is. The universe functions according to general rules laid out by its Creator, but it is not detached from its Creator's free and gracious will and creatively sustaining presence. God made things in such a way that they bump and collide their way through what we might call a "randomly ordered" existence. We are subject to "time and chance," yet we believe, as Christians, that our loving God uses these very real, and often painful happenstances of "time and chance" to mysteriously and graciously bring us out of darkness into his marvelous light.

Always faithful

The "God" of Plato and Aristotle could not change, because for "God" to change would mean that "God" was not already perfect. So "God" was called the "unmoved mover." But the God of the Bible has no problem with changing whenever he decides to, and he remains perfect and perfectly God all the while. He haggled with Abraham over the fate of Sodom, agreeing to change his plan under certain conditions (Genesis 18:16-33).

God changed his mind about saving the Israelites when they started worshiping the calf at Mount Sinai, then allowed Moses to talk him out of killing them all and starting the whole plan over with Moses' children (Exodus 32:7-14). He accommodated himself to Israel's desire for a king even though they were making a mistake, and he would still ultimately deliver them from their rebellion (1 Samuel 8; Hosea 11:9; 14:4). He changed his plan regarding wicked King Ahab's punishment (1 Kings 21:27-29).

God is sovereign, but God, who is Father, Son and Spirit, is sovereign the way he chooses to be, not the way the greatest human thinkers conclude the ultimate cause of all things must logically be. God will be who God will be, and he has revealed himself to be, for us and with us, the Father of Jesus Christ, the Sender of the Holy Spirit, the Forgiver of sins, the Lover of souls, our Savior, our Deliverer, our Comforter, our Advocate, our

Helper, our Strengthener, our Righteousness, our Peace, our Hope, our Life, our Light, our Friend and many other good and wonderful things.

God is smarter than we are, and our ideas about God aren't always correct. God doesn't behave the way we would expect. We cannot package him to make him more appealing. We cannot mold him into our imagined idea of what a proper and respectable, board-certified God ought to be like. God is not an unmoved mover who created a windup world of preprogrammed automatons. Nor is God "way out there," merely looking down and watching and judging us as some detached Super-being.

He is the immanent one, that is, God with us. He is here, has been all along, and always will be, simply because he wants to be. Because he loves us. Because he made us real, to be real with him and in him and through him. Far from some platonic impersonal "other," this God is always active and involved in his creation. He gets his hands dirty. He takes this reeking and sin-infested hovel we have turned the world into, and by the power of the bloody and unjust crucifixion of his own incarnate self, he cleans, redeems, transforms and ushers us and it into the joy of his eternal kingdom.

In Christ Jesus, God brings humanity into union and communion with the essence of who he is. We are one with him by his action on our behalf, not for our own sakes, but for the sake of Christ, who became for us the perfect human. If we are in him, we are in union with God, not as Gods, but as humans in union with the God/man, Jesus, who is human and divine for our sakes. Our continual communion, or fellowship, with him is a continual confirmation of and participation in that grand truth—we are God's children in Christ.

Free in God's faithfulness

We must not get the idea that God has to create, or that creation necessarily (that is, automatically, like a fire must necessarily produce heat) flows from him. God creates entirely in his divine freedom, not because he is a creation machine. Nor must we get the idea that God creates because he is lonely, or because there was something "missing" in God that compelled him to create. God is not lonely. The triune God is complete in every way, including in love, joy and perfection, without the creation.

God does not need the creation. God does not depend on the creation. The creation does not add anything to God that God "lacked." The creation happened because God freely made it happen in the abundance of his joy and love, not because he had to or needed to, but simply because he wanted to.

So when we talk about God's covenant faithfulness, we can begin to see how certain our trust in God can be. God brought the world into being for the sheer joy of it, redeemed humanity because he loved the people he made, and holds all things, all existence, including yours and mine, in the palm of his hand.

We can trust him because we know we exist only because he says so. If he has gone to all the trouble, while we were still his enemies, to redeem us through the cross (the hard part), how much more certain can we be that he will see our salvation through to the end (the easy part) now that we are his friends (Romans 5:8-11)?

God creates and God redeems because he wants to, not because we asked him to, or got him to, or talked him into it, or convinced him to, or behaved really well. He did it because he is good, because he is love, because he is who he is. Your behavior is not going to change who God is, nor who God is toward you. If it could, he would not be God, because God cannot be changed by any incantations or spells or nice or naughty deeds you can throw at him.

You cannot manipulate God or coerce him. You can only trust him and receive the good things he has given you, or not trust him and refuse the good things he has given you. You have that freedom, a created freedom that reflects and derives from God's own uncreated divine freedom. It is freedom to trust him, to commune with him, to love him. You can turn it into freedom to reject him if you want, but you don't have to.

Assurance of salvation

Since the blood of Christ covers all sin, and he atoned for the whole world (1 John 2:1-2), then predestination, or election, in the sense of being chosen by God to be his people, applies to everyone through Christ (Ephesians 1:9-10). It is received and enjoyed only by those who accept it in faith, but it applies to everyone.

Some people are called to faith in Christ and experience his redemption before others do (verse 12). Those called to faith early are a living testament to the grace God has poured out on the world, a grace that will come fully into view at the appearing of Christ (Titus 2:11-14).

It is all done according to the foreknowledge of the God of grace who has been working out in Christ his gracious plan for humanity from the beginning (Matthew 25:34). When it comes to assurance of salvation, we trust in God who justifies the ungodly, which we are. We are saved by grace alone, not by our works, so our assurance rests in the sure word of the God of free grace.

Here is what, by the testimony of Jesus Christ, we know to be certain: God loves us, and we do not have to fear that we won't be saved. He saves us in spite of our sins because he is faithful and full of grace. The only people who will not enjoy his salvation are those who do not want it.

Someone may say that in this treatment of predestination we have oversimplified a complex theological matter, and no doubt we have. But this we know: God calls on us to trust him. If you and I are to trust him, we have to know that our relationship with him matters. We have to know that we are more than cogs in a deterministic machine of human pain, sorrow and tragedy. We have to know that God loves us, that he loves us so much that he sent his own Son to bail us out of a lifetime of horrible decisions and sin by taking all of it on himself in our place, even though we didn't deserve such mercy.

Without a doubt, we can trust a God like that. We can throw in our lot with him and follow him to the ends of the earth, because we owe him our lives now and forever.

J. Michael Feazell

Jesus — The Complete Salvation Package

Near the end of his Gospel, the apostle John made these intriguing comments:

> Jesus performed many other signs in the presence of his disciples, which are not recorded in this book.... If every one of them were written down, I suppose that even the whole world would not have room for the books that would be written. (John 20:30; 21:25)

Given these comments, and noting differences among the four Gospels, we conclude that these accounts were not written to be exhaustive records of Jesus' life. John says his purpose in writing was that "you may believe that Jesus is the Messiah, the Son of God, and that by believing you may have life in his name" (John 20:31). The focus of the Gospels is to tell the good news about Jesus and the salvation that is ours in him.

Though in verse 31 John attributes salvation (life) to the name of Jesus, it's common for Christians to speak of being saved by Jesus' death. Though this short-hand statement is correct, relating salvation exclusively to Jesus' death can stunt our understanding of the fullness of who Jesus is and all he has done to save us. The events of Holy Week remind us that Jesus' death, though vital, is part of a larger story that includes our Lord's incarnation, death, resurrection and ascension. All these are intrinsic, inseparable milestones of Jesus' one redemptive work — the work that gives us life in his name. Let's look to Jesus — the complete salvation package.

Incarnation

Jesus' birth was not the ordinary birth of an ordinary person. Unique in every way, it was the beginning of the Incarnation of God himself. In Jesus' birth, God came among us as a human in the way all humans since Adam have been born. Remaining what he was, the eternal Son of God took on a whole human life, from beginning to end — birth to death. In his one Person, Jesus is both fully divine and fully human. In this stunning statement we find an eternity's worth of significance that merits an eternity of appreciation.

Through the Incarnation, the eternal Son of God stepped out of eternity and into his creation of space and time to become a man of flesh and blood: "The Word became flesh and made his dwelling among us. We have seen his glory, the glory of the one and only Son, who came from the Father, full of grace and truth" (John 1:14). Jesus was indeed a genuine full-fledged man, but at the same time he was fully God — one in being with the Father and Spirit. The birth of Jesus fulfills many prophecies and is the promise of our salvation.

The Incarnation did not end with Jesus' birth — it continued throughout his earthly life, and continues today in his glorified human life. The Son of God incarnate (in the flesh), remains one in being with the Father and Spirit — the fullness of the whole God is present and active in Jesus — making the human life of Jesus uniquely significant. As Romans 8:3-4 says,

> What the law was powerless to do because it was weakened by the flesh, God did by sending his own Son in the likeness of sinful flesh to be a sin offering. And so he condemned sin in the flesh, in order that the righteous requirement of the law might be fully met in us, who do not live according to the flesh but according to the Spirit.

Paul further explains that we are "saved through his life" (Romans 5:10). The life and work of Jesus are inseparable — they are all part of the Incarnation. The God-man Jesus is the perfect high priest and mediator between God and humanity because he partook of human nature and reclaimed humanity by living a sinless life. His sinless life helps us understand how he can maintain a relationship with both God and other humans. While we typically celebrate his birth at Christmas, the events in Jesus' whole life are always part of our worship. His life reveals the relational nature of our salvation. Jesus brought together, in his own person, God and humanity in perfect relationship.

Death

For some, the short-hand declaration, we are saved by Jesus' death, carries with it the unfortunate misconception that Jesus' death was a sacrifice that conditioned God into being gracious. I pray that we all see the fallacy of this notion.

T.F. Torrance writes that with a proper understanding of the Old Testament sacrifices, we will see Jesus' death not as a pagan offering for the sake of forgiveness, but as a powerful witness to the will of a merciful God (*Atonement: The Person and Work of Christ,* pages 38-39). Pagan systems of sacrifice were based on retribution, but Israel's was based on reconciliation. Under Israel's system, rather than sacrifices and offerings being given to earn forgiveness, God provided them to cover for and remove the people's sin so that they would be reconciled to God.

Israel's sacrificial system was designed to make manifest and to witness to God's love and mercy, pointing to the purpose of Jesus' death, which is reconciliation with the Father. His death also defeated Satan and the power of death: "Since the children have flesh and blood, he too shared in their humanity so that by his death he might break the power of him who holds the power of death—that is, the devil—and free those who all their lives were held in slavery by their fear of death" (Hebrews 2:14-15). Paul adds that Jesus "must reign until he has put all his enemies under his feet. The last enemy to be destroyed is death" (1 Corinthians 15:25-26). Jesus' death is the atoning part of our salvation.

Resurrection

Each Easter Sunday, we celebrate Jesus' resurrection, which fulfills many Old Testament prophecies. The author of Hebrews tells us that Isaac being saved from death is a picture of resurrection (Hebrews 11:18-19). The book of Jonah tells us that Jonah was inside the sea monster "three days and three nights" (Jonah 1:17). Jesus related that event to his death, burial and resurrection (Matthew 12:39-40; Matthew 16:4, 21; John 2:18-22).

We celebrate Jesus' resurrection with great joy because it reminds us that death is not permanent. It's a temporary step toward our future—eternal life in communion with God. At Easter we celebrate Jesus' victory over death and the new life we will have in him. We look forward to the time spoken of in Revelation 21:4: "He will wipe every tear from their eyes. There will be no more death or mourning or crying or pain, for the old order of things has passed away." The resurrection is the hope of our salvation.

Ascension

Jesus' birth led to his life, and his life led to his death. But we cannot divorce his death from his resurrection and we cannot separate his resurrection from his ascension. Jesus didn't just come out of the grave and live as a human being. Now a glorified human, Jesus ascended to the Father, and it was not until that great event occurred that he finished the work he started.

In the introduction to Torrance's book *Atonement,* Robert Walker wrote this: "The ascension is Jesus' taking of our humanity in his person into the presence of God into the union and communion of the love of the Trinity." C.S. Lewis put it this way: "In the Christian story God descends to re-ascend" (*Miracles,* chapter 14, paragraph 5). The glorious good news is that in ascending, Jesus took us up with him: "God raised us up with Christ and seated us with him in the heavenly realms in Christ Jesus, in order that in the coming ages he might show the incomparable riches of his grace, expressed in his kindness to us in Christ Jesus" (Ephesians 2:6-7).

Incarnation, death, resurrection and ascension —all vital parts of our salvation and thus our worship. These milestones point to all that Jesus has accomplished for us through his whole life and whole work. Let's take in more and more of who Jesus is and all of what he has done for us. He is the complete salvation package.

Joseph Tkach

Christ's Resurrection: Our Hope of Salvation

"If Christ has not been raised," the apostle Paul taught, "your faith is futile; you are still in your sins" (1 Corinthians 15:17). The resurrection of Jesus Christ is of momentous importance for every Christian, indeed for everyone on this planet. Because Jesus Christ conquered death, we, too, will live again — and so will our friends and relatives who have already died. That is why the most exhilarating message human ears have yet heard was the one announced to some astonished women outside a rock tomb in first-century Jerusalem: "Why do you look for the living among the dead? He is not here; he has risen!" (Luke 24:5-6).

A foundational teaching

The resurrection of Christ has always been the central teaching of Christianity. "If the resurrection is not historic fact, then the power of death remains unbroken, and with it the effect of sin" (James Hastings, *A Dictionary of Christ and the Gospels,* vol. 2, page 514).

Michael Green in *Man Alive* is emphatic: "Without faith in the resurrection there would be no Christianity at all." W. Robertson Nicolls, quoting another writer, puts it plainly: "The empty tomb of Christ has been the cradle of the church" (*The Church's One Foundation,* page 150).

Anchored to history

To mention Jesus Christ and his life, death and resurrection is to get to the root of the Christian faith, for Christianity claims a basis in historical fact. "There are ancient myths in pagan literature about dying gods who attained some form of resurrection," writes Philip Rosenbaum, "but no other sacred writing intersects human history the way the Bible does. For it is the historical fact of Christ's life, death, and resurrection that separate God's Word from all others" (*How to Enjoy the Boring Parts of the Bible,* page 116).

But the New Testament accounts have come under intense scrutiny and attack. Scottish philosopher David Hume argued in the 1700s that miracles — including Christ's resurrection — violated all known workings of natural law. In our century, theologian Rudolph Bultmann concluded, "An historical fact which involves a resurrection from the dead is utterly inconceivable." In light of such arguments from rationalists and critics, it is no wonder that theories have been devised for the events of crucifixion week:

- The Swoon Theory: The idea that Jesus didn't really die but faked a death on the cross, then tricked his disciples into thinking that he had conquered death, only to live out his life elsewhere.
- The Theft Theory: The idea that the disciples, other sympathizers, perhaps robbers or someone else, stole the corpse. This is the oldest and most widespread argument against Christ's resurrection.

These are bold contentions, almost as bold as the resurrection claim itself. They are rhetorical daggers aimed at the very vitals of the Christian faith. Peter wrote, "We did not follow cleverly invented stories…but we were eyewitnesses" (2 Peter 1:16).

Who is right?

What about the Swoon Theory? This theory suggests that Jesus Christ plotted — for whatever reasons — the biggest hoax in history. Did Jesus, by some amazingly cunning strategy, fake a death on the cross? Let's keep in mind that the four Gospels are the primary documented evidence for Christ's death, burial and resurrection. We have good internal evidence for believing. These writings are emphatic that Jesus Christ's execution was a public and state-certified spectacle (Mark 15:29).

"This thing was not done in a corner," Paul argued before King Agrippa, the most influential Jewish official of his day (Acts 26:26, New King James Version). How right he was. Jesus Christ's mortal enemies — the leadership elite of his nation — were on the scene. They were watchfully determined to stamp out the Jesus movement (John 11:46-53). That is why they schemed behind closed doors to carry out their plot, at risk to their own standing among the people (John 7:25-52). It had to be the perfect crime.

Pontius Pilate, the chief Roman official on the scene, double-checked to verify if Christ had died (Mark 15:44-45). The testimony of John 19:23 and Mark 15:39 indicates that at least four Roman soldiers, including a centurion, carried out the execution. You can be sure that Roman occupation troops of the first century knew what death was.

Consider this: Would Christ's foes — opponents eager to crush out the infant Christian movement — have allowed Christ, once in their clutches, to fake a death? This hardly seems logical or consistent with their motives and with the biblical narrative. John Stott demolished the Swoon Theory with common sense. He asks if we can really believe

> that after the rigours and pains of trial, mockery, flogging and crucifixion he could survive…in a stone sepulcher with neither warmth nor food nor medical care? That he could then rally sufficiently to perform the superhuman feat of shifting the boulder which secured the mouth of the tomb…without disturbing the Roman guard? That he could appear to the disciples in such a way as to give them the impression that he had vanquished death? … Such credulity is more incredible than Thomas' unbelief. (*Basic Christianity*, page 49)

First-century propaganda

The oldest argument advanced against Christ's resurrection is the intriguing theory that Christ's body was stolen. This is a significant claim. The one crowning blow to disprove Christ's resurrection would have been a public display of his body. A display of the corpse would quickly end any "myth" that was developing about the resurrection of Jesus.

Public exhumings have happened more than once in history; why didn't the rulers of first-century Judea do that? There was a good reason: The body could not be found. Christ had been bodily resurrected. The Gospel account makes the most sense.

The rulers of Jerusalem "gave the soldiers a large sum of money" to circulate the story that Jesus' disciples stole his body (Matthew 28:11-15). The Theft Theory is indefensible, no matter who the robbers supposedly were. If the guards were sleeping, how did they know who had stolen the body? Second, the Jerusalem hierarchy had outsmarted themselves — they had posted a guard to prevent this very sort of thing from happening.

As Paul Little asks in *Know Why You Believe:* "What judge would listen to you if you said that while you were asleep, your neighbor came into your house and stole your television set? Who knows what goes on while he's asleep? Testimony like this would be laughed out of any court."

In his book *The Resurrection and the Life,* George Hanson made this point: "The simple faith of the Christian who believes in the Resurrection is nothing compared to the credulity of the skeptic who will accept the wildest and most improbable romances rather than admit the plain witness of historical certainties."

Any explanation, to be credible, must fit all the facts. The Theft Theory doesn't. The case against it is devastating. Even the existence of the New Testament church is evidence that something happened in Jerusalem, something no adversary could explain. There is no doubt that these defenses of the resurrection ring true. Sincere and learned scholars have labored hard to nullify the claims made against Jesus Christ's resurrection.

A question of faith

Christianity is more than a series of clever arguments. It is more than a list of intellectual debating points that can be argued back and forth. This is why the validity of the Gospel testimony does not remain at the mercy of the latest "debunking" best-seller or archaeological find in the Middle East. In the end, Christianity rests on faith, faith based on a living and ongoing relationship with Jesus Christ, a living Savior!

Thomas wanted the strongest form of proof: "Unless I see the nail marks in his hands and put my finger where the nails were…I will not believe it" (John 20:25). Thomas saw, he tested, and then he believed (verses 26-28). Yet Jesus followed this dramatic encounter with the words: "Because you have seen me, you have believed; blessed are those who have not seen and yet have believed" (verse 29).

As Oliver Barclay wrote: "The historical Jesus Christ was an amazing power in the lives of men years after his death. It is not so much the fact that a miracle happened…. The chief reason that the disciples spoke so often about it was that Jesus was alive and with them again" (*Reasons for Faith*, page 115). This is why the disciples came storming out of Jerusalem and so influenced the world with their message (Acts 17:6). The living Christ had changed their lives. He can do the same for you.

Neil Earle

The Incarnation: The Greatest Miracle

Which is the greatest miracle of all? Many Christians would point to the resurrection of Jesus after his death on the cross. The crucifixion-resurrection event is, after all, the basis for our salvation. But why would we consider the death and resurrection of Jesus so great event? Others have died and risen again, such as Lazarus. Why is the resurrection of Jesus a greater event? Lazarus eventually died again, but Jesus rose to eternal life and glory. When Lazarus rose, a great deal changed for him, but little changed for the world. But when Jesus rose, everything changed.

What was so different about Jesus' resurrection? The key lies in who died and rose. In the case of Lazarus, a man died and rose again to continue his mortal life. But in the case of Jesus, someone much more than a man died and rose again. Jesus was a man, but not just a man. He was the God-man — God in the flesh, God incarnate, both God and human in one.

The reason his death and resurrection have such power is not because resurrection is the greatest miracle. Rather it is because his death and resurrection had been preceded by the miracle that is truly the greatest of all: the miracle of the incarnation. The incarnation means his resurrection is new. Billions will eventually die and be resurrected into eternal life and glory; the incarnation, however, will remain unique.

C.S. Lewis called the incarnation "the Grand Miracle." He wrote: "The central miracle asserted by Christians is the Incarnation.... Every other miracle prepares for this, or exhibits this, or results from this.... It was the central event in the history of the Earth — the very thing that the whole story has been about" (*Miracles,* chapter 14).

By a miracle that passes human comprehension, the Creator entered his creation, the Eternal entered time, God became human — in order to die and rise again for the salvation of all people.

He comes down; down from the heights of absolute being into time and space, down into humanity; down further still...[to] the womb...down to the very roots and sea-bed of the Nature He has created. But He goes down to come up again and bring the whole ruined world up with Him. (ibid.)

The greatest miracle of all is that wonderful, incomprehensible act by which God became a human, and was born to a young Jewish girl named Mary, in a stable in Bethlehem, about 2,000 years ago during the reign of Herod the Great.

The power of the life, teaching, death and resurrection of Jesus Christ does not lie in the events themselves. The power of the events derives from the person of Jesus: who and what he was and is. His words have power and authority because they are the words of God incarnate. His life has power because it is the life of God incarnate. His death and resurrection have power because they are the death and resurrection of God incarnate.

Three of the four Gospels begin their record of Jesus' work by emphasizing the wonder of his incarnation. Matthew records how Jesus was miraculously conceived in the womb of Mary by the power of the Holy Spirit, and that he was "God with us." Luke stated that Jesus was the Son of God. John described how the Eternal Word, who is God, had become flesh as Jesus Christ to dwell among us.

However, some Christians take little notice of this greatest of all miracles. A spirit of commercialism has become attached to the Christmas season. Disturbed by these things, some avoid the festival. But too often, they also forget to dedicate time to think about the message Christmas was intended to remind us of: the message of God's greatest miracle. What a pity that, as a result, some forgot to rejoice in this greatest of all miracles, the birth of Jesus.

Let us not miss the opportunity to celebrate the great miracle: to come in wonder and worship before the One who humbled himself to become a baby, a child, a human; who descended into his own creation so that by ascending again he might lift it up with him from decay and bondage into glory and freedom.

The Birth of Jesus: A Story of Shame

Jesus' birth involves more humiliation than glory. The Son of God was in glory, but he saw us living in the slimepit of sin, and he loved us so much that he came into this slimepit to save us. He gave up his glory and he lived in humble circumstances. When Jesus was born, people were not amazed by his glory. There was no glory in putting a baby in an animal's feed trough.

Jesus didn't deserve any shame, but he was willing to live in it, until we killed him. That is the example God has given us. It shows us what love is. It shows us what God is like. Jesus told Philip, "If you have seen me, you have seen the Father" (John 14:9). He wasn't talking about appearance, but about love and humility.

When Christ became flesh, it was not some strange deviation in his character. Rather, it shows what God is like all the time. God is always so loving that he is willing to come to our slimepit to rescue us. He is always willing to put his own comfort and glory aside so he can rescue us. This is true greatness. Glory is not about power and bright lights. True greatness is not in strength or money. True greatness is humility and service, and that is just as true of God as it is for us. God's greatness is seen in his love, in his willingness to serve. The birth of Jesus shows that.

To put it in human terms, it would be like Pharaoh decided to give up the throne, give away his wealth and join the Hebrew slaves in the claypits, trying to make bricks without straw – not just for a day, but for 30 some years. If any Pharaoh actually did this, we would think he was insane, but God did this on an even greater scale. He gave up more, and he descended even more – and this is what God is like all the time. His glory and greatness is seen in how much he is willing to give up, not in how much he has now.

A birth in shame

Think about the circumstances of Jesus' birth. He did not come when the Jewish people were a strong nation. Rather, he came when they were despised and ruled by a pagan empire. He did not come to the most important city – he grew up in a region called "Galilee of the Gentiles."

Jesus was born in embarrassing circumstances, less than nine months after Mary and Joseph married. God could have easily caused the conception after Mary and Joseph were married. It would have been just as easy for the Holy Spirit to create a baby in a married woman as in an unmarried woman. It would have been easy to avoid the appearance of evil, but God did not. Even before Jesus was born, Jesus was in a compromised situation.

Luke tells us that Joseph went to Bethlehem because everyone was supposed to go to their family's city to be counted for the census (Luke 2:3-4). I don't know, but it seems that Joseph would have had at least a few brothers or cousins in the family of David who would have gone to Bethlehem, too. But we hear nothing of them, about how they might have helped Joseph and

Mary. They were on their own.

God loved the world so much that he gave them his only Son—and the world didn't want him. They knew God only as a God of power and wealth; they had forgotten about the God who walked in the garden of Eden calling for his wayward children. They had forgotten about the God who had a still, soft voice.

The world didn't want God, but God still loved the world. Even when we were sinners, even when we were ungodly, God loved us and sent his Son to die for us (Romans 5:6, 8, 10). That is what God is always like. The birth of Jesus should remind us of that. Christmas should remind us of his great humility.

A touch of glory

The angels were a touch of glory in the nativity story. Here were the bright shining lights, the heavenly choir singing praises to God. But where did they appear? Outside of town, with shepherds, the lowest level of society. Shepherds were so despised that they couldn't even testify in court. No one trusted them because they moved from one town to another. But God sent his angels to shepherds, not to priests and kings.

Some of the king's advisors in Jerusalem knew that the Messiah would be born in Bethlehem (Matthew 2:4-6), but they didn't bother to make the five-mile trip. God was drawing the far-off, but the ones who were close, couldn't even see the star. The glory of Christmas was so hidden that only a few people from the east could take the hint.

Not long after this, an angel warned the family: "Flee for your life. The king is out to kill you." The Christ child was taken to Egypt, becoming a refugee in the land the Jews had left—the land of slavery, the land of outcasts. This is the glory of being poor, persecuted, rejected by the people you have come to save. This is not the way we usually think of glory, but it is God's kind of glory—the glory of love and self-sacrifice. Whoever wants to be great, Jesus said, let him become a servant. This is true greatness because this is the way God is.

Just like Jesus

God is like a king who steps into the mud to help us make bricks without straw. He is like a king who sends his Son to his people even though he knows they will kill him. God is like someone who sacrifices himself to keep his enemies (that's us) from being punished. God is like Jesus—all the time. He is like a person who loves children, touches lepers and socializes with tax collectors and prostitutes. God is like someone who was hated without a cause, beaten without mercy and crucified without committing a crime.

God lets people hate him and beat up on him—not because he is a fool, but because he knows the best way for us to come to our senses is to see what selfishness really leads to. He knows that the best way to overcome evil is not by force, but by persistent love.

Thankfully, God has the power to pull it off. He is not hurt by our flailings. He does not get depressed when we reject him. He does not get vindictive when we insult him. He is bigger than that, so much bigger that he can be patient with us. He can be a helpless baby, he can be a crucified criminal, he can stoop that low because he loves us.

In this way, Christmas shows us what God is like. It shows us how much he loves us. It shows us the extreme that he went to in order to save us. God is so glorious that he left his glory and came down into the slimepit to save us. He was willing to be a baby conceived before marriage. He was willing to be born in a stable, to be rejected, to flee to Egypt. He was willing to give it all up, even his life, for us.

A lesson for us

God wants us to be like he is, to be like Jesus was. Not in appearance, not in power, but in love and humility. He set the example for us, and Christmas, or the birth of Jesus, has a message for us in how we behave toward one another. Jesus said that a servant is not greater than the master. If he, our lord and teacher, has served us, we should also serve one another (Matthew 20:26-28). Whoever wants to be great should become a servant. Jesus wants us to go out of our way to help others. We are to use our time and our resources to help others. Jesus also said, "If you want to follow me, take up your cross." Be willing to lose, even your life, and you will be great.

This is the way we are to follow Jesus' example, to let him live in us. We don't follow his example in keeping Hanukkah, in cleansing the temple, or in going to synagogues on the Sabbath. But he specifically says that we are to follow his example in serving others. That's the message of Christmas and the path of true glory.

We need to identify with that baby in the manger, to be like he is. We need to identify with the woman who had to give birth in a stable, and with the family who were refugees in another nation. Our role model is someone who loved his enemies, who was rejected time and again, and yet loved them. He was taken advantage of, ridiculed, despised and convicted of a crime, all because he wanted to help us. That is truly praiseworthy, truly worth celebrating!

Joseph Tkach

Appreciating Christ's Sacrifice

While reading a list of the 100 best novels written since 1900, I noted that there were two by Vladimir Nabokov. Not being familiar with this author, I checked him out on Google (ah, the marvels of search engines!) and found that in addition to being a famous novelist, he is known for coining the term doughnut truth, which refers to truths with holes in them, making them less than the full truth. It struck me that some of the current explanations of Christ's sacrifice are doughnut truths. Let me explain.

"Jesus died to appease the wrath of God brought about by your sins" is a message being given from many pulpits. The idea is that Jesus had to place himself between God and us and suffer in order to absorb all of God's wrath towards sinful humanity. Many Christians accept this penal-substitution theory of the atonement (sometimes called the forensic theory) as the Bible's primary teaching on the topic. Sadly, an overemphasis on this theory leaves the impression that Christ died not as a substitute for sinners, but as a substitute object for God's punishment. The mistaken idea is that God the Father had to take his anger out on someone—as if inflicting pain and suffering on someone would make things right.

There are significant problems with this theory (model) of the atonement. One is that the Bible uses not one but several models to describe the riches of Christ's atoning work on our behalf, including the sacrificial model, the economic model of exchange (redemption), the familial or filial model of family (reconciliation), the marital model (fidelity), and the healing model (peace, shalom). As Gustaf Aulen points out in *Christus Victor: An Historical Study of the Three Main Types of the Idea of Atonement*, the Bible also presents a Christ the victor (Christus victor) model of the atonement, which was the primary one taught by the early church fathers.

According to this model, "The work of Christ is first and foremost a victory over the powers which hold mankind in bondage: sin, death and the devil" (*Christus Victor*, p. 20). Rather than going to the cross to appease God's wrath, Christ did so to claim victory over the bondage of sin, the threat of death and the power of the devil, thus making all things subject to himself. Just as God delivered Israel from the bondage of oppression into liberty, so God delivers us from these terrible forms of oppression into true freedom in Christ.

Some theologians, such as Gregory Boyd and Scot McKnight, teach that the Christ the victor model should be seen as the Bible's central model of atonement, and the forensic model should be viewed as only one of several. Some theologians who support the centrality of the forensic model offer cautions about doing so. J.I. Packer warns that it should not be based singularly on human models of justice (which often is retaliatory or reciprocal) and should not be understood as an automatic explanation of how penal substitution really works. John Stott, in *The Cross of Christ*, lists multiple cautions about misrepresenting the nature of the atonement.

Problems with penal substitution

It is true that Christ's death paid the price, the cost, the debt and even the penalty of our sin. Jesus rescued us from the consequences of our sin and experienced those consequences in order to overcome them and transform them on our behalf. But the penal substitution model of the atonement can be taken too far. Here are some common ways:

- Misrepresenting the Father as forcing the Son to do what he didn't want to do—making the will of God divided and opposed between the Father and the Son.
- Misrepresenting the Son as manipulating, appeasing or cajoling the Father into changing his mind about condemning humanity—again, making the will of God divided.
- Characterizing the Father's wrath as being pitted against the love of Christ. This mistake pits God against God as if the character and purpose of God are divided, at odds.

- Modeling the atonement after human models of retribution or vengeance, which are rooted in violence and tend to look more like child abuse than grace—as if human wrath "works the righteousness of God," when it does not.
- Portraying the sinner as the object of God's wrath instead of the sinner's sin being the object of his wrath. This mistaken approach loses sight of the biblical truth that God's aim is to separate the sinner from the sin, so that the sin can be done away with and the sinner redeemed.
- Viewing the Old Testament sacrifices as God pouring out his wrath on the animals used for sacrifice—sending them to "hell" on behalf of Israel. The sacrificial animals were not being punished, but as unblemished creatures were sacrificially giving their lives so that there might be life in others where there was only death.
- Misrepresenting forgiveness as God making exceptions for sin in the lives of some. The truth is that God is implacably opposed to all sin everywhere, and through Christ made a way to condemn all sin, yet rescue sinners, giving them new, regenerated natures and making everything new.
- Portraying God as being absolutely separate from sinners. This misrepresentation flies in the face of God dwelling among Israel and the entire story of the Incarnation.
- Attributing to God a role that actually is Satan's (whose name means "accuser"), thus making God out to be the accuser of humanity (because humanity is unholy and unworthy) and portraying God as desiring sinners' condemnation rather than their repentance (the mistake made by Jonah!).
- Viewing grace as a secondary, separate and optional work of God after his primary and necessary work of judicial justice has been accomplished.
- Separating God's justice from God's love; his righteousness from his mercy and grace.
- Portraying God as more bound by his own rules of retributive justice (punishing the bad and rewarding the good) than by his restorative righteousness and desire for the reconciliation of his covenant love (where God's righteousness aims to put things right).
- Placing an exclusive emphasis on sinners being saved from the penalty or consequences of sin, rather than on the sinner being saved from sin and being given a share in Christ's renewed and glorified human nature. The truth is that we are saved *from* sin and *for* a right relationship of holy love with God as his beloved children.
- Overlooking the incarnation, the cross and the resurrection, and thus the truth that the Son of God became the new Adam—the new head of humanity—who came to reconcile the world to God on behalf of the Father and in the Holy Spirit, and not to condemn the world.

Keep the whole story

Faithful and accurate consideration of the atoning work of Christ will take into account the whole of the biblical story and teaching. When one aspect of that truth is singled out and developed in isolation, distortion inevitably results. But when we assemble all the pieces, giving all of them full weight while keeping Jesus at the center, we're on the right track. That holistic approach keeps clearly in mind Christ's relationship to the Father and the Spirit, and his relationship to us, and why he came.

The apostle Paul did this when he wrote that God poured his love out lavishly upon us in Jesus Christ in order to condemn sin in his flesh so that we might have his new life and love in us by the Spirit (Ephesians 1:7-8; Romans 8:3-4). The author of Hebrews adds that Jesus Christ paid the price to bring this reconciliation about freely and gladly, united in heart, mind and will with the Father and the Holy Spirit (Hebrews 12:2; 9:14). The Bible teaches that Jesus' atoning work was an act of the eternal, divine love of the Father, Son and Spirit.

We understand God and his lavish love for us through Jesus' life and especially through his self-giving death. As T.F. Torrance notes in *The Mediation of Christ*, "the cross is a window opened into the very heart of God." The cross reveals a God who is passionately in love with the world, not one who is furiously angry with it. God so loved the world that he gave his Son.

God hates sin – he hates it because it hurts the world that he loves; it hurts his beloved creation. God does not pour out his wrath on the object of his love—Jesus or any of his other children. Jesus did not go to the cross to appease an angry God, but to show clearly the unconditional love of a Father, Son and Spirit whose greatest desire is to be in relationship with us. That's not doughnut truth—it is whole, gospel truth!

Joseph Tkach

It Isn't Just About How He Died

I didn't see Mel Gibson's *The Passion of the Christ* when it first came out, and I still haven't. I don't want to. Hearing that the movie is grisly, sparing us no detail of the crucifixion, is enough for me. People say it leaves an indelible "special effects" impression of how Jesus died. I wonder whether that is a good thing.

Crucifixion was brutal, and that anyone would deliberately put himself at risk of the cross for others is, of itself, an impressive demonstration of love. But the fact that Jesus was crucified is, to some extent, just a detail. If he had been born a Roman citizen he would have been beheaded. If he had lived in another time or place he could have been hanged, stoned or shot. Today we would have electrocuted him, or strapped him to a gurney for a lethal injection, probably after spending several years on Death Row.

The graphic details of crucifixion focus primarily on making us feel sorry for Jesus, and therefore on wanting us to feel that we "owe it to him" to accept him after all he went through. Many people say that's the effect the movie had on them. But it seems that the emotion it stirred up was temporary. The movie was touted as "the greatest evangelistic tool for 2000 years," but it has had a minimal impact on church attendance. Wallowing in the blow-by-blow details of Jesus' scourging and crucifixion is not as persuasive as some had hoped.

Besides, Jesus and his Father want us to follow him because he lives, because as one of us he not only died, but was raised from the dead and dwells in the joy of perfect communion with the Father and wants to share that joy and communion with us. He's not looking for your sympathy; he's looking for you to come home to the love of your heavenly Father and your older Brother. That's why he took away our sins — to give us life, to call us home — not to garner our pity.

Jesus, the Son of God, the One through whom all things were made and who upholds all things by the word of his power (Hebrews 1:2) became human for us and died. Maybe it is simply this fact that demonstrates most dramatically the depth and meaning of his sacrifice. For Jesus to face death in any way and in any form was utterly foreign to all that he is.

"In him was life," John's Gospel tells us. "That life was the light of us all." C.S. Lewis, in a discussion about what it meant for Jesus to come and live as a human being, wrote: "The Eternal being who knows everything and who created the whole universe, became not only a man, but (before that) a baby, and before that a fetus inside a woman's body. If you want to get the hang of it, think how you would like to become a slug or a crab" (*Mere Christianity*, chapter 5). For about 30 years the Creator and Architect of human life shared in its limitations. Then he allowed his life to be ended in a brutal display of cruelty. For three days, the one who was life lay in a cold dark tomb.

I have a friend who has been for many years in

a maximum security prison. He has become used to it, and manages to live a productive Christian life. I love and respect my friend, and visit when I can. But the thought of spending even one night in his environment is frightening. It helps me understand just a little bit the sacrifice Jesus made.

Instead of focusing on the depth of Jesus' sacrifice by remembering how he died, perhaps simply the fact *that* he died underscores the depth of his love for us. He made our burden his, so that he could make his joy ours. He shared our experience, including death, in order to destroy the power of death over us. Jesus did not ask us to remember his death by dwelling on the grisly details. Instead, he gave us a simple ceremony. At the end of what we call "The Last Supper," he took some of the leftovers and established the simple ritual that we call communion. "Do it in remembrance of me," he said.

Communion: the word means "to join with." To join with others — a reminder of our commitment to love as we have been loved. To share, serve, tolerate and regard our neighbor's needs as highly as we do our own. Communion is not an empty religious ritual. Nor is it an outburst of emotion after exposure to some masterfully wrought special effects. Communion is something Christians do again and again. But it should never become routine. Each time we accept the symbols of Jesus' body and blood we commit ourselves to him and to all that he stands for.

John Halford

Don't Cry for Jesus

"Don't Cry for Jesus" was one of the most memorable sermons I have ever heard. It was given by Dr. Lewis Smedes (1921-2002) at a Fuller Seminary chapel service. I was there as a student during Holy Week in hopes of being better prepared to fully appreciate Christ's crucifixion and resurrection. My prayers were answered that day. I heard a message that has stuck with me ever since.

What was Professor Smedes getting at that struck me as being so profoundly right? He wanted us to see as clearly and precisely as possible that Jesus was no victim and that he didn't want us to pity him or feel sorry for him. I thought at the time, "What? How can we not feel sorry for him, after all he went through for us?" As Smedes developed the message I saw what he meant and how true it was. Professor Smedes had us consider two things: first, the way the story of Jesus is told to us by the New Testament writers and second, a comparison of Jesus with the Greek tragic heroes like the demigod Achilles.

Let me first briefly recount for you the upshot of that comparison. The Greek gods suffered often because of their own immoral activities and those involving the other gods. But their greatest sufferings were tragic because they were due to circumstances beyond their own control. These gods were born with their various strengths and weaknesses. No one of them "had it all." They were always born into situations not of their own making and often involving jealousies, revenge plots and grabs for power between various other gods.

These tragic heroes were always victims of their circumstances as the inevitable wheel of fate turned against them at some point. It was their vulnerabilities that would lead to their most tragic suffering and defeat, like Achilles' lamentable heel. Were it not for the fact that despite all his armor, Achilles' heel was exposed and that his goddess mother was prevented by her unwitting mortal father from completing the daily rituals that would have made Achilles immortal, Paris' arrow would never have found its fatal target. In some versions of the myth, the god Apollo, for his own reasons, intervened and guided that arrow to pierce Achilles just at that one and only tiny unprotected point. How can you not feel sorry for Achilles? The unfairness of it all. Through no fault of his own, the greatest of all Greek warriors was brought down.

Though we don't think of Jesus as a Greek tragic hero, I realized upon further reflection that his cross is often described in tragic terms. Jesus is often portrayed as a victim of circumstances that go all the way back to the fall of humanity. Jesus is sent to be our Savior because humanity has rebelled and needs to be reconciled and regenerated if we are to share in God's eternal and triune fellowship and communion and for God's original intention at creation to be realized.

In the New Testament we find Jesus, the Son of God, living at a time when the Jewish nation is occupied by the pagan Romans. Among his own people, the Pharisees and Sadducees are involved in their own disputes with each other. Yet they manage to form an alliance to plot Jesus' arrest and execution. Closer to him, there is a traitor among his own disciples, Judas, who betrays him—with a kiss, no less. Jesus is betrayed first into the hands of the court of the high priests and then into the hands of Pilate, who is himself caught between the rival forces of the Emperor and the potentially riotous crowds. Finally, Jesus suffers the brutally cruel treatment of the Roman soldiers who strip, mock and whip him, then lead him to Golgotha, where he is put to death on the machinery of Roman execution, a cross.

Given these tragic circumstances surrounding Jesus' sacrifice, why should we not consider Jesus a tragic victim? Not because he didn't pay an unimaginably high price for us and our salvation. Not because he didn't actually suffer and die. But simply because he was no victim of those circumstances and because he had no fatal flaw!

The cost of our salvation was foreseen and anticipated before the foundations of the earth were even laid. God was not taken by surprise at the Fall nor by our subsequent need for costly deliverance. But our God, Father, Son and Holy Spirit, counted the cost (as it were) from all eternity and agreed they were ready and willing to gladly pay the price for our deliverance from evil and for our reconciliation. So the plan for creation was carried out knowing full well the price to be paid to put things right, for God's righteousness to be done.

Jesus knew why he had come and what his saving work would cost. His mission was freely chosen. He was freely sent and freely given by the Father out of their joint abounding love for the world. Jesus repeatedly told his disciples what he would have to go through, even though they could not imagine his being so completely rejected by their religious leaders and political authorities that it would lead to his death. Jesus was anything but unaware or naive about the path he would have to take to make all things new.

Jesus tells us that, like a good shepherd, when danger comes to his sheep, he lays his life down—and also takes it up (John 10:17). Jesus freely, voluntarily, not only gives up his life but also receives it back. When Pilate reminds Jesus that he has the power of life and death over him, Jesus reminds Pilate that he has no power except what has been allowed him by God, his Father (John 19:10-11).

In the garden, when one of his disciples takes it upon himself to defend Jesus with a sword, Jesus reminds them that all of his Father's angelic hosts are available to protect him at any moment if he were to call on them (Matthew 26:53). Jesus is no victim of fate, of circumstances, or of powers greater than himself. He is in charge. He goes forth to Jerusalem only when his hour has come—not sooner, not later.

Jesus' suffering is not the result of any large or small flaw in him. Far from it. There is not even a fleeting shadow of personal weakness evident in his confident exercise of divine omnipotence as he fulfills his redemptive mission. Rather, it is by means of his strength and authority operating in full concert with his Father that he arrives at the right moment to exert saving power over sin, evil and death itself. His act of self-giving is a work of deliberate might based on the strength of his holy love. Jesus is no tragic hero, but the willing, omnipotent, Lord and Savior.

Perhaps most astonishing are Jesus' words spoken on the way to Golgotha, even as he bore the heavy weight of the cross-beam of his own crucifixion. Seeing the women standing by, no doubt exceedingly distraught and anguished, welling up from the depths of his compassion, Jesus found the strength to tell them something they and we need to know: "Daughters of Jerusalem, *don't weep for me*" (Luke 23:28).

Jesus does not want us to pity him as a hapless victim who suffers because it couldn't be avoided, because it was inevitable, destined by forces he could not resist. He is not looking for our pity—he trod that road, the Via Dolorosa as it is called, on purpose, by divine design. He intentionally took that journey and nothing, not even torture at the violent hands of human wickedness, could stop him. We may weep for ourselves, if we must, that is, be sorrowful for our sins. But Jesus didn't come looking to gather our tears. Rather, his costly love calls for giving him our thanks, our praise, our gratitude, our love, our absolute trust and loyalty—indeed our very lives in eternal worship.

Jesus not only freely but also gladly gave his life that we might have resurrected life in him. So the author of Hebrews sums it up: "For the joy set before him, he endured the cross" (Hebrews 12:2). For joy? Yes, for joy. But how can that be? In short, because Jesus was no fool. The price he paid was worth it and he knew it. He has no regrets! He did not enjoy the suffering. Not at all. It was excruciating. But he rejoiced in what he with the Father and Spirit would accomplish by means of his extravagant self-sacrifice. Jesus was no victim but the victor. The surety of his victory gave him a great joy that saw him through his agonies. Crucifixion would lead by the grace and power of God to resurrection and a new heaven and earth.

Jesus was no reluctant Savior, but the conquering Servant-King of all creation. That's the good news that Professor Smedes preached, and from that moment on, I saw that I could no longer think, preach or teach as if Jesus was a victim that we should feel sorry for.

All those illustrations of the cross that I had heard in both liberal and conservative Christian contexts that made it seem that Jesus was a victim, I had to forswear. These made Jesus out to be anything and everything—from a mother rabbit frozen in a blizzard to save her little bunny child, to an innocent toddler run over by a train or ground up in the gears of a drawbridge—all this occurring while his helpless father looks on in horror from a distance. Somehow caught off-guard and facing a horrible dilemma, this father-victim had to choose between his son and humanity. And so he pulls the lever that seals their respective fates. In these illustrations both the Son and the Father are depicted as victims of circumstances and of their own limitations that call for our pity. As tragic characters they match, if not exceed, the sorry state memorialized in the myth of Achilles.

Perhaps more theological than these misguided analogies are certain interpretations of the cross that pit the Father against the Son. The Father is sometimes said to be taking his wrath out on the Son—punishing him to satisfy his righteousness. In this case, the tragedy occurs between the Father and the Son (some, who have rejected the idea of the cross altogether, have gone so far as to claim that if so, the Father is the victimizer and the Son the victim!). Or the Son is depicted as having to overcome the resistance of the Father to being merciful and forgiving by appealing to his own suffering to gain the Father's pity and so get him to relent of his wrath. From these perspectives, the wills, attitudes and aims of the Father and the Son are at odds and can be resolved only by the Son's suffering. How tragic! "Only that it wasn't so!" we reply out of pity.

Sometimes we imagine a modern adversarial court scene where the Father is represented as the judge who wants to condemn the guilty party, and Jesus is the defense lawyer hoping to help the defendant avoid the penalty required by the law. Fortunately, Jesus figures out a way to keep us from the punishment we deserve. It's a plan that the Father can't argue with since it doesn't seem to involve any violation of the law. Finding no grounds for objection, the Father-Judge has to concede: Jesus wins the court case for us.

But the biblical revelation shows us the Father, Son and Holy Spirit are of one mind, one purpose, united in being, acting for the one and same end: our salvation. The Father sends the Son in the power of the Spirit. The Son freely comes and serves out of love for the Father and with joy in the Spirit. The Holy Spirit empowers the Son to overcome temptation and undo evil itself in order to set free the captives, open the eyes of the blind, set at liberty those who are oppressed and bring in the Lord's promised Jubilee (Luke 4:18-19).

At the cross, no exception is made. Our sin is judged and condemned in Jesus. The wrath of God aims to burn away evil and the sin in us that has corrupted our very natures. Dying in him, we are separated and rescued from the evil in us for eternal life. We are given a share in Christ's restored and sanctified humanity. God's wrath serves his mercy. His righteousness serves his love. There is no tension between the attributes of God nor between the Father and the Son. There is no tragic relationship at the heart of the gospel. At the cross the Son "through the eternal Spirit offered himself unblemished [without flaw] to God" (Hebrews 9:14). Our salvation is the united work of the whole Triune God, our Savior—Father, Son and Holy Spirit.

At the foot of the cross, Christ doesn't call us to join him in a great pity-party: the Father feeling sorry for the Son, the Son feeling sorry for the Father, Jesus feeling sorry for us and we feeling oh so sorry for him. For Jesus was no tragic victim. Rather, we gather at the foot of the cross to worship in unspeakable awe, with adoration, thanksgiving, praise and prayer for the costly victory of Christ. By his joyful and freely given life, he righteously restored us to fellowship and eternal communion with God our Triune Redeemer.

Gary Deddo

A Theology of the Holy Spirit
Part 3

This is a continuation. Parts 1 and 2 were in *40 Days of Purpose, Volume 2*.

The Triune God: one in being, three distinct Divine Persons

Earlier, we saw that God is one in being and yet exists eternally as three distinct Divine Persons: Father, Son and Holy Spirit. In seeking to communicate this truth about God, some use the catch-phrase, one-in-three and three-in-one. Though it's not wrong, it can be misleading if people understand it to mean that God is both three and one of the exact same thing. But God is not one and three beings; nor is he one and three Persons. The "oneness" and the "threeness" of God refer to two aspects of who God is. "One" refers to God's one being while "three" refers to the three Divine Persons.

To more accurately convey this truth, I recommend this statement: God is one in being and three in Divine Persons. Now let's unpack that statement and begin to focus on the main topic of this essay: the Divine Person known as the Holy Spirit.

Three Divine Persons

When we say "three Divine Persons," we don't mean "persons" exactly like you and me. We humans are created in the image of God, but God is not an image of us. Divine Persons are not exactly the same as human persons. If God was three persons exactly like we are, then God would be three beings, since human persons are separate beings. When speaking about God, we're not using the word "person" in exactly the same way we do about ourselves.

Recall that the discipline of theology is to make sure we don't talk about God as if God was a creature. We have to avoid projecting human ideas on God. This discipline of theology takes a while for people to catch on to, but that is why we're teaching people to think about God according to God's nature, not to think about God, for example, as a big human being in the sky!

In speaking of the Father, Son and Holy Spirit as Divine (not human) Persons, we are affirming that these personal names and personal relationships between them reveal to us the reality of God. God knows himself as Father, Son and Spirit. There are real and eternal relationships in God. Elsewhere in Scripture these relationships are also characterized as a mutual knowing, loving, glorifying and oneness.

What we think about human persons in living, loving and holy relationship with each other does, to a certain degree, reflect the truth about God. God is more like a community of three human persons than like any other created thing. Or, it would be better to switch this around and say that the Father, Son and Holy Spirit are the original and real Persons, and since we are somewhat like them, we can borrow the term "person" to speak of ourselves as individual human creatures! God is not more like a single, lonely, isolated individual. He is not, as the philosopher Leibnitz declared, a Monad!

Perichoresis and triunity

Reflecting on the unity and distinction of the Divine Persons, some down through the ages have thought of the church as imaging the Trinity: one in Christ, yet many members. But the church does not and cannot have the same kind of unity as do the three Divine Persons. Their unity is their oneness of being. Our unity cannot match that. The kind of unity that God has is revealed to us in Jesus Christ. It is a unity so unique that early church teachers eventually coined a word to represent that one-of-a-kind divine unity. That word is *perichoresis.* This Greek word is often not translated because it has a unique meaning that can't be translated easily. It means, most literally, to envelope one another or to make space for one another. It has also been translated as mutually indwelling each other, or having a co-inherence in each other, or in-existing in one another.

The language of perichoresis represents Jesus' teaching that he is "in the Father and the Father is in [him]" (John 14:11). It is also just what we see lived out in the Gospels as we watch and hear Jesus in his dynamic relationship with the Father and the Spirit. This unique unity has been also explained by saying that the whole of God, all three Persons, are present in each of the Persons. Each, though fully God in being, is distinct in Person so that there is a real relationship and exchange going on from all eternity between the three Divine Persons. As one fairly early creed (The Athanasian Creed) summed it up: the unity of God is a Trinity and the Trinity of God is a Unity. We can try to put this truth into a single word: triunity.

Everything we can say about the Father we can say about the Son and we can say about the Spirit except that they are not each other. Why? Because they mutually indwell one another and are equally God, sharing all the divine attributes together as one God. They have an absolutely unique kind of unity so that they are distinct in Divine Person but united in being. Unlike creatures, the unity of being doesn't undo the difference of Person, and the distinction of Person doesn't undo the unity of being. Remembering this will help us get our language squared away so that we don't grossly misrepresent God.

What kind of God?

The meaning of what we're saying here about God is, of course, deep and profound. It's beyond our most descriptive words, for words are incapable of fully explaining the nature of God. The early church understood that the purpose of words (as in our doctrinal formulations) was to protect the mystery of God's nature, not explain it away. Nevertheless our words about God are important, as far as they go, in faithfully identifying who God is. When carefully stated in the context of all of Scripture, they show us something significant about the kind of God this God is. They point to the fact that God has his being by being a fellowship, a communion of Divine Persons. Along with the biblical writers, we can sum up the quality of those relationships as all being forms of love. Begetting, being begotten and proceeding are all relationships of loving exchange.

This is why we can say with John, "God is love." We can see what Jesus means and why he says he loves the Father and the Father has loved him from all eternity. It makes sense then that Jesus tells us that as the Father has loved him, so he loves us. Further, as he has loved us, so we ought to love one another. No wonder then that the ways of the people of God can be comprehensively summed up in the two commands to love God and love neighbor.

Those relationships, internal and eternal to God, are filled with holy loving. God is a fellowship kind of God—a communion kind of God. God is not just a lonely being floating out there from all eternity "looking for someone to love." God is the fullness of holy love, the fullness of fellowship and communion. Bringing it all together, we can say the Father and Son have their fellowship and communion in the Spirit.

This God of love, fellowship and communion is very different than an isolated individual God who can't love until there's something else outside of God to love. The Triune God is very different from a god who exists with no internal and eternal relationships, one in whom there is no exchange, no giving and receiving, in whom there is no reciprocity of knowing, loving and glorifying of one another. Such a god would be very different from the God we come to know through Jesus Christ, according to Scripture.

To summarize: the Christian God is a fellowship, a communion. God the Trinity has his being by being in relationships of holy loving. Those relationships are eternally begetting, being begotten and proceeding—each a unique form of holy, loving exchange. Those are the key words that we have to point to this amazing reality of who God is.

Those are the essentials to remember if we're going to talk about the Holy Spirit. We have to remember who the Spirit is. If the Spirit first exists in relationship with the Father and the Son, then that's the first thing, not the Spirit's relationship to us or our relationship to the Spirit. Those come afterwards. There was a time when nothing other than God existed and the Holy Spirit was perfectly happy being the Spirit of the Father and the Son. The Spirit doesn't need us to be the Spirit. There was a time when there was no creation. God was then the fullness of fellowship in Father, Son and the Holy Spirit. While we want to talk about the Spirit's relationship to us, we should remember that that's a secondary matter. The being of the Spirit is being one with the Father and the Son.

Having completed an introduction to Trinitarian doctrine, what can we go on to say about the Holy Spirit?

Who is the Holy Spirit?

Who is the Spirit? The simplest answer is that the Spirit is the Spirit of the Father and the Son. That means that whenever we speak of the Father and Son, or hear about them in the Scripture, since God is one in being, the Spirit is also involved in some way, whether we know it or not or explicitly say so. The Spirit always has something to do with the Father and Son. We don't always remember this connection, and we probably should make it more explicit more often. So, when speaking of the Father or the Son we do not exclude the Spirit, because the Spirit is the Spirit of the Father and the Son. Reference to the Son involves the Spirit and the other way around. We can't talk about the Holy Spirit apart from the Son because the Holy Spirit is the Spirit of the Son.

If we assume we can think of one without the other, we're misrepresenting who the Spirit is, because the Spirit has his being, he is the Person he is, by being in an essential relationship to the Father and Son. We don't always spell this out, but nevertheless we should remember to make the connections. A full understanding will always seek to grasp each of the divine Persons in their relationships with each other.

The who, not how of the Spirit

Seeking further understanding, we often look for answers to "how" questions. This is particularly the case when the topic is the Holy Spirit. We ask "how" questions like, How does God operate his providence over all of history and nature and everything else? Or, How did Jesus become united to a human nature? Or, How did God save us? Or, How does God perfect us? Or, How does God communicate his word and will to us? Or How do we receive the gifts and fruit of the Spirit or the help of the Spirit in prayer?

Many of the "how" questions about God are actually answered by a "who" answer, which points to the Spirit. The answer to "how" God does something often is, simply, "by the Spirit." Such a "who" answer, although naming one of the Triune Persons, often is regarded as insufficient. The follow-up questions reveal why. We want to know the mechanisms, the machinery. We want to know the chain of cause and effect. Somehow we have come to believe that simply identifying the agent responsible for what takes place does not constitute an intelligible answer. So we press on to the "how" question. But often in Scripture, the only answer given to a "how" question, is simply the identification of the agency of the Holy Spirit. We are simply told who does something and in many cases, that is the full extent of the explanation. Question: How? Answer: By the Holy Spirit! We can know the "who," without knowing the "how"!

Did Jesus tell Nicodemus the mechanism of how one becomes born from above? Did he offer him a technique? Did he list a bunch of rules that if we do this and that and the other, then bingo, it happens? No. He explained that, because the Spirit works more like the wind, no explanation like that can be given. The working of the Spirit can't be controlled or predicted by us. That's the nature of the Spirit — both who he is and how he works!

Many of our questions, especially those regarding the Christian life, are answered simply by identifying the agency of the Holy Spirit. And that's it. But we always seem to want more, that involves some mechanism, technique or steps. We feel that there needs to be some combination of conditions filled in order to get the Spirit to work. There is quite a bit of teaching in Christian circles these days that speculates and even invents techniques and methods to fill in the gap between what biblical revelation teaches and what we, like Nicodemus, often want—answers to our "how" questions that specify exactly what conditions we need to fill to get the Spirit to work, or work more effectively. However, shouldn't we stop where Scripture stops rather than carry on with mere speculations?

Many of the current controversies or differences of emphasis between various teachings and ministries actually have to do with their lining up behind a favorite technique or mechanism or a particular list of conditions needed to get what we're looking for from the Spirit. The arguments and controversies are most often over which teaching offers the best "how to." But if we go down that road, we've already forgotten most of who the Spirit is. On that path we can easily be tempted to start asking all kinds of questions. Some can mistakenly assume God can be divided up. So the question arises, "Can you have the Spirit without having the Son?" Or, "Can you have the Son without having the Spirit?"

Others assume that the presence and blessing of the Spirit comes not by grace but by technique or by fulfilling certain conditions, and so they ask, "What steps do we need to take before we can effectively have and use the gifts of the Spirit?" But such an approach makes the grace of the Holy Spirit dependent on our works, our efforts! The result is that we then approach the Spirit by works rather than by faith in God's grace! We replay the same error that Paul wrote the church in Galatia about.

"By the Spirit of the Father and Son" answers these "how" questions. We can try to use all kinds of Bible verses to work out answers to these questions and controversies. But the problem with that approach is that the nature and character of the Holy Spirit is forgotten, even lost. For example, if the Father, Son and Holy Spirit are one in being, can you then have one without the other? No, you can't, not in an exclusive way. You can't have one completely without the other. The unity of the Persons in action is indicated in biblical revelation where we are told that no one truly proclaims Jesus is Lord except by the Spirit (1 Corinthians 12:3). We are told that when the Spirit of sonship comes upon us, we cry out "Abba, Father" (Romans 8:15; Galatians 4:6). God doesn't split up, with the Son heading off saying, "Goodbye, Spirit. I hope you catch up later." God is one in being but also God is one in action. They act and work together.

Many if not most current controversies have forgotten some of the most fundamental things about who God the Holy Spirit is. Our thoughts can then head in all sorts of wrong directions, and we end up speculating in order to answer misguided questions. We grab random Bible verses and try to throw them together to come up with an answer. As a result, different groups ended up gravitating toward certain verses to prove their points. But in doing so, they left behind the more fundamental teaching that points to the reality of who the Spirit is. The fundamental thing, the answer to the "who" question regarding the Spirit, is often forgotten, and so the answers promoted are inconsistent with the deeper, more central truth of the Spirit, who is one in being and one in working with the Father and the Son and who ministers by grace.

Biblical revelation about the ministry of the Spirit is often presented in connection with the mention of at least one other Divine Person.

Scripture tells us that only the Holy Spirit can break into a person's pride and enable them to recognize that Jesus is their Lord and Savior, come in the flesh as one of us (1 John 4:2). It tells us that we only have the Spirit because he is sent by the Son, from the Father (John 15:26). It also says that if anyone is convicted by the message of the gospel, it is because the Spirit is at work (1 Thessalonians 1:3-5). Scripture declares that Jesus sends the Spirit to bring persons to an acknowledgment of sin and the need for judgment and righteousness (John 16:8).

When the "Spirit of sonship" comes upon us, we cry out "Abba, Father," Paul tells us (Romans 8:15; Galatians 4:6). Why do we cry out "Abba, Father"? If we know who the Spirit is, the answer is clear — because God is one in being and one in action. That's amazing! The whole Trinity is involved in that one simple and profound cry of our hearts. When the Spirit acts, he doesn't act apart from the Father but with the Son, too—he brings our worship all together.

So when Jesus says "Go out and baptize them in the name" (singular) and then gives them the one name: "Father, Son and Holy Spirit," we should not be surprised. The name we're given matches the reality: Father, Son and Holy Spirit is the one name of God. A simple way to say this is that God is the Father-Son-Holy-Spirit-God, as if it's one name instead of three names, because it really isn't three separate names, but a threefold-name. We're baptized into the one Name of the three Divine Persons. Jesus' instruction makes sense if that's who God is, and therefore that's how he acts and has his being as the Triune God—one in being and three in Divine Persons.

All our thinking about the Holy Spirit needs to be contained within these Trinitarian boundaries. That will help us interpret Scripture properly and also see more deeply into Scripture so that we come to know the reality of who the Spirit is ever more profoundly. Good theology doesn't take us away from Scripture—it helps us see how it comes together even more coherently. Good theology doesn't answer every question we might have, but it does answer the questions God most wants us to grasp and proclaim. So, we want to help others read Scripture, interpret Scripture and bring all the pieces of Scripture together.

In the next section, we'll look further at the importance of the Holy Spirit.

A Theology of the Holy Spirit, Part 4A

The importance of the Spirit

Why the need to talk about the Spirit beyond simply acknowledging him? First, because a disconnection between the Divine Persons can develop in our understandings of the Father and the Son and the Spirit. Many churches end up emphasizing and talking almost exclusively about the Father. Others restrict their focus to the Son, while others have a tendency to put the spotlight on the Spirit. Such understandings are fragmented, but that doesn't mean God is fragmented. Misunderstandings can trip us up in our faith and in our lived relationship to God. We want our understanding to be faithful and coherent with the truth of God as all three persons, not dividing them up.

As faith seeks understanding, we aim to improve our understanding so that it more faithfully matches the reality. You can recognize and interact with things better when you have improved understanding. As we gain a clearer understanding of the Spirit in relationship to the Father and Son, we'll better recognize the ministry of the Spirit. We can more joyfully and peacefully join in with the Spirit when our understanding matches who the Spirit is and then how we're involved in what the Spirit is doing.

What theological understanding of the Spirit can offer

Theological work aims to fix things on our side, not fix things on God's side. We can grow in understanding even if the reality is not changed by our better grasp. If we have misunderstandings, it will be good to clear them up. As the Holy Spirit is working, it is far better to be aware of that work compared to being unaware. But our better understanding does not make something real or change the nature of the Spirit's working. God does not all of a sudden become the Holy Spirit when we recognize the Spirit. The Holy Spirit is not tied up, unable to do anything until we figure him out. That would be like saying the wind is tied up until we can figure it out. No, the Spirit still works, but we may not recognize it. And by recognizing it we may more fully participate, we become more involved, become more in tune with the truth and reality of who God is. So we're trying to make sure our understanding matches the truth about who God is, such as the Spirit has been revealed to us.

Our understanding may be fragmented, but God is not fragmented. Our understanding of the working in the ministry of the Spirit may be fragmented, but that doesn't mean the actual working of the Spirit is fragmented. We're not controlling God by our understanding. If that were the case, then God would be dependent on us. We want to sort this all out and let our understanding be as full as it can be.

How do we fix the problem of a lack of awareness and understanding of the Spirit? How do we bring our understanding of the ministry of the Spirit up to speed in a way that recognizes the Spirit is one of the three Divine Persons of the Trinity? Some are concerned about the need to speak proportionately about the Holy Spirit, giving the Holy Spirit equal time or equal emphasis. What's behind that concern?

There are situations where our faith and understanding of the Spirit is lacking, and so lags behind the Father and Son. Wherever we find this situation, it ought to be set right. We should become familiar with all that's been revealed to us about the Spirit and then pass that on to others. In those cases, additional teaching and focus on the Spirit is called for (although this should never be the exclusive focus). In that way our faith and knowledge of the Spirit will become better aligned with the other Divine Persons.

Objections to pursuing the Holy Spirit

In pursuing this kind of correction, we may run into some obstacles that contributed to the unbalanced situation in the first place. For example, some persons might not be interested in the Spirit and so have neglected the topic. Hopefully they will come around and see that the Holy Spirit is no less important than the Father and Son.

Others may not want to know or have much to do with the Holy Spirit because the Spirit seems kind of, well, spooky. We usually don't want to be around ghosts, especially one you can't control or that you can't identify or you can't nail down, can't make a part of your program and who is like the wind (or maybe a typhoon!).

Some people may be avoiding the Spirit because they have worries. That's not the best reason not to have an interest in the Holy Spirit. Their fears may be based in part (or perhaps in whole) on ignorance or misinformation about the nature of the power and working of the Holy Spirit. Those who have misgivings may not have a good grasp on who the Holy Spirit is. The Spirit isn't like a ghost or something to be fearful of in the sense that it might do us harm.

Helping people know that the Spirit is Holy, is good, is crucial. The best way to do this is to emphasize regularly that the Spirit has the same character and purpose as Jesus. There is no slippage in mind, attitude, or aim between the two. The best way to identify the working of the Spirit is to compare it to what we know about Jesus. It is his Spirit. If it doesn't feel, sound, taste and work like Jesus, then it is not his Spirit. Knowing Jesus is how we best discern the spirits, that is, which is the Holy Spirit.

Some could think the Spirit is now irrelevant to our current situation or no long available to us, at least as in the days of the early church. That would be another poor reason to have little or no interest in the Spirit. While it's acceptable to raise questions about the working of the Spirit today, there is no biblical teaching designed to inform us that the Spirit cannot or will not continue to work as in the days of the early church. This does not mean that the Spirit cannot adjust the mode of his ministry as, in his wisdom, he sees fit from time to time and place to place. He can in his sovereign grace make adjustments. However, there is no reason that the Spirit could not continue to work today as in the days of the New Testament. That is up to the Spirit.

Those who dogmatically conclude that the Spirit does not work and cannot work in the same manner have argued from their own experience, and on that basis they have selected and interpreted Scripture to explain their lack of experiencing the working of the Spirit. But such arguments do not have binding authority in the church—and especially upon the Spirit! It might simply be that the Spirit at some times and places chooses to work behind the scenes, mostly undetected even perhaps by Christians—and that's why the church's experience of the Spirit is not evenly distributed all the time.

Thinking that the ministry and manifestation of the Spirit depends on us, what we do, what condition we're in, what we want, or on our level of understanding, is to put the cart way before the horse. If the Spirit depends on us in these ways, then the Spirit does not (cannot?) minister by grace. The ministry of the Spirit is being regarded as a reward for works. Whatever the Spirit does and however he works, it is all of grace. We do not condition the Spirit to act. The Spirit is faithful whether or not we are.

Some are concerned about abuses and misrepresentations of the Spirit. There are legitimate reasons for folks to be cautious or concerned. There have been, since the days of the New Testament, abuses, misuses and misleading teaching about the Spirit. There are many cases where an emphasis on the Holy Spirit has contributed to conflict and church splits. There have been deceitful things said and done in the name of the Holy Spirit. In connection with an emphasis on the Spirit, some things have occurred that are bizarre and in some cases even abusive. Are these good reasons to neglect the Spirit? No. Any good thing can be misused. As an ancient maxim states: abuse does not rule out proper use.

If these things can be guarded against, all the while coming to understand and welcome the ministry of the Spirit, I think the way can be clear to address any imbalance. But checks and balances, spiritual discipline and discernment need to be in place provided by wise pastors and elders ministering under the authority of the whole teaching of Scripture. That is a legitimate requirement to guard against spiritual pride and abuse, disunity and division. There are real dangers.

Equal proportions?

Given all that, setting up a goal of equality of emphasis or parity of focus on the three Divine Persons is not the best way to go about making a healthy correction if there is an imbalance or ignorance about the Spirit. There are valid reasons why there necessarily always will be a certain kind of faithful disproportion or inequality of emphasis or focus on the Spirit compared to the other two Persons of the Trinity. The reason has to do with the nature and character of the Spirit.

There are good reasons why the church down through the ages has had less to say and did not give equal concentration or time to the Spirit. Here are some good reasons why the Spirit will not get equal time or focus in our level of explanation or concentration of attention.

First, there is less biblical information about the Holy Spirit. In the Gospels there are plenty of references to the Spirit, but many more concerning Jesus and his relationship with the Father. Jesus speaks of the Spirit and not just as side comments. The Spirit is an essential element to his message and life, and is not less important. But he talks and tells much more in detail about the Father and his relationship with him.

The same goes for Paul's epistles. There is plenty of important teaching there about the Spirit and living in relationship with the Spirit. But there as well, we find significantly more discussion and detail about the person and work of the Son and his connection to the Father. The disproportionate detailed treatment does not signal an inequality of importance, since it is clear that faith in the Holy Spirit and his ministry is not only important, but vitally connected to the ministry of Jesus.

In the Old Testament there are significant references to the Spirit, including landmark prophecies about the Spirit in Joel and Ezekiel. Yet, throughout the Old Testament there is far more consideration given to God the creator, covenant maker and deliverer of Israel. Again, this disproportion does not indicate that the Spirit is less important. We simply are given less detailed information about this important subject.

Though the Father and Spirit are named together in Scripture, we are given little detail about their relationship. The Spirit is said to "proceed" from the Father and is "sent" from the Father in the Son's name. We find their actions described in a way that indicates they are coordinated with each other. When Jesus acts he does so in or by the Spirit, including on the cross (Hebrews 9:14). But we do not have a detailed description of the Spirit's interaction with the Father like we find for the Son, for instance, in Jesus' prayer in John 17.

Given the whole of biblical revelation, we do not have near as much written about the Spirit as we do about God the Father and the Son. Though the information given is unequal, disproportional, that is no excuse not to pay careful attention to the insight we are given about the Spirit. That may be a problem that needs to be corrected. Perhaps we should give more care to what has been made available to us. But if our speech and understanding are going to remain dependent upon biblical revelation, then we shouldn't be surprised that our considerations will follow the same unequal pattern. So having less to say does not necessarily demonstrate neglect or fear or disinterest in the Spirit.

A Theology of the Holy Spirit, Part 4B

Misguided attempts at correction

Given that the Scripture revelation is disproportional, we could artificially try to give the Spirit "equal time" by extending what we say through the fabrication of long chains of argumentation leading to various conclusions. But such speculations about the Spirit, even if they start with a bit of Scripture, can offer nothing secure, since logical inferences (even from some true starting point) are never necessarily true. In fact, that's where a lot of heresy and bad teaching about the Spirit comes from.

Some preachers and teachers have taken a few biblical verses and then made strings of logical arguments from them, often not paying attention to other biblical teaching regarding the Spirit. But the conclusions reached in that way are speculative. In reaching them a lot had to added, such as making someone's experience (and their understanding of it!) normative for all Christians, in order to establish a purportedly doctrinal statement. But all that additional information, and the logical chains developed on them, do not amount to reliable Christian doctrine.

So giving the Spirit more attention by generating more information than we actually have been given is not a recommended or reliable procedure. But sometimes a desire to rebalance things and give greater emphasis to the Spirit has resulted in such practices. We should not follow suit.

Why is less revealed about the Spirit?

Is there some reason why there is unequal information about the Holy Spirit in Scripture? It seems to me the disproportion ought to be expected because of what we do find out about the Spirit. Given the very nature of the Spirit and the nature of his work, it makes sense that there is less to say concretely and authoritatively about the Spirit than the Father or the Son.

First, the Spirit is not incarnate. We don't have an embodied revelation of the Holy Spirit. The Spirit remains undetectable himself, but is identified indirectly by the effects of his working (like the wind). The Holy Spirit doesn't show up on the incarnate stage of history like Jesus does. The Son is the only triune Person who becomes incarnate. There's no incarnate description of the Spirit. That's the main reason why we have a lot more to say about the Son. The purpose of his coming in human form was to be the self-revelation of God. He is the Word of God to us.

The Spirit doesn't have his own incarnation. The Spirit doesn't have his own independent word. Jesus is the Logos, the intelligibility, the communication, the living interpretation of God to us. Without the incarnate life and teaching of Jesus, we would know far less about the Spirit, for the Son reveals not only himself, but the Father and the Spirit to us. The Incarnate Son takes us to the Father and sends us the Spirit, so we approach the Spirit through the mediation of the Son.

Even when the Spirit is active within creation, he doesn't establish his own revelation and doesn't convey his own self-explanation. The Spirit remains the Spirit. He remains unincarnate while present to and within creation. The Spirit's remaining unincarnate serves a positive purpose. It prevents us from reducing God simply to a creature or thinking that we can understand God entirely in terms of creaturely realities. It preserves the transcendence, the spirituality of God. God is not a creature, so we cannot explain God as if God were a creature subject to creaturely ways and limitations. We cannot simply read back onto God the incarnated nature of Jesus.

Some people mistakenly think that when the Son of God took on human form, the Father (or God) turned into a human, a creature. There are two mistakes in that. First, it was the Son of God who became incarnate, not the Father (nor the Spirit). Second, the Son of God did not cease being the eternal, divine, Son of God when he took on human being. He remained what he was but also added to himself a fully human nature and lived a human life. He didn't stop being something he was and turn into something else, a man. Early church teachers put it this way: "The eternal Son of God, remaining what he was, assumed also a human nature to himself." You can recognize this kind of confusion when, considering the possibility of the incarnation, people ask, "Then who is running the universe?"

How the eternal Son of God can be incarnate in human form is a mystery. We can't imagine how such a change of that order could be true for human beings. But remember: God is not a creature. Admittedly, it is easier to think of Jesus' incarnation as his turning into what he was not and ceasing to be what he was. If A becomes B, then it ceases to be A. It's now B. That's easy to think, because that's how most creaturely things work. However, such thinking just doesn't apply to the truth about who the Son of God is. He remains what he was, the eternal Son of God, assuming a human nature as well.

The Spirit never took on a human nature himself. If you ask, "How was Jesus conceived in the womb of Mary?" The answer is, by the Spirit. The agency of the Spirit is the answer to the "how" question. But this answer doesn't tell us the mechanisms involved. No mention of DNA or what happened with the chromosomes. We don't get that type of explanation. Instead, we are told who the agent was. He knows how! I suppose if we asked the Spirit and he thought it was important for us to know, the Spirit could explain it to us if we were educated and intelligent enough to grasp it. But apparently, it's far more important to know *by whom* it occurred rather than how.

But we learn something about the Spirit in this event. The Spirit can interact in time and space, with flesh and blood, without being incarnate himself. The Spirit is able to be present and active at the deepest levels of creaturely existence, down to the DNA and chromosomes if need be. The Spirit is not absent but able to be present to creation. That's one way God can work within creation — by the Spirit. Recognizing that God is the Spirit and the Spirit is God and he remains the Holy Spirit prevents us from thinking of God as merely being a creature. The Spirit doesn't have to be incarnate to have a ministry to us. As Jesus said, he is sending another Comforter who was with us, but will be in us (John 14:17).

There is another reason why there is a disproportion in the amount of information we have about the Spirit in the biblical portrayal. This distinction is not one of importance, but of the extent of the revelation. If what we say and teach about the Spirit depends on that revelation, then this will make a difference in how much we can say and how much we can understand about the Spirit. This second reason has to do with the character of the Spirit and of his ministry. It seems that the purpose and character of the ministry of the Holy Spirit is to always direct attention away from, not bring it to himself. The ministry of the Spirit, Jesus tells us, is to direct us to Jesus (John 15:26). He doesn't come with his own independent message, but bears witness to the truth spoken by the Son. The Spirit does not glorify himself, but he glorifies Jesus by taking his words and declaring them to us (John 16:13-14). That is the glory of the Spirit!

The Holy Spirit isn't saying, "Jesus, you've had the microphone for plenty of time. Now, it's my turn to tell people about myself." No. When the Holy Spirit "gets the microphone," what does he announce? He helps us recall all that Jesus taught, the truth that he taught. He, perhaps annoyingly, passes up his opportunity to shed light on himself. The Holy Spirit doesn't draw attention to himself. Rather, he points away from himself. Why? Because that's his ministry, so that we see who Jesus is, who reveals to us the Father. The early church put it this way: The Holy Spirit is like light. He shines light on the face of Jesus, who has a flesh-and-blood human face. When the Holy Spirit's light shines on the face of Jesus, what do we see mirrored in the face of Jesus? The face of the Father. Isn't that a beautiful thing?

The Holy Spirit doesn't say, "Hey, look at me. I'm the light. I'm shining. Can't you see how bright I am?" Not at all. The reason for the Spirit's shining is so that when we look at the face of Jesus, we see the face of the Father. That's the point of the light. The light doesn't draw attention to itself.

That doesn't mean the Spirit's not important, but the contrary! If the light didn't shine, what would result? We wouldn't see the face of the Father in the face of the Son. There wouldn't even be a face of the Son incarnate if the Spirit hadn't been involved in the conception of the Son in the womb of Mary. The Spirit has a coordinated but different mission and ministry than the Son. But that ministry would be compromised and would not demonstrate the true nature and character of the Spirit if it drew attention to itself.

One theologian has said, if you add the biblical picture up, the Spirit is the "shy one" of the Trinity or the "retiring one." We could even say the Holy Spirit displays the humility of God, because he serves the Father and the Son. Theologian Thomas Torrance brings out this point regarding the character of the Spirit. Relatively speaking, he stays in the background.

Should we conclude that the Holy Spirit serves the Father and Son rather than himself? Absolutely. We'd be somewhat impoverished if we didn't know that. We are learning something about the Spirit when we see that he doesn't draw attention to himself! Whenever we find revelation concerning the Spirit, we discover more references to the Father and the Son. The Spirit actually promotes the disproportion of detailed understanding about the Triune Persons, because that's the ministry of the Spirit. The Spirit says, "You saw the face of the Father and the face of the Son. Wonderful. That's what I do. That's why I'm here."

In the next section, we'll look at the Spirit's work in the church and in the lives of individual believers.

A Theology of the Holy Spirit, Part 5

The Spirit in relationship to the church

What is the Holy Spirit's work in the life of the church, in the life of the believer? Think of times when we repent, as a whole church or as individuals. Our repentance is the result of the ministry of the Spirit, who brings us the conviction of sin. Why does anyone ever repent and not hang on to their pride and remain in self-justification mode all their existence? Because the Holy Spirit works. We don't see the Holy Spirit working in a direct way. Most of the work of the Holy Spirit is deep and internal to persons, speaking with their spirits, as Paul put it (1 Corinthians 2:9-11). We don't see the Holy Spirit acting, but we see the results of the working of the Holy Spirit, like the wind.

So we see evidences of the ministry of the Spirit. When we're hearing God speaking his word, when we're seeing the face of the Father in the face of the Son, when we're repenting, when we're grasping the Word of God, when we're interpreting the Scripture as God intends, then we're experiencing the effects of the Spirit. But we don't see the gears turning—we don't watch the machine running. We see the results, the outcome. Most of the work of the Holy Spirit is invisible to us. What we see is the result, the effect. The Spirit seems to deliberately not draw attention to himself. He is the shy one, the humble one, the retiring one, or as T.F. Torrance put it, the "self-effacing one." He doesn't show us his own face. The Spirit is not worried about that. Each person of the Trinity gives glory to the others. The Spirit has his own way of giving glory.

Even in the names of the Divine Persons, we find an asymmetry. Father and Son are mutually referential terms that speak of a concrete Father-Son relationship. Thus these terms are easier to think about than is Holy Spirit, which does not lend itself as easily to being described using creaturely terms. Has the Holy Spirit been short-changed once again? Maybe not. Perhaps that's how it's supposed to be. Maybe being given that name is not a mistake. Maybe the name, the Holy Spirit, is given in order to prevent us from trying to nail down his identity in the same way we might the Father and Son. Perhaps that "inequality" is meant to lead us to identify with and pay primary attention first to the Father and Son. Perhaps by being named Holy Spirit, we are kept from reducing the Father and Son to creaturely definitions, thinking God is Father and Son in just the way human beings are. After all, Scripture can refer to the whole God as Spirit. The Holy Spirit reminds us of the transcendence, the sovereignty, the irreducibility of God to an idol made by human hands or minds and imaginations.

Given the pattern and content of biblical revelation about the Spirit, we should not expect to be able to have as much to say, or be able to say in as much detail as we can say about the Father and the Son. Though we see some disproportion, it does not indicate inequality of importance among the Divine Persons.

Why not correct by focusing on the Spirit?

If we have under-represented the Spirit up to this point, not making use of what we have been given to go on, why not take time to shift our focus of attention to the Spirit—attempting to bring about a proper balance? Why not attempt to make up for lost time, giving the Spirit his turn on stage, even if just a temporary one? The danger to watch out for in attempting to correct in this way is giving the Spirit independent consideration, in isolation from the revelation of the Son and of the Father in him.

Why is this a problem? Because the Spirit doesn't have an independent ministry. The Holy Spirit's ministry is to deliver to us all the benefits of the work of Christ — the benefits he accomplished as the Son of the Father, sent from him and returning to him that we might know him. This work of the Spirit can't be grasped apart from the working of the Father and Son. The working of the Father and Son must include sooner or later an appreciation for the "behind the scenes" working of the Spirit. So the best way is to move in our understanding from the Son to the Father and then in a more focused way to the Spirit, bringing all three into coordination.

To be a little facetious, it isn't as if the Spirit says, "Jesus, you did that awesome work on the cross. You took your turn and accomplished that great task. I know everyone will praise you for it, but now it's my time to get some attention. I'm going to take my turn to accomplish my own mission, and so make my own addition to what you've done."

That kind of thinking regards God as dividing up his work and will into a division of labor, each separate from the others. But the will and working of God can't be sliced up that way. That splits God into parts and separate roles or tasks, as creatures might have. It obscures the oneness of God in being and in action. A simple way to point to the unity of the working of God—while allowing for distinction of contribution to the one whole work—is to say that what Christ has done for us according to the will of the Father, the Holy Spirit does in us. That's about the simplest way you can put it, not that more couldn't be said, and probably should be said.

When we say that the Spirit takes all of what Christ has done for us in his humanity and delivers it to us, does that amount to little or nothing? No, not at all. From the Holy Spirit's point of view, that's everything! The Holy Spirit cannot accomplish his deepest work except on the basis of what Jesus, the Son Incarnate, accomplished for us in the name of the Father. They are one God. They are all together Savior. The Father sends the Son. The Son sends the Spirit. This was all done so we might have the life of the whole Triune God over us, with us and in us.

As T.F. Torrance has expressed it, it seems that rebellious human beings can share in God's kind of life (eternal life) only after it has been worked out in such a way that it can fit us fallen creatures. We first need to be reconciled to God and, second, have our human nature regenerated, sanctified, made new. That's what God accomplished in the incarnate Son, who assumed our human nature. He reconciled and transformed it, perfecting our human nature, so that the Holy Spirit could indwell us and make us share in Jesus' sanctified humanity. The Holy Spirit could not come and take up residence in us ("indwell" is the old theological word) until the Son has completed his incarnate work in our fallen humanity.

We're not leaving out the Holy Spirit when we say that the Spirit takes what the Son has done and delivers and builds it into us. It would be senseless for the Spirit to say, "I need my own ministry apart from the Son." They're one in being. They're one in act. They're one in mind, one in heart, perfectly coordinated in their ministry to give us a share in God's own life, and each contributes in his own way.

The whole God is Savior God—Father, Son and Spirit. The Spirit leads in working out in us what Christ has accomplished for us in his humanity. That's a marvel. The Spirit works in us in unique ways. That is why Jesus says it's an advantage that another Comforter come to us, to deliver to us and within us his life, by the indwelling of the Spirit—the Spirit who is the Spirit of Jesus, the One who has accomplished everything for us in his human nature.

You can see the problem if, wanting to give the Spirit equal time, we were to say, "Yes, Jesus did this, but the Spirit does that," then focus on "that" as if it were an independent mission. But there is no independent mission—the Father, Son and Spirit always work together in an ordered and coordinated fashion. That insight ought to guide our thinking, our explanations, our preaching and teaching about the Spirit. Describing their joint mission requires referring to one another, because the Spirit is the Spirit of the Son and the Spirit of the Father. That's who the Holy Spirit is. The working of the Spirit is to work out in us what the Son has done for us. That's an amazing, glorious thing.

Unique manifestations of the working of God by the Spirit

There are particular manifestations of the

Spirit's work—times and ways in which he is active at the leading edge, as it were, of what the Triune God is doing. The Spirit's relationship to creation, after Christ's incarnate ministry, is dynamic and variable, rather than static, fixed or mechanical. His ministry is personal and relational. This was seen at Pentecost when the Spirit came down. No human agency initiated, conditioned or controlled that event. No believer set it up, orchestrated it, or made it more or less likely to occur. Rather, Jesus had promised its fulfillment in the name of the Father. His work, promise and sending is what pre-conditioned that mighty, longed-for event pointed to by the prophets. Jesus indicated that this would be at the Father's initiative, according to his timing. The church was simply to wait.

Why at that particular time? Because Christ in his earthly form had finished his dimension of the saving work that God was accomplishing. The Spirit was promised by the Son, and perfectly coordinated, he showed up on time. But notice what happened when the Spirit descended. The people started talking about the great and mighty things that God had done to accomplish their salvation in Jesus. They didn't just focus on the amazing event they had just experienced! They related to each other in new and amazing ways, just as the Spirit was working in them in new ways. But they didn't just focus on the Spirit, or their experience of the Spirit. Their view was larger, much more comprehensive of all that God had done, was doing and would do.

Pentecost is a primary example of a manifestation of the working of the Spirit that is dynamic, variable, not static, not fixed, not mechanical, but personal and relational. In Paul's admonitions to not quench the Spirit or not grieve the Spirit and to be continually filled with the Spirit, we also see anticipation of a dynamic interaction with the Holy Spirit. Paul is not thinking of a situation in which the switch to the Holy Spirit is sometimes in the "on" position and at other times in the "off" position. In Paul's view, the Spirit is never completely absent as though he were a billion miles away, having nothing to do with anything and then immediately near and causing everything to happen, almost magically. The Spirit does not operate in that way. Instead, there is a dynamic interaction between God's people and the Spirit. He can be present in a wide array of ways, or at least in a range of ways that have a wide array of effects we can notice.

"Being continually filled with the Spirit" is a good way to understand the places in his letters where Paul talks about our relationship with the Spirit. The Spirit should not be approached as if he's a vending machine: put in the right coins, push the right button and get your soda or your candy bar or something else. No, it's not contractual or automatic. The relationship is not simply a matter of being "on" or "off." It's not a mechanical relationship. It is dynamic. It's like the wind blowing.

Let's look at another aspect of the manifestation of the working of the Spirit in the church—the gifts of the Spirit. These too involve dynamic interactions. Paul encourages believers to use them in certain ways: let the person with the gift of giving, he says, give with liberality; those who give aid, with zeal; those who do acts of mercy, with cheerfulness (Romans 12:6-8). Gifts can be used well or misused. They are to be received and then used well, rightly, faithfully. That is a dynamic process, not a magical chain of effects impersonally sparked.

It's easier to think of the working of the Spirit in mechanical terms, especially if we think of the Spirit as an "it"—an impersonal power or energy, like electricity. Just on or off; here but not there; near or far. But God is not like that. We could say that the Spirit, especially, is not like that!

There is a particular dynamic to living in the Spirit. The Spirit is living and moving—acting as an intelligent agent; interacting with us in a deep and personal way—even acting in ways of which we aren't aware. Often, by the time we become aware, the Spirit may have already moved on to another thing. We'll likely recognize his activity and proclaim, "The Spirit was working and we were blessed!" But by the time we do, the Spirit may already have moved on to another "project." The Spirit is active and moving!

There is a variability, a change, a dynamic, an

ebb and flow to the activity and manifestation and interaction with the Spirit in relationship to the church and in relationship to the world. We ought not think of the Holy Spirit as an impersonal force, a vending machine or conveyor belt. Another way we can think mistakenly of the Spirit is as a genie or a magician. In this case we approach the Spirit thinking, "If I'm going to be blessed by the Spirit, I'll have to do things just right. I'm going to have to rub the lamp exactly three times and say just the right words and then the power of the spirit-genie will work." But that's an impersonal, mechanical approach that is just as misguided as the idea that we must take the initiative, believing that the working of the Spirit is unlocked (or not) by us. Unfortunately it's not difficult to find erroneous teachings like this—ones suggesting that we should act towards the Holy Spirit as if "it" was a magical power, much like a genie. To get the Spirit to work we have to fulfill certain conditions just right—then (like magic!) the Spirit is set free to accomplish his ministry on our behalf.

The special techniques promoted by some for activating the Spirit don't involve rubbing a lamp. Other conditions are laid out, some sequence of events under our control are specified in order to "prime the pump" or to "release the Spirit" to work. If the Spirit doesn't show up, the explanation will be: "You didn't get things quite right. You weren't sincere enough. You didn't have enough faith. You weren't humble enough. You were stuck in your head and thinking too much. You didn't 'let go' enough to 'let God.'" In essence, such explanations say the spirit-genie is not going to come out because you said "abracadabro" instead of "abracadabra." Or you said it with the wrong accent! Or..., or..., or.... Any number of conditions might be specified. Each teacher of such false views will specialize in describing and prescribing exactly which conditions are called for.

These wrong-headed approaches put us in charge, making the Spirit dependent upon us with little to say for himself. Such approaches make our relationship with the Spirit one that is legal (contractual), mechanical and conditional. Like a genie or some mechanical power, the Spirit has no more choice in the matter than electricity has when you plug in your TV or turn on your lights. Imagined here is a cause-effect relationship from us to the Spirit. Only when the conditions are just right can the Spirit do its work, and when the conditions are set just right, apparently the Spirit is unable to decide, "No, I'm not going to do your bidding!" We set the agenda and the Spirit somehow comes under obligation to us!

Unfortunately, we can think about the Spirit in these impersonal ways—as an "it" rather than the very personal God that he is. Sadly, we can easily find teachers who lead us in those wrong directions. But we don't need to go down those dead-end paths. We can have more faithful understandings that stay more closely tied to the actual teaching about the nature and character of the Spirit in relationship to the Father and Son as made known in Scripture and experienced in the church of the New Testament times.

Next, we will look at various issues related to the Holy Spirit's continuing ministry.

Gary W. Deddo

Parts 6 and 7 are not part of this 40 days of discipleship, but they are included in the appendix, if you wish to finish reading the series.

Scripture: God's Gift – Part 5

This is a continuation. Parts 1–4 were in *40 Days of Purpose, Volume 2.*

Reality and the meaning of Scripture

This article is part of a series by Gary Deddo on interpreting Scripture. For parts one through four, see *40 Days of Discipleship: The Second 40 Days*. This article covers several more aspects of listening to, studying and interpreting Scripture that honors its God-given nature and purpose. As we examine these, perhaps we'll find some habits that need to be unlearned.

Discovering the meaning that is there

Often when we hear Scripture read or preached or study it for ourselves, we approach it thinking we're going to "try to make sense of it." But I think that's really not the best way to put it. Rather, we come to realize that as God speaks to us in Scripture it reads *us*, it makes sense of us! God's Word sheds light on our lives. God's Word is living and active and not a passive collection of data that we probe, organize, arrange and apply and then announce what we've made of it. Rather, as we listen to Scripture, we are acted upon by the Word and the Spirit. It comes with its own meaning and sense. So, we don't give it meaning and make sense of it. We *discover* its meaning and sense.

Listening to and studying Scripture is a matter of discovery, not creativity, innovation or theorizing. Hearing Scripture in a way that fosters faith calls for a receptiveness on our part, allowing it to speak to us. We do not sit in critical judgment on it, deciding ahead of time what we will or won't hear or whether we will or won't live by it. St. Augustine long ago realized there was a huge difference in approaching Scripture as users, compared to being receivers who are prepared to enjoy and live under the Word we hear. He advised, just like the book of James does, that we take the posture of hearers of the Word of God, receiving and even delighting in it.

Receptivity, the proper subjectivity

We don't have to guess or sort through a lot of hypothetical options to discover what attitude of receptivity we should have towards God's Word. First, Jesus, in his own responsiveness to his Father and the Spirit, demonstrates the proper personal and internal (subjective) orientation we are to have to the Word. Second, the apostles whom Jesus chose, including Paul, embodied the spirit of responsiveness that reflected Jesus' own receptivity. These apostles were not chosen merely because they could be relied upon to convey accurate information (facts). They were appointed because they also had the right kind of receptivity (subjective orientation) to the truth that they were given. If we are to hear the Word of God, we must stand in their place, taking up their attitude of receptivity. We must have ears to hear in order to grasp what they are saying—to hear what they heard.

Often we think that the biblical revelation given to us by its authors is simply a collection of data, information that sits objectively on the page, neutrally and in that sense objectively (we say). We then take over that "data," mining it for ourselves with whatever subjective orientation we please, including the attempt to rid ourselves of any subjective element. But the biblical preservers of revelation do not simply offer objective information that we then decide how or whether to appropriate or receive. No, the biblical revelation includes the revelation of the nature of its own proper receptivity, its own orientation and attitude. That subjective aspect is embodied in Jesus and his apostles and is also conveyed in their preserved writings. Revelation as revelation cannot be gained apart from this kind of receptivity because it is included in it.

This subjective orientation is not neutral or abstractly objective. The receptive orientation of the biblical writers is one of trust, readiness to repent, a desire for reconciliation and confidence in the power and faithfulness of God to redeem, renew and put right all things. Revelation includes both objective and subjective elements perfectly coordinated with each other. How the revelation is received is perfectly harmonized with what is revealed. The revelation cannot be grasped at all except in and through that subjective orientation. God does not approach us neutrally, but passionately and redemptively. So we cannot approach God neutrally and dispassionately if we are to receive the content and benefits of his revealed redemption. The receptivity that is resident in Jesus and resonant in the apostles is given to us as a gift of the Spirit so that we might receive the revelation of God that the apostles of Jesus Christ passed on to the whole church for all time.

The false objectivity of abstract thinking

Much of the information we get, some of which is called scientific, is abstract. It is disconnected from the source of the information, from the object being investigated. Such input can seem to be simply words, concepts, ideas, principles or numbers and mathematical formulas. Sometimes the information comes to us as a line of argument made up of a chain of logical connections. To use an analogy, it would be like studying the wake made by a boat that has long since passed by, but not learning much about the boat itself—which is really what we want to know. Such information rarely helps us relate to or interact with the object, the reality itself, since it's only indirectly connected to it. We're looking at the effects of something, not the source or cause of the effects.

Often in Christian teaching we're led to consider evidences of something (the wake, the effects) but aren't directed to think about the reality itself (the boat, cause or source of the effects). For example, we might be presented evidences for the empty tomb, or for the possibility of Jesus' miracles, but not give much consideration to Jesus himself. Following that path we may learn something about him, but we don't get to know Jesus himself.

This abstract approach is often what we get from "experts." Sometimes we are impressed by the knowledge and insight they impart. But at other times, their abstract information and principles annoy us and leave us cold. It can seem that such information has nothing practical to do with life. We suspect that what they are sharing is the product of overactive minds fueled by over-sized egos!

Though not always, this abstract approach is often characteristic of theological or philosophical thinking, which provides ideas or concepts about God. Doctrine then becomes a mere collection of ideas or concepts to believe in (or not!). This reduces Christianity to merely understanding Christian ideas—ideas derived from the Bible. But this abstracting and conceptualizing approach sets us up for the disaster that is common in modernity and postmodernity (two periods now existing side-by-side). The modern mindset tends to regard faith as bias that distorts any true knowledge of the reality. The postmodern mindset tends to see faith, like all forms of knowing, as governed by personal/subjective factors (such as race, gender, class, etc.). With this postmodern perspective, all knowledge collapses into self-knowing, agnosticism or, more often, a knowledge controlled by the will-to-power.

A biblically formed mindset acknowledges these barriers to knowing truth, including knowing God. From the biblical perspective, we fallen humans are seen as idolaters who create gods in our own image in order to justify ourselves and our own kind. The prophets of Israel spoke out against this idolatry, which is our attempt to recreate God in our own image or images that we can control and use. The golden calf in Moses' time is an example. All Scripture teaches that God cannot be found by sheer human effort and that we will only end up deluded by the results of such misguided efforts. Jesus declared, "No one knows the Son except the Father, and no one knows the Father except the Son" (Matthew 11:27). As the early church used to put it: "Only God knows God…" But that does not mean God cannot be known, for it does not eliminate the possibility that God is smart enough and motivated enough to figure out how to make himself known. So the early church saying continued: "And only God reveals God." That is what Jesus goes on to say: "…and those to whom the Son chooses to reveal him."

The God of the Bible can and wants to make himself known. He's the Good Shepherd who knows how to get through to the dumb sheep. God's act of self-revelation is required if we are to know God himself, personally and deeply (*epignosis* is the Greek word used in the New Testament).

Revelation, especially the self-revelation of God in Christ, that was borne witness to by Jesus' personally selected apostles and the working of the Spirit, can't be approached in either the modern or postmodern way, by either eliminating the subjective element or declaring that it always hides or distorts the truth. Knowing God in his act of self-revelation calls for a subjective orientation that correlates with the nature and purpose of the revelation, namely being reconciled to God. It calls for humility and a mustard seed's worth of faith/trust to get the ball rolling. We have to be willing to orient our ways of knowing, both its objective and subjective elements, to the nature of the revelation. Knowing God calls for a readiness to repent and a desire to be reconciled to God. God's self-revelation rules out the twin errors of either attempting to remove all subjectivity (a false objectivity) or assuming that any subjective stance we might prefer would suffice (a false subjectivity).

Listening in this way to the Living Word through the Written Word by the Spirit puts us into contact with the reality itself, with the living God. In and through Scripture, with Christ at the center, we're not being given information about God, but hearing a Word from God who makes himself known as Lord and Savior through the medium of those witnesses preserved for us. If we approach Scripture as simply a set of concepts, ideas or principles about God and his ways, we will be missing the boat! Scripture, by the Word and Spirit, does not primarily enable us to know about God or his will for us, but to know God, himself, in person. That is the case because God is a living God and a speaking God and has not become mute since the days of Jesus. Listening to and studying Scripture with humility and trust/faith in the God of the Bible is a vital aspect of our living in relationship, communication, and communion with God. If we miss this we miss receiving the gift of God.

Taking the Bible realistically

Some in the church and its various seminaries have attempted to correct such an abstract approach to the Bible by emphasizing that they take the Bible "literally." Their aim is to achieve a more "objective" approach. Others have recommended that we fix the problem on the subjective side of things by taking Scripture more seriously, more imaginatively, in a more narrative way. Or those seeing the problem on the subjective side might gravitate toward interpreting it more ethically (either personally or socio-politically), more pragmatically or with greater conviction, courage and commitment. While well-intentioned, these commendations seem to me to fall short of what is hoped for and don't align as closely with the actual nature and character of God's Word as we might think.

There are other theologians, notably Thomas F. Torrance, who said that we need to take the Bible realistically. When we listen to or study Scripture, we are hearing from those who, by the inspiration of the Spirit of Jesus, are telling us about the reality of who God is and what God has done, is doing and will do. Scripture tells us about the nature of reality – reality we can have contact with and can access, for example creation, and also reality that we cannot directly access but that can contact us, e.g. the Living Word by the Spirit. The words of Scripture point to, inform us and put us into contact with the reality of who God is and who we are in relationship to him and to creation. By them God tells us what the real situation is. In listening to Scripture we are getting to know God himself because God is able to use, by the Spirit, the created medium of divinely appointed human communication to speak to us through it. When interacting with Scripture, we're dealing with the "boat" itself, not the wake it leaves behind.

So the question we ought to ask in reading any text of Scripture is this: "What reality is this passage telling me about?" This ought to be the central and controlling question, whether it's a historical event or a didactic teaching, a narrative or parable, a simile, a metaphor or symbol, a historical person or a hypothetical and representative character. Of every passage we need to ask these questions: What am I being told about the nature of reality, of God, of human nature, of our relationship with God, of right relationship with each other? Of course, by "reality" we do not mean simply that which human creatures can see, taste, touch, measure, weigh and calculate. Those features only have to do with empirical realities, part of what we call nature, considered as causal and mechanical and impersonal things. But Scripture puts us in touch with realities that cannot be investigated by empirical means. The most important reality is the nature, character and reality of God the Father and God the Holy Spirit and what he has done for us in Jesus. These are not natural or earthly realities. The living and speaking God continues to reveal the true nature of these realities through his Written Word with the Living Word as its center.

Faith comes by hearing

How do we discover these, to us, invisible realities if we can't see them, touch them, weigh them or experiment with them? The answer is that we hear about them from reliable, personal sources or authorities. We encounter their objective reality through being told about them by those who know. We can know about things we cannot empirically explore by being told about them. By having ears to hear, we can see with spiritual eyes (the eyes of our heart – Ephesians 1:18; Acts 26:18). Jesus' eternal relationship with the Father and the Spirit is an example of such a reality. Other examples are the prophetic words from Jesus and his apostles about God's future intentions for his creation, namely, that God will give us a renewed heavens and earth and that every tear will be wiped away by God's final restorative working. By means of hearing from those who know, we can know and also interact with creaturely and divine realities that cannot be seen and cannot be empirically discovered. Speaking and hearing can be an objective event that conveys to us and thus puts us into contact with a divine transcendent reality. By the Spirit, this encounter corrects our wrong notions and arrogant attitudes. We can know, love, trust, obey and pray to God, who speaks an objective word to us in and through his Word.

So we listen to Scripture as a way of getting to know and interact with divine and creaturely reality, not just to have correct truths, ideas, concepts, ideals or doctrines. By hearing, we come into contact with the truth and reality of who God is and who we are, and discover the true nature of created things. Taking all of Scripture realistically tells us who and how things really were, are and will be.

The meaning of Scripture

Another connection that probably needs to be made, although it perhaps sounds self-evident when articulated, is that what the Bible means is the reality to which it refers. The words of the Bible point beyond themselves by referring to and, by the Spirit, disclosing to us the reality itself, e.g., who God is. The words of the Bible have their significance (they signify or point to) realities. So when we take Holy Scripture realistically, we are asking after the meaning and significance of the words. The words don't refer to or mean other words or ideas. The words refer beyond themselves and indicate realities that are far greater than the words themselves. The realities cannot be reduced to the words, but faithful and accurate words authorized by God through the Spirit can put us in contact with the reality. We want to know what realities the words point to, for that reality is their meaning. We are not attempting to find or create or give meaning to Scripture or make the Bible meaningful to us or others. Rather, we're discovering the meaning and significance it already has as we recognize the realities to which the words point and, by the Spirit, put us into contact with. That's what God's revelation intends to do and can do.

Meaning beyond the words through the words

An implication of Scripture's meaning is that the fullness, meaning and significance of the reality exceed the words used to point to it. Even words that are indispensable for discovering and relating to the reality, like biblical revelation, can never substitute for the reality itself. The reality of God especially cannot be reduced to words, even biblical words. But those inspired words are not arbitrary or dispensable. They are the gift of God, the God-given means empowered by the Spirit to refer us to and reveal those realities. The Bible is like a unique and authoritative map that is essential to guiding us to our destination—which is not a point on the map, but a location in reality. The meaning of the texts will always be found beyond the words themselves, although never discovered in any authoritative way except in and through the words spoken to us. That is why Scripture is indispensable to the Christian church, though we don't worship the Bible. We don't pray to the Bible and we don't believe that the Bible will, on the last day, raise us from the dead. The object of our worship, love and faith is not the Bible, but the God who speaks to us uniquely through his written Word.

Our own words (in writing, preaching and teaching), including our doctrines, ought to be evaluated by how well they point to the same reality that Scripture points to. We don't want to be drawn into arguments about our words or those used by others. Rather, we listen for their meaning—the reality to which they point—realizing that words fall short of the transcendent and divine reality itself. We look for the most faithful words we can find, often with the help of others, in faith hoping to add our non-authoritative witness and testimony to the reality that the words of Scripture point to authoritatively.

These points about reality and the meaning of Scripture are large overarching concerns. But if Scripture is taken to offer simply concepts or ideas about God, or if we think our job is to make sense of it, or think the meaning of the words of Scripture are simply other words or ideas, we'll go off in an unhelpful and confusing direction that will not easily contribute to our faith relationship with its Giver.

There are a few more detailed, nitty-gritty suggestions we can touch on to wrap up this series of articles on listening to and studying Scripture. But we'll wait to take them up in our last installment.

Scripture: God's Gift – Part 6

Concluding Principles

We now conclude this series with several principles that help us interpret Scripture in ways that honor its God-given nature and purpose.

The written form of biblical texts

God's gift comes to us in the form of writings that were preserved down through the ages in the form of written texts in human languages. To honor Scripture is to honor the form in which is it given to us, not just the content. Thus to pay careful attention to the Bible, we have to take into consideration its historical, linguistic and literary forms. Our methods have to be able to attune us to the communication offered in those forms. But the methods used to engage the forms of communication cannot be allowed to take over and determine what we are able or are allowed to hear. That's how modern biblical studies and criticism have often gone wrong. However, we can selectively use methods attuned to the form of Scripture in ways that enable us to hear the words as references to the realities that disclose to us its meaning and significance. Methods that impose their own meanings and significance must be set aside; otherwise we are granting them final authority over Scripture, placing our ultimate trust in them and not in the living Word of God.

What are some implications of recognizing the importance of the form of biblical revelation? First, a knowledge of the biblical languages can be helpful for those translating it into other languages (missionary translators), for those translating it into other historical-cultural contexts (pastors and teachers) and for those who equip others to communicate the biblical message and meaning. A familiarity with the customs, the culture, the time period of history and the original audience addressed when the various texts were written is also useful. A grasp of the various literary forms used and how they function as means of communication (e.g., history, wisdom literature, letters, Gospels, apocalyptic etc.) also helps us better listen to God's Word. Much of scholarship is devoted to these elements of biblical studies. There are a number of good books that assist us in discerning the genre of the various biblical writings and how to approach them.

Methods must serve the message and meaning of the texts

However, the methods have to always be in service of and subservient to the message and the meaning (realities to which they refer) of the biblical revelation. Whatever methods we use should not: 1) impede our hearing the message or 2) call into question the possibility of actually knowing those realities or 3) impose their own philosophical presuppositions on what we can expect to know or hear before we've listened, or 4) draw us into a false sense of objectivity (which promotes a seeming neutrality or abstract distance between us and the object of revelation's disclosure). Methods that do so would need to be ruled out, rejected and repented of. For in those cases the methods have become our religion, our primary object of trust, the authoritative source of our most fundamental assumptions about reality. They will have become the controlling reality and therefore serve as conceptual idols that make us into users of and lords over the Word of God.

They may do this under the cover of our assumed powers that we have and need for "knowing good and evil." (Just what the serpent tempted Adam and Eve to think they needed.) But such dangers need not rule out a proper use of methods that are ordered to the nature and ends of the good gift of Scripture. We honor the creaturely form of Scripture when our methods correspond to it rather than rule over it. Such methods pay careful attention to the genre of the various biblical texts as well as the language and historical and cultural background. A resource such as the *IVP Bible Background Commentary* provides such information to assist anyone on any passage of Scripture.

Whole literary units

Another simple implication is that the form of biblical revelation is for the most part conveyed to us as whole literary pieces. The books of the Bible were written, collected and arranged as whole pieces. Thus, harkening back to what we said about interpreting the parts in terms of the whole and the whole as made up of all the parts, we should always consider the whole of the literary unit in which Scripture was written and preserved for us to ascertain the meaning and significance of the various sub-units within.

Individual passages or even chapters should be interpreted in the light of the whole book and the location and order in which each verse, paragraph or section appears in the book. Failing to do so takes the parts out of context and does not honor the coherent form in which God has given and preserved his written word for us. On any topic, every book of the Bible must be taken into consideration along with its location in the history of God's revelation and in relation to its revelatory center in Jesus Christ. But that process must start by studying the biblical books as whole units written or collected and arranged as wholes. In that way we have many pointers, some clearer than others, guiding us to know and properly relate to the realities that God intends them to disclose to us.

Indicatives of grace are the foundation for the imperatives of grace

I have become alert to another bad habit that somehow has sneaked into our biblical interpretation that could use some corrective attention. We are often under conviction that the Bible is there primarily to tell us what to do for God or how to do certain things for God. This is especially true for those who have already become believing people, members of a church. This pull of being obligated to do things for God becomes so strong that often we are drawn into bad habits of biblical interpretation. We end up not really hearing the Word and inadvertently distort what we hear. We end up thinking God is essentially a taskmaster and we are his slaves or worker-bees!

The problem arises when we take something that is simply declared to us so that we might trust in its truth and reality, and then turn it into something we are to do, or accomplish or somehow make actual or real. In shorthand, using grammatical terms, we turn indicatives of grace into imperatives (commands) of works.

For example, in the Beatitudes in Jesus' Sermon on the Mount (Matthew 5), we turn the indicatives that tell us that God has blessed certain folks (the poor in spirit, the meek, those who thirst for righteousness and those who are peacemakers) into commands telling us to try harder to become these things. But Jesus was not using imperatives to command his listeners to work harder to do those things or to become those things. Rather, he was indicating what God already has done in blessing his people. God blessed some listening to Jesus right then and there. Jesus was inviting them (and us!) to recognize and marvel at what God had done by his Spirit in his people.

A little later in the Sermon, Jesus does give a command—he issues an unconditional imperative at the end of the Beatitudes: "Rejoice and be glad!" Yes, that's what we are obligated to do for God! Why? Jesus tells us: because God has blessed his people so that some are meek, some are longing for righteousness, some are peacemakers. God is a blessing God…rejoice and be glad! But when the indicatives of this passage are twisted into imperatives, by the time we get to the actual imperative in the sermon, we're too burdened down with guilt to even hear Jesus' command. Or if we do hear, we don't obey. "Right," we say, "rejoice and be glad. No way! He can't be serious after haranguing us like that—disappointed that we're not doing all that we're supposed to do." When we follow that faulty line of reasoning, taking what we think might be the "harder road," we've dismissed the truth of Jesus' message about the blessings of God and missed the actual response he intends to elicit from us!

The Ten Commandments in perspective

I could multiply examples where people take a description in Scripture of what God has done or what he can be trusted for and convert that description (indicative) into an obligation or a command (imperative). This mistake comes from our anxiety to do things for God. The supposed commands are seen as conditions for getting God's approval or his blessing. But as you study Scripture, look to see if it isn't the case that underneath or behind every command there isn't some indication of who God is or what God can be trusted for, which supplies the foundation and motive for those commands. God does not need to be conditioned to be faithful to himself and his promises to us.

Let me give another example. Let's go back to the Old Testament, to the Ten Commandments given to Israel. Notice that it is not given until 430 years after God established his covenant with Abraham. It amounted to a promise: "I will be your God and you shall be my people." "Through you all the nations of the earth shall be blessed." Exodus chapter 20 does not begin with "Thou shalt nots." Note verse 2: "I am the Lord your God who brought you out of Egypt, out of the land of slavery." This verse indicates who God is and what he can be trusted for. It points out that the God who commands is the kind of God who rescues, redeems, sets free, delivers and saves! Why would Israel have an interest in other gods? Did the frog god do such for them? Did the fly god? The Nile River god? The cow god? The sun god? No, all the gods of Egypt became curses and led to death, not life.

As long as Israel trusted their God to be true to his character as revealed and indicated in the great Exodus, they would not even be tempted to turn to these idols, much less make images of them! Who God is in his nature and character is the foundation and the freedom for obeying his commands that follow. When this God is obeyed by faith in his character as revealed in his acts of deliverance, his commands are easy to obey. They are difficult and perhaps impossible to obey only if and when we don't trust God to be true to his character, the same character we see revealed supremely and in person in Jesus Christ, our ultimate Deliverer.

Look for the indicatives of grace upholding every command of grace

So the simple interpretive rule here is: Always interpret the commands of God in terms of indicatives of God's grace and faithful character. Never grab a command apart from its foundation on the indicatives that reveal and remind us who God is. Whenever you find a command, stop and find the indicative of grace upon which it rests and then interpret them together. It should be somewhere nearby, either before or after the command. It might be the whole first half of the book, like Romans, where chapters 1–11 lay out the grace of God and chapters 12-16 present the proper response to that grace. Don't turn the indicatives of grace into an obligation of works. Doing so violates the form (grammar, in this case) and meaning of the words of Scripture. Don't let your guilt, fears and anxieties tempt you to turn a truth about God into an obligation to be laid on yourself or others.

Where do warnings come from?

Another bad habit I have run into and been guilty of myself in years past regards how we interpret the warnings in Scripture. For some reason, I don't know why, when reading the warnings in the Bible, many have the habit of thinking that it indicates that God has a mean streak (should I say "spirit"?) and wants the horrible outcome spoken of to come to pass. So we might be tempted to think that Jesus wants and delights in sending away those not prepared for the wedding feast, or that he wants the rich man who mistreated Lazarus to suffer eternally, etc. After reading a warning we often conclude, "See, we knew there was a dark and unforgiving side of God—look at that warning right there in Scripture! He delights just as much in punishing, rejecting and being wrathful as in saving, reconciling and restoring." But what is the meaning, the reality of these warnings? How should we interpret them in the context of all of Scripture and in light of the character of God revealed in our Lord and Savior Jesus Christ?

First, warnings are not the first word God gives. Warnings come as the last word offered to those who reject all the other words of promise and blessing that call for trust in and worship of God alone. The warnings are mostly directed at self-righteous and haughty religious people, not those who are unbelieving and not a part of the community of worshippers.

Then, what is the purpose or aim of a warning and why would someone give a warning? The purpose is to *prevent* the outcome pictured from happening! It is not given to assure that it happens. It is given because the outcome is not wanted, is not desired but to be averted. It is given to *help* the person being warned of the danger. Warnings are a sign of love, not rejection. Perhaps it is the last sign given, but nevertheless it is still one of love. If God didn't care or wanted the anticipated negative outcome to occur, there would no reason for him to issue a warning. Why even bother? But, no, warnings are the last words of love to prevent the potential outcome.

Other biblical teaching tells us that God does not delight in the punishment of the wicked (Ezekiel 33:11) and he wants no one to perish but to turn and repent (2 Peter 3:9). Jesus' own explanation that he came not to condemn the world but to save it (John 3:14-18) backs up this understanding of biblical warnings. We have Scripture that tells us how God regards the unbeliever, the unrepentant ones. God does not take delight in seeing his good creation come to ruin. Warnings are expressions of love when nothing else has worked. They are not threats God can't wait to carry out. So we ought to interpret biblical warnings in terms of the character of God shown in Christ and according to the purpose of warnings meant to prevent the potential disastrous outcome to those God loves.

Interpret deeds in the light of the interpretive words

Finally, one last bad habit of interpretation to consider. In listening to and studying Scripture, we can fall into the trap of interpreting an action of God or of God's people apart from the accompanying words that indicate its meaning. The revelation of God involves a word-deed event. God does things and has his people do certain things, but the deeds cannot be understood apart from the word given that interprets it. Deeds do not interpret themselves.

The significance and meaning of a particular deed is revealed through words that explain what was behind that action. Often we read of God doing something, especially in the Old Testament but sometimes in the New, and immediately react and draw conclusions about what that deed must say about God or his purposes or mind. For example, we read that the Egyptians drowned in the Red Sea or that God hardened Pharaoh's heart. Or we read of Jesus driving out the money-changers from the temple, or cursing the fig tree, or warning those who have not repented, or instructing the disciples to shake the dust off their feet from those villages that refuse to welcome them. Instead of looking for the prophetic and apostolic interpretation of these deeds—seeking to understand what they point to and how they are fulfilled and perfected (brought to their right and true end or purpose)—we interpret them in the context of what *we* might mean if we were to do these things today (or perhaps what the worst and meanest person we can think of might mean by it!).

In making this mistake, we are substituting our imagined context for the biblical context and explanation. Although sometimes it's not obvious in every text, when the whole picture is assembled, we find that the ultimate purpose of the text is redemption, reconciliation, deliverance—the salvation that is fulfilled in Jesus. Deciding on what a deed of God or his people means apart from God's character and words that interpret such deeds is another way of taking Scripture out of context—it is the grasping of an individual part that is disconnected from the whole. Deeds must never be understood apart from their revealed explanations.

Jesus, God's final word and deed

While there are other words surrounding and interpreting for us those deeds mentioned above, I want to conclude by reminding us that Jesus Christ himself is the final deed and word of God. Jesus had to interpret his deeds even to his own disciples for them to know what they meant. This is especially true of the saving significance of his death and the hope of the resurrection. Without hearing his spoken words, we would not know the meaning of his actions. Both must be taken together.

All the deeds of God in the Bible and other prophetic words should be interpreted in terms of who Jesus is, the final word-deed. The Exodus and Pharaoh must be interpreted in terms of Jesus and his revelation of the heart and mind of God toward all his human creatures. He embodies and explains his purpose to save. As the Son of God and the Son of Man, he worked out that purpose by assuming our human nature as the second Adam and becoming the new head of the race.

Jesus' deeds must be interpreted in terms of his words, not in terms of our words, thoughts, or imaginations. All his deeds or work must be interpreted in the light of his person—in the light of who Jesus is. We must interpret his works in terms of his person. Who is Jesus in his being and nature? He is the Son of the Father, our Savior, Redeemer and Reconciler. That's what the name *Jesus* means—the name given to him by his heavenly Father. All of Jesus' deeds indicate who he is as the eternal Son of the Father, become our Brother, Lord and Servant King in order to make us his beloved children. As God's final word and deed, Jesus is the key to interpreting every word and deed in Scripture—the written word belongs to Jesus and comes from him, God's Living Word to us.

This is what was occurring when Jesus stayed with those he met on the road to Emmaus following his resurrection: "Beginning with Moses and all the Prophets, he interpreted to them in all the Scriptures the things concerning himself" (Luke 24:27, ESV). You'll recall Jesus' admonition to the Pharisees: "You search the Scriptures because you think that in them you have eternal life; and it is they that bear witness about me; yet you refuse to come to me that you may have life" (John 5:39-40, ESV).

Interpretation of Scripture is the church's responsibility

There is one last word to consider before we end this series. The task of interpreting Scripture is not the responsibility of isolated individuals, but the task of the whole church, involving its various members with their gifts and callings, including those gifted as teachers and preachers. Proper interpretation of Scripture takes account of how particular passages of Scripture have been understood by many down through the history of the church and into our own times. We'll want to pay more attention to those teachers and interpreters who follow the kind of guidelines we have laid out in this series.

In presenting this series, I am indebted to many who have gone before me. I have not footnoted these references, but I could have. It is good to consult others before we make final determinations of what a given passage of Scripture means or what a collection of Scriptures add up to mean. We should look for precedents—paying attention to those who have been called by God to assist the church in listening to and understanding Scripture. We ought to be skeptical about esoteric interpretations that have little or no continuity with what the orthodox church as a whole has historically understood. This does not mean that deeper understanding could not be obtained as we stand on the shoulders of those who have gone before. But that understanding should be deeper and fuller than what has gone before, not a departure or wholesale discount of it.

God has many laborers working by faith to understand Scripture. We must not be so arrogant as to think that we alone, individually, can have an independent and final say. While the approach advocated in this series will not guarantee uniformity of interpretation throughout the church, it will help us avoid falling into traps, especially those already identified centuries ago! God gives his Word and his Spirit to the church as a whole. We must not despise others who approach it with the same honor with which we regard it, for in doing so we would be rejecting some of the good gifts that God has given to the church in the past for our benefit today.

With those words then, I end this series with the hope that more questions have been answered than raised; more light shed than heat generated.

May the Lord himself sanctify all these words to you. Amen.

Gary Deddo

Be Devoted to Scripture

One of Christianity's most important doctrines is that of the authority of Scripture. Scripture is the basis for what we teach. Faith is an important part of Christianity—an essential part. But not just any faith will do—our faith must be in something that is true. Faith must not be a false hope—it must be based on evidence—and such evidence needs to be taught. The church Jesus founded is to be a teaching church, and his people are to be people who are learning. (The word "disciple" means "one who learns.")

People who believe in a Savior will be eager to learn more about him. They will hunger and thirst not just for a feeling about God, but also for knowledge of God that involves facts. They will want to learn. Doctrine is important—the New Testament makes that clear. Jesus told the church to teach. The book of Acts tells us that the apostles gave teaching a high priority. Paul wrote that teaching was important. Teaching is an important part of our work.

The importance of the ministry of the word

After Jesus ascended into heaven, the Holy Spirit filled the disciples and the church began to grow by the thousands. What did the people do? "They devoted themselves to the apostles' teaching and to the fellowship, to the breaking of bread and to prayer" (Acts 2:42). Teaching was important.

There were many unusual needs, partly because some of the people had come to Jerusalem for the festival of Pentecost and ended up staying for months longer than they expected. How did the people respond to this need? "Selling their possessions and goods, they gave to anyone as he had need" (verse 45).

Can we imagine what it must have been like? A new community was being formed—new leaders, new followers and new structures. The old social system did not work for these people. Many were cut off from family and former friends, so new ties had to be forged. At first, everyone's needs were taken care of informally. But eventually a system was created to meet the needs. Donations were given to the apostles for redistribution to the needy (Acts 4:34-35).

As important as this charitable work was, the apostles did not spend all their time with it. They continued to focus their attention on teaching: "Day after day, in the temple courts and from house to house, they never stopped teaching and proclaiming the good news that Jesus is the Christ" (Acts 5:42).

Apparently the apostles delegated to other believers the responsibility of taking care of the poor. However, some people began to complain. The system wasn't working fairly, they said (Acts 6:1). If we had been apostles, we might have been tempted to step in to make sure that things ran right. But the Twelve resisted that temptation. They allowed lay members to take care of this need.

Why did the apostles back away from this important need? "It would not be right for us to neglect the ministry of the word of God in order to wait on tables.... We will...give our attention to prayer and the ministry of the word" (verses 2-4).

Note the priority set by these spiritual leaders: praying, teaching and preaching. This priority still exists. Spiritual leaders should not get bogged down in things that take them away from prayer and the Word of God. Our primary role in the church is teaching and preaching, and we cannot do that without a firm foundation in prayer and study.

That is easier said than done. Many pastors face seemingly never-ending demands on their time. Often the requests are for legitimate needs, and each would be a good use of time—but when added all together they become an unmanageable burden. As much as pastors would like to help everyone who approaches them, they must prioritize their time and delegate some of the responsibilities. High on the priority list is prayer, and a ministry of the word.

Here I want to emphasize the importance of "the ministry of the word." This phrase includes diligent study of Scripture, careful thought about the messages, systematic teaching, and persuasive preaching.

Teaching and preaching

Scripture emphasizes the importance of doctrine, of teaching, of truth. Jesus' commission to the church includes teaching (Matthew 28:20). A concordance will quickly show that "teaching" was a large part of Jesus' own ministry. It is the truth that sets people free, and the truth needs to be taught. Good feelings and pleasant words are not enough.

In the early church, the apostles preached and taught:

- "The apostles were teaching the people and proclaiming in Jesus the resurrection of the dead" (Acts 4:2).
- "At daybreak they entered the temple courts…and began to teach the people" (Acts 5:21).
- "They never stopped teaching and proclaiming the good news that Jesus is the Christ" (verse 42).
- "Barnabas and Saul met with the church and taught great numbers of people" (Acts 11:26).
- "Paul and Barnabas remained in Antioch, where they and many others taught and preached the word of the Lord" (Acts 15:35).
- "Paul stayed for a year and a half, teaching them the word of God" (Acts 18:11).
- "I have not hesitated to preach anything that would be helpful to you but have taught you publicly and from house to house" (Acts 20:20).
- "He preached the kingdom of God and taught about the Lord Jesus Christ" (Acts 28:31).

The apostle Paul

Paul called himself a teacher (1 Timothy 2:7; 2 Timothy 1:11). He taught in all his churches (1 Corinthians 4:17), and the Holy Spirit also moved him to write to many of his churches. Throughout his letters, he teaches about the gospel. His letters are examples of the teaching that the early church was built on and immersed in. These letters were read in the churches and were the foundation of faith and practice.

Paul urged the Thessalonians to "stand firm and hold to the teachings we passed on to you, whether by word of mouth or by letter" (2 Thessalonians 2:15). He told the Ephesians that they "were taught…in accordance with the truth that is in Jesus" (Ephesians 4:21). He told the Colossians, "We proclaim [Christ], admonishing and teaching everyone…. Continue to live in him, rooted and built up in him, strengthened in the faith as you were taught…. Let the word of Christ dwell in you richly as you teach and admonish one another with all wisdom" (Colossians 1:28; 2:6-7; 3:16).

Paul told the Corinthians that everything in their worship meetings should be done for edifying—building the body of Christ (1 Corinthians 14:26). No matter what spiritual gift is being used, it should be used to edify. Edification is the priority. The only words we speak should be "helpful for building others up according to their needs, that it may benefit those who listen" (Ephesians 4:29).

Everything Paul did was for the purpose of edification (2 Corinthians 12:19). "Make every effort to do what leads to peace and to mutual edification" (Romans 14:19). "Encourage one another and build each other up" (1 Thessalonians 5:11). This continues to be an important part of our work today. We have the God-given responsibility to teach our members.

The Pastoral Epistles

After Paul had preached the gospel, raised up churches, corrected doctrinal errors, and trained assistants, he passed the baton of leadership to others. The letters to Timothy and Titus also tell us that the church leaders have an important responsibility:

- "Devote yourself to the public reading of Scripture, to preaching and to teaching" (1 Timothy 4:13).
- "Watch your life and doctrine closely. Persevere in them, because if you do, you will save both yourself and your hearers" (verse 16).
- "These are the things you are to teach and urge on them" (1 Timothy 6:2).
- "The things you have heard me say in the presence of many witnesses entrust to reliable people who will also be qualified to teach others" (2 Timothy 2:2).
- "All Scripture is God-breathed and is useful for teaching, rebuking, correcting and training in righteousness" (2 Timothy 3:16).
- "Preach the word; be prepared in season and out of season; correct, rebuke and encourage—with great patience and careful instruction. For the time will come when people will not put up with sound doctrine" (2 Timothy 4:2-3).
- A church leader "must hold firmly to the trustworthy message as it has been taught, so that he can encourage others by sound doctrine and refute those who oppose it" (Titus 1:9).
- "You must teach what is in accord with sound doctrine" (Titus 2:1).

These verses show that doctrine is important. We need solid teaching, based on diligent and accurate study of Scripture. We do not need anyone's pet theories, but rather teaching that has been tested against the ideas of other faithful Christians. Solid teaching doesn't necessarily make us feel good. Solid teaching sometimes challenges our comfort zones. This is sometimes what we need.

Work is required

It is arrogant and dangerous for any one person to make his or her own interpretation the final word, and to proclaim that all who disagree are incorrect and therefore not led by the Holy Spirit. No, when we approach Scripture it is helpful to do it in the context of the believing community today as well as the historic Christian church. Just as we hope that others learn from us, we also hope that we can learn from others through their Christian experiences and discussions of Scripture.

Often, one group or school of thought can identify errors that another school of thought cannot see. So with caution, we can learn from others, and in some cases, they can point out areas in which we need further research. That doesn't mean that we blindly accept what others say. If we wanted to do that, we would find it impossible, because some ideas contradict others. We cannot believe them all! So what is the standard of truth? It is Scripture. That is why it is essential that we strengthen our foundation in Scripture.

The ministry of the Word takes work. It takes time. Pastors need to spend a considerable amount of time studying, researching and preparing sermons that have a solid foundation behind them. Most of this work will never be seen, but it is necessary. We should have a library, but we do not bring the library with us when we preach. We do not cite every fact we've found. We do not quote every Greek word we've examined. We take time to distill the message of Scripture, to point out its relevance for modern life, and to present it in an interesting way.

Pastors must be active and "at home" in a study, with reference works and technical resources. They must also be active and "at home" in the marketplace, where those to whom they serve live and work. Their role is to bridge the gap between the two—to translate and explain the gospel clearly and in an interesting, compelling way. Pastors have the responsibility to teach the members—and members of the church have the responsibility to study. Let us devote ourselves to prayer and study, preaching and teaching.

Joseph Tkach

Tips on Biblical Exegesis

In our booklet *The God Revealed in Jesus Christ*, we have sought to address typical questions and objections (see pages 7-14 of this volume) that arise as people consider Trinitarian theology. Other verses bring similar questions or objections. We have sought to demonstrate a Trinitarian, Christ-centered approach to reading and interpreting all passages of Holy Scripture.

Some object to the idea of interpreting Scripture. They say, "I just let the Bible say what it means." This idea, though admirable, is not accurate, nor possible. The act of reading is, necessarily, an act of interpretation. The issue is not whether to interpret; it is this: What criteria do we use in interpreting as we read?

We always bring to Scripture certain ideas and advance assumptions. What we are urging here is that we come to Scripture with the truth of who Jesus Christ is as the beginning point and the ongoing criterion by which we read and interpret the Holy Scriptures. Jesus must be the "lens" through which all Scripture is read.

Therefore, in reading Scripture, we recommend thinking about the following questions:

- How does this passage line up with the gospel, which answers its central question, "Who is Jesus?"
- Is this passage referring to the universal, objective salvation of all humanity in Jesus, or is it referring to the personal, subjective experience of accepting or rejecting that salvation?
- What is the historical, cultural, and literary context?
- How is this passage worded in other translations? Other translations can sometimes help us see passages from different perspectives. It's also helpful to check Greek lexicons and other translation helps, because some of the richness and subtleties of the Greek New Testament are lost in translations into other languages.

For a guide to biblical exegesis, you may find it helpful to consult *How to Read the Bible for All Its Worth*, by Gordon D. Fee and Douglas Stuart (Zondervan, 2014) or *Elements of Biblical Exegesis: A Basic Guide for Students and Ministers*, by Michael J. Gorman (Baker, 2010). See also the book *A Guided Tour of the Bible*, by John Halford, Michael Morrison, and Gary Deddo.

Timeless Truths in Cultural Clothes

The Authority of the New Testament Writings

Most Christians accept the Bible as authoritative, as a book that gives reliable spiritual guidance. If we took a survey of Christians, asking them, "Do you believe the Bible?," most of them would say, "Yes" — or at least they would try to say yes to some portion of the Bible, such as the New Testament, or the teachings about loving one another. They want to say in some sense that they believe the Bible, that they accept it as an authority in their faith.

Protestants in particular respect the Bible as the basis for the Christian faith — the basis for their beliefs about God, Jesus, salvation and the church. Even though they may not have read the Bible, they tend to assume that it is true. Their faith in Christ leads them to accept the book that tells them about Christ. A preacher can say, "The Bible says…" with the expectation that the audience will give favorable weight to a biblical citation. The general tendency is for Christians to trust the Bible.

Some Christians view the Bible skeptically, but this is a more intellectually challenging (and therefore less common) position. It is not immediately apparent to new believers how a person can combine trust and mistrust — faith in Christianity with skepticism about the book that has been the traditional basis of that faith. They might view it as like sawing off the limb on which one's ladder is resting.

Limits to belief

Christians do not automatically believe everything that the Bible says. For example, if the preacher says, "The Bible says to destroy houses with persistent mildew," most Christians would not take it seriously. Although the Bible does say that (Leviticus 14:43-45), most Christians would not accept it. Their reasons might vary in sophistication: 1) That would be stupid. 2) No other Christians believe that, so it can't be right. 3) Jesus never said anything like that. 4) That has nothing to do with going to heaven. 5) Old Testament laws don't apply to Christians.

Most Christians reject the teaching about mildew. They are using a filter on the Bible — a filter that in most cases they haven't thought much about. They say they accept the Bible as an authority for their beliefs and practices, yet they do not accept part of the Bible. In this case, the common sense of most Christians functions as more authoritative than the original meaning of Scripture.

I am not saying that houses should be destroyed. Nor am I saying that we should routinely ignore the Bible and follow our common sense. We do not have to choose between such extremes. But Christians should think about the kind of authority the Bible has. If we openly disobey some of its teachings, then in what sense can we say that it is authoritative? Whether we like to think about such tensions or not, we do not read far in the Bible before we are faced with the issue. Why do we stand on some parts of the Bible, but not others? To use the ladder analogy again, we want to be sure that our ladder is resting on the correct branch, a branch that will not be broken by the winds of additional thought.

Let's use a New Testament example. Paul says four times, "Greet one another with a holy kiss" (Romans 16:16; 1 Corinthians 16:20; 2 Corinthians 13:12; 1 Thessalonians 5:26, NRSV), and Peter also says it (1 Peter 5:14). Nevertheless, the vast majority of Christians who claim to accept the Bible as authoritative do not accept this command as required for Christians today. They greet one another, but not with a holy kiss. Why? Nothing in Scripture says that we can ignore what Peter and Paul wrote. There is no "Third Testament" to tell us that this part of the New Testament is obsolete. So the question remains: How can we say that the

Bible is authoritative, and yet consider parts of it as not authoritative? In what way is the authority of the Bible limited?

Accidents of history

Christians often call the Bible the Word of God. They view it as revelation from God to humans. The writers "spoke from God" as they were "moved by the Holy Spirit" (2 Peter 1:21). The Scriptures were "inspired by God" (2 Timothy 3:16). The New Testament is believed to be inspired in the same way as the Old.

But the Bible is not the supreme revelation of God — Jesus Christ is. The letter to the Hebrews begins by noting that difference: "God spoke to our ancestors in many and various ways by the prophets, but in these last days he has spoken to us by a Son" (Hebrews 1:1-2). And Jesus, the Son, reveals God perfectly: "He is…the exact imprint of God's very being" (verse 3). "The whole fullness of deity dwells bodily" in Christ (Colossians 2:9). Jesus reveals God so well that whoever has seen Jesus has seen the Father (John 14:9).

But this supreme revelation of God came in a very specific form. His hair was a certain color, his skin was a certain color, he wore a certain style of clothes and spoke specific human languages. He was a male Jew living in Galilee and Judea at a particular time in history. So, is this what the Father looks like? Are we to identify a particular style of clothing and language as more God-like than other styles? No, those things do not reveal God to us — they are accidents of history. In speech, dress, and personal appearance, Jesus probably looked much like Judas Iscariot — and in such incidentals, Jesus reveals no more to us about God than Judas does.

Jesus, the supreme revelation of God, came to us in a specific cultural form, and when we discuss the way in which Jesus reveals the Father, we must distinguish between form and substance, between culture and principle. Sometimes it is easy to distinguish Jesus from his culture. But in other cases, Jesus participated in his culture — he went to Jerusalem for Jewish festivals, he told someone to follow a Jewish ritual, he told Peter to pay a tax, he told stories about kings and vineyards, he ate fish and drank wine, and called God Abba (John 7:14; 10:22; Matthew 8:4; 17:27; Luke 24:43; Mark 14:36). Did he do these things by conviction, or by custom? Are Christians today to follow his example in these things, or do we overlook them as cultural accidents?

Jesus must be seen within his culture. We do not go to the extreme of imitating everything Jesus did, nor do we go to the other extreme of ignoring everything. We call Jesus our Lord, and we feel that we should obey his teachings, but we also make various exceptions. We do not "sell everything you have and give to the poor" (Luke 18:22). Some of Jesus' teachings were limited to a particular time and place, or even to a specific person. Although Jesus has supreme authority, we filter his teachings. We want to ensure that we are responding to the right teachings, not a command intended for someone else. We want to make sure that our ladder is resting against the correct branch of the tree.

Scripture likewise limited

Jesus, the supreme revelation of God, must be interpreted with some allowance for the specifics of his culture. How much more so must the Bible, a less direct revelation! Each writing was given at a particular time and place, in a particular language with words of a particular nuance. Sometimes the text addresses one specific situation only. We do not need to obey all the commands God gave to Noah, or to Abraham, or to Moses, or even to Jesus' disciples or to the believers in Corinth.

The command, "Bring my cloak and parchments" (2 Timothy 4:13), was given to a specific person. So was the command, "Use a little wine because of your stomach" (1 Timothy 5:23). The same letter says, "Let a widow be put on the list if she is not less than sixty years old and has been married only once" (verse 9). Such commands are rarely obeyed now, even by those who say they accept the Bible as authoritative.

Scripture is not a collection of timeless truths. Although some of its truths are timeless, other parts of the Bible are designed for a specific situation in a specific culture, and it would be wrong for us to take them out of that context and impose them on modern situations. First-century men were advised to pray with their hands raised (1 Timothy 2:8). Slaves were advised to submit even to harsh masters (1 Peter 2:18). Virgins were advised to remain virgins (1 Corinthians 7:26). Women were told how to dress when they prayed (1 Corinthians 11:5), and men were given advice regarding hair length (verse 14). Similarly, people were told to greet one another with a kiss.

These behaviors were appropriate in first-century Mediterranean culture, but are not necessary in Western culture today. Just as the New Testament was written with Greek words, but we do not have to repeat those Greek words in our worship, so also the New Testament was written with a particular culture in mind, but we do not have to repeat all the cultural details. Just as we recognize that the command to destroy mildewed houses was given to a specific people at a specific time, and does not apply to us today, we can also recognize that the command to kiss one another was also given to a specific people at a specific time, and we are not those people. Despite the fact that the command is given five times in the New Testament, it is not a command for us today.

The apostle Paul used one style of message in the synagogue and a different style at the Areopagus. If he could speak in our culture, he would change his style again (1 Corinthians 9:19-23). He might cite Old Testament scriptures in a different way, or different scriptures, or at least give a longer explanation of how the verse is relevant to his argument. Parables might refer to urban life more often than to agricultural customs. Advice about slavery would not be included; modern situations would be addressed. The Bible was written in a different culture and for a different culture. Its truths were given with words and styles shaped by the culture it was given in.

Scripture does not warn us when a culturally-specific command is being given. When we read, we do not know in advance which verses are going to be culturally conditioned, so we cannot rule out the possibility in advance. We have to consider the possibility for all verses. This may complicate our approach to Scripture, but it is unavoidable, for this is the way Scripture was inspired. It came with certain extraneous details, just as Jesus had certain personal details about himself that were not essential to his revealing God to us.

Everything in Scripture had an original setting, but we do not conclude that the Bible had value only in its original setting. It continues to have value. Even the New Testament, which declares much of the Old Testament obsolete (Hebrews 8:13), nevertheless says that the Old Testament continues to be useful for Christian doctrine and training in righteousness (2 Timothy 3:16). The New Testament often quotes the Old Testament not just as an authority about history, but for a principle that continues to be important for Christians. The New Testament is not advocating a wholesale application of old covenant laws, but it is saying that the Old Testament has a less specific but no less important usefulness, a usefulness rooted more in principles and concepts than in specific laws or specific words.

Why have I spent so much time on the Old Testament? Because, when the New Testament speaks of the inspiration and authority of Scripture, it has the Old Testament in view. Our understanding of inspiration for the entire Bible is built on scriptures that are about the Old Testament. The New Testament is inspired in the same way as the Old Testament. Just as with the Old, the authority of the New Testament is not in the specific cultural situations it happens to mention, but in the principles and concepts that lay behind the writings.

It is beyond the scope of this article to explain how to distinguish cultural details from timeless truths. In some cases the difference will be obvious. In other cases it will take more work to determine whether a teaching applies in other cultures, and in some cases it will be debatable. The point here is simply that a discrimination is necessary. There are obsolete instructions in the New Testament. The authority of the New Testament must be sought not in a literalistic application of every word (e.g., kiss), but in the level of principles (e.g., greet with affection).

Let me use the analogy of the ladder again. Many new Christians see that the tree is solid and well-rooted. They assume that all its branches are equally solid — even the smallest twigs — and they place their ladder against the tree without realizing that those twigs were never designed to carry such weight. Small branches may support the ladder for a while, but when a wind or an extra weight comes along, the ladder becomes unstable and possibly dangerous.

Now let me suggest a safer approach: New Christians need to begin at the trunk of the tree, and move out on branches only after testing them for stability. Some parts of the Bible (mildew, kisses, clothing styles) are good for decoration, as it were, but not for support. They are useful, but not always in the way we assume. They were inspired for one purpose, and we go wrong if we try to make them serve a different purpose. We need to focus on the purpose.

Authority of Scripture

So far, I have shown that Scripture has limitations, in particular the fact that it was written in and for other cultures. Some people use that fact to dismiss large portions of the Bible, perhaps Scripture itself. It is easy to show that biblical authority must be qualified in some way, but we do not jump from there into the opposite view, to say it has no authority at all. We are not forced to choose between all or nothing.

Let me mention some evidence that supports biblical authority. First, Scripture claims to be inspired by God. Writers such as Paul claimed to write with authority derived from his commission from God. God is the ultimate authority; Scripture is a derivative authority, but an authority nonetheless because it comes from God and testifies about Christ. This is a faith claim, not a proof. There is no way to prove the Bible's authority beyond all question; not even Jesus convinced everyone.

Tradition supports biblical authority. Christians throughout the centuries have found these writings to be useful and reliable, for both faith and practice. These books tell us what sort of God we believe in, what he did for us, and how we should respond. The biblical Jesus is the only one we have; other reconstructions are based more on presuppositions than on new evidence. Tradition also tells us which books are in the Bible; we trust that God ensured that the right books were included. Since God went to the extreme of revealing himself in flesh, we believe that he would also ensure that the revelation be faithfully preserved. This cannot be proved, but is based on our understanding of what God is doing with us.

History also shows that Scripture has been useful as a corrective to abuses within the church (e.g., in the Middle Ages) and within society (e.g., slavery, Nazism). The fact that a moral authority is needed does not prove that the Bible *is* that authority, but history shows that the Bible was useful in reforming some problems, and its usefulness came because people accepted it as an authority.

Personal experience also helps us understand that the Bible has authority. This is the book that has the courage and honesty to tell us about our own depravity, and the grace to offer us a cleansed conscience. It gives us moral strength not through rules and commands, but in an unexpected way — through grace and the ignominious death of our Lord. The Bible testifies to the love, joy and peace we may have through faith — feelings that are, just as the Bible describes, beyond our ability to put into words. This book gives us meaning and purpose in life by telling us of divine creation and redemption. These aspects of biblical authority cannot be proven to skeptics, but they help authenticate the writings that tell us these things we consider true.

The Bible does not sugar-coat its heroes, and this also helps us accept it as honest. It tells us about the failings of Abraham, Moses, David, the nation of Israel, and the bumbling disciples. The Bible is a message of grace, and grace resists manipulation. Although some use Scripture as a club, the Bible itself gives the message that undercuts such misuse of its authority. The Bible is a word that bears witness to a more authoritative Word, the Word made flesh, and the good news of God's grace.

The Bible's complexity is impressive. It is not simplistic; it does not take the easy way out. The New Testament claims both continuity and radical discontinuity with the old covenant. It would be simpler to eliminate one or the other, but it is more thought-provoking to have both. Likewise, Jesus is presented as both human and divine, a combination that does not fit well into Hebrew, Greek or modern thought. This complexity was not created through naïveté of the philosophical problems, but in spite of them. The Bible is a challenging book, not likely to be the result of peasants attempting a fraud or trying to make sense of hallucinations.

The disciples firmly believed Jesus to have been resurrected, and the most likely explanation for their belief is that Jesus was actually raised from the dead. (Fraud, hallucination, and mistake are all implausible.) Jesus' resurrection then gives additional weight to the book that announces such a phenomenal event. It gives additional weight to the testimony of the disciples as to who Jesus was and to the unexpected logic of conquering death through a death.

Repeatedly, the Bible challenges our thinking about God, ourselves, life, right and wrong. It commands respect not so much through outright command, but by conveying truths to us we do not obtain elsewhere. The testimony of Scripture, of tradition, of personal experience and reason all support the authority of the Bible — yet it is an authority given in a particular historical context. The fact that it is able to speak across cultures, to address situations that never existed when it was written, is also a testimony to its abiding authority. Its timeless truths are given to us in cultural clothes.

Bibliography

The literature on biblical authority is enormous, often technical, and often contradictory. I recommend here a few introductory books. Perhaps one of these titles will pique your interest, should you want to explore this subject a little more:

Achtemeier, Paul. *Inspiration and Authority*. Hendrickson, 1999.

Marshall, I. Howard. *Biblical Inspiration*. Eerdmans, 1982.

McKnight, Scot, ed. *Introducing New Testament Interpretation*. Baker, 1989.

McKnight, Scot. *The Blue Parakeet: Rethinking How You Read the Bible*. Zondervan, 2008.

McQuilken, Robertson. *Understanding and Applying the Bible*. Moody, 1992.

Mickelsen, A.B. and A.M. Mickelsen. *Understanding Scripture*. Hendrickson, 1992.

Stott, John. *Understanding the Bible*. Zondervan, 1984, 1999.

Thompson, Alden. *Inspiration*. Review & Herald, 1991.

Wright, N.T. *Scripture and the Authority of God: How to Read the Bible Today*. HarperOne, 2013.

Wright, N.T. *Surprised by Scripture: Engaging Contemporary Issues*. HarperOne, 2015.

Michael Morrison

What Jesus Said About Himself

Jesus preached the kingdom of God. However, the early church preached mostly about Jesus. Is there a contradiction in this? Did the early church get things turned around, preaching about the messenger but neglecting his message? Let's go to the four Gospels to see whether the early church's focus on Jesus is compatible with Jesus' own teaching. Did Jesus actually preach about himself?

1. Near the end of the Sermon on the Mount, how does Jesus describe the people who enter the kingdom of God? Matthew 7:21-23. Is it appropriate to call Jesus Lord? Is it appropriate to do good works in his name? What else is needed? Verse 21. In verse 23, who is acting as Judge? Whose words are we to put into practice? Verse 24.

Comment: Throughout the Sermon on the Mount, Jesus spoke with personal authority. People are blessed or not blessed in relation to him. He indicated that his own words were on the same level as Scripture. He said that people should put Jesus' words into practice just as seriously as they obey God.

2. Did Jesus claim to be able to forgive sins? Matthew 9:2-6. Did he heal for the purpose of showing this authority?

Comment: I can forgive sins that are committed against me, but I do not have authority to forgive s sins that they commit against someone else. But Jesus claims to forgive all sins, even in terms of a person's relationship to God. In this passage, Jesus is teaching something about himself. This is one aspect of the message God the Father wanted Jesus to preach: that forgiveness comes through Jesus Christ. This means that entry into the kingdom is through Jesus Christ. The kingdom of God is good news for those who accept Jesus' authority.

3. If a person does not accept Jesus, how will that affect the person's relationship with God? Matthew 10:32-33. Is Jesus claiming to be Judge of our eternity? Does Jesus promise eternal rewards? Verse 42. Does he pronounce judgments about the future? Matthew 11:22. Which is worse—the sin of Sodom, or the sin of rejecting Jesus? Verse 24.

4. What did Jesus claim about his own knowledge and authority? Matthew 11:27. Did he claim to be more important than Solomon, more important than Jonah, more important than the temple, more important than the Sabbath? Matthew 12:5-8, 41-42.

Comment: As part of his mission, Jesus claimed an authority and knowledge that was much greater than any other person ever had. He claimed to be the key to eternal life in the kingdom of God. He was teaching about himself.

5. Did Jesus want his disciples to know who he was? Matthew 16:13-15. Did God the Father want them to know? Verses 16-17. Did Jesus have authority to give the keys to the kingdom of God? Verse 19. Is obedience to Jesus more important than life itself? Verse 25.

Comment: If ordinary people said this, we would consider them either crazy or dangerous cult leaders. But Jesus said it about himself. He was extraordinary. He preached the kingdom of God, but he also preached about himself as the decisive factor as to whether a person is in the kingdom. For the gospel to be communicated accurately, it is essential that people know about who Jesus is and what he taught.

6. Jesus called himself the Son of Man. Did he also claim that he would have the Father's glory? Matthew 16:27. Would he also be the Judge, the one who gives eternal rewards? Did he claim to give authority to his disciples? Matthew 18:18; 19:28. If

Jesus can give that kind of authority, does it imply that he has even more authority than that — more than heaven and earth?

7. Did Jesus claim that his life was worth more than all other people? Matthew 20:28. Did he take a psalm about God and apply it to himself? Matthew 21:16; Psalm 8:2. Does he claim to have angels, whom he can send throughout the universe? Matthew 24:30-31. Does he claim that his words are infallible, greater than the universe? Verse 35.

Comment: These claims are astonishing in scope. Jesus is teaching that he is as great as God.

8. In a parable, Jesus again claimed to be the Judge, sitting on a throne in heavenly glory. Will he control the eternity of all human beings? Matthew 25:31-32. Will he have authority to give eternal life in the kingdom of God? Verse 34. Will he have the authority to condemn people? Verse 41.

9. Did Jesus claim to institute a new covenant between God and his people? Matthew 26:28. Does this covenant bring forgiveness? Whose blood made it possible?

Comment: Jesus taught that he was the sacrifice that enabled people to live in the kingdom of God, the ransom that could set them free. He claimed to do this by his death, and yet he also claimed that he would live forever. In all these things, Jesus was teaching something about himself.

10. Does Jesus again claim universal authority? Matthew 28:18. Does he put himself on the same level as the Father? Verse 19. Does he put his own commands on the same level as the Father's? Verse 20. Does he claim to be present with believers throughout the world and throughout the ages?

11. Did Jesus give his disciples power over all things? Luke 10:19. Did he claim authority to give the kingdom of God and to give the highest positions? Luke 22:29. Even on the cross, did he claim authority to judge whether a person would be saved? Luke 23:43. Did he have the authority to send the power of God? Luke 24:49.

12. When Jesus approached Jerusalem, did he equate his own coming with "the time of God's coming"? Luke 19:41-44. Did he acknowledge being the Son of God? Luke 22:70. Did he claim to be the fulfillment of the Old Testament Scriptures? Luke 24:44. Was this what he taught before his crucifixion, too? Same verse, first part.

Comment: The first-century Jews were looking forward to an earthly kingdom, with land, laws, king and subjects. If Jesus preached this kind of kingdom, most people would have found it normal, and not objectionable. But Jesus caused controversy by the things he taught about himself. This was what caused the Jewish leaders to accuse him of blasphemy and to crucify him. This was an important part of his message.

13. Jesus' identity is more explicit in the Gospel of John. What does he claim about himself? John 3:13-16, 35. Did his audience understand that he was claiming to be equal to God? John 5:17-19. Can the Son give eternal life? Verse 21. Is he the Judge of the world? Verse 22. Should Jesus be honored in the same way as the Father — with worship? Verse 23.

14. Did Jesus teach that he had life within himself? John 5:25. Is he the one who gives eternal life? John 6:27. Is he the one who raises the dead? Verse 40. Is eternal life uniquely dependent on Jesus? Verse 51. Is he the key to eternal life? John 11:25-26.

15. Did Jesus teach that he existed before Abraham? John 8:58. That he had glory with God before the world began? John 17:5. That he is able to resurrect himself? John 10:18. That he is equal with God? Verse 30. That he is the perfect representation of what God is? John 14:9-10.

Comment: Jesus did not begin his sermons with, "Let me tell you about how great I am." Nevertheless, in his preaching and teaching, Jesus often taught about himself. He taught that he had an extraordinary greatness, and our eternal future hinges on whether we accept him for who he is. He is the key to the kingdom. We must believe in him before we can experience his forgiveness and life in his kingdom.

Jesus' disciples didn't always understand what Jesus taught. He often chided them for being slow of heart and of little faith. They did not understand Jesus' role as Savior until after the resurrection. They seem to have misunderstood who he was, despite all the things he taught. There were some things that he specifically told them to be quiet about until after his resurrection (Mark 9:9).

After Jesus ascended into heaven and the Holy Spirit empowered the apostles, they understood much more about Jesus and his kingdom. They were inspired to see even more clearly that Jesus' teachings about himself were of supreme importance. People can have many misunderstandings about the kingdom and still be saved, but in order for them to experience salvation, it is crucial that they accept Jesus as Lord and Savior. He is the most important part of the message. People need to know about Jesus.

Jesus taught about his own death and resurrection, and he taught that forgiveness comes through him. That also formed the focus of the preaching of the early church in the book of Acts. The apostles did not contradict their Master. What we see is continuity and greater clarity, not contradiction. The gospel focuses on who Jesus is and what he did so that we might be saved in God's kingdom.

When we compare the different sermons in the book of Acts, we see different ways to preach the gospel. When we see the different parables and sayings of Jesus, we also see a variety of ways to preach the gospel of salvation. When we examine the letters of Paul, we will again see some differences, as well as continuity in the most important points.

Michael Morrison

Good News in an Alabaster Jar

Matthew 26 records an interesting episode in the life of Jesus, just two days before he was killed. This was an action-packed week, filled with highly significant events — and this event is no exception. In Matthew 26, we find a description of Jesus being anointed with perfume. The story begins in verses 1-2:

> When Jesus had finished saying all these things, he said to his disciples, "As you know, the Passover is two days away — and the Son of Man will be handed over to be crucified." (NIV 1984)

Jesus knows that his time is short – he has only two days to live – but his disciples seem to be unaware of it. Jesus will soon be given another opportunity to tell his disciples about his impending death. Then there is an abrupt change of scene, in which Matthew tells us what is happening in another place at about the same time:

> The chief priests and the elders of the people assembled in the palace of the high priest, whose name was Caiaphas, and they plotted to arrest Jesus in some sly way and kill him. "But not during the Feast," they said, "or there may be a riot among the people." (verses 3-5)

Jesus anointed with perfume

Matthew then takes us back to Jesus:

> While Jesus was in Bethany [two miles east of Jerusalem] in the home of a man known as Simon the Leper, a woman came to him with an alabaster jar of very expensive perfume, which she poured on his head as he was reclining at the table. (verses 6-7)

A whole jar of perfume! The smell would have filled the entire room.

> When the disciples saw this, they were indignant. "Why this waste?" they asked. "This perfume could have been sold at a high price and the money given to the poor."

Aware of this, Jesus said to them, "Why are you bothering this woman? She has done a beautiful thing to me. The poor you will always have with you, but you will not always have me. When she poured this perfume on my body, she did it to prepare me for burial."

Then Jesus, with special emphasis, said,

> I tell you the truth, wherever this gospel is preached throughout the world, what she has done will also be told, in memory of her. (verses 8-13)

Why is this so important?

I would like to ask a follow-up question: Why is this story so important that it will be told wherever the gospel message goes?

The woman had done a nice favor for Jesus, and it was appropriate for Jesus to thank her in a nice way. But surely this does not mean that the disciples, no matter where they went in the world, would have to tell this story everywhere they told the gospel? If the disciples were running short of time, couldn't they just preach the gospel and skip this particular story? No, said Jesus. Wherever the gospel is preached, this story must be told, too. It is practically as important as the gospel itself!

When the disciples were inspired to write the stories of what Jesus did, they also wrote the story of what this woman did. In the Gospel accounts, it is on an equal level with the teachings and miracles of Jesus. What this woman did is an essential part of the story of Jesus. That is not just long ago and far away. It also applies right now, and right here. Wherever the gospel goes, this story must be told, too. Why is that?

The context: Jesus' death

This section of Matthew is about Jesus' death. It begins in verse 2 with Jesus mentioning his death. It moves in verse 3 to the conspiracy to kill Jesus. And in verse 12, Jesus connects the anointing with his burial.

Right after Jesus says that this story will be told around the world, Matthew tells us in verse 14 that Judas went out and conspired with the chief priests to betray Jesus. This anointing with perfume was the last straw for Judas. He was so upset about this waste of money that he went out to betray his master for 30 pieces of silver – ironically, money that he himself would waste. He eventually saw that there was something more important than money – but that is a different story. Our focus today is on the story of what the woman did. That is the story that must be told everywhere the gospel goes.

The story is set in the context of Jesus' death. It is part of the introduction to what is called "the passion" – Jesus' suffering and death. That helps make the story significant. There are several points of resemblance between what this woman did and what Jesus did on the cross. Her action was in some ways a parable, a drama that portrayed spiritual truth about Jesus.

Many of Jesus' own actions were object lessons for spiritual truths. He did many more miracles than could be recorded in the Bible, but some are reported to us because they have special significance.

The miracle of feeding 5,000 people, for example, helps show that Jesus is the bread of life. Just as he gives food for physical life, so also he gives what we need for eternal life. The fact that he could do something we can see, gives us assurance that he can do something we cannot see. Just as he heals diseases, so also he forgives sins. The physical action pictures a spiritual truth.

This is also true of what this woman did for Jesus. What she did illustrates for us some lessons about the sacrifice of Jesus Christ. It also pictures the way that we should respond to Jesus. What this woman did is a miniature picture of the gospel. That is why this story is so important that it has become part of the gospel message. It can help us explain the nature of the gospel.

A powerful devotion

Let's give this woman a name. John 12 tells us that she was Mary, sister of Lazarus, and that this was shortly after Jesus had raised Lazarus from the dead. The story can be told without that particular fact — the action is more important than the name of the person who did it — but it does help us understand a little more of what went on behind the scenes. (It is not certain that the story in John 12 is the same incident as we read about in Matthew 26, but that question does not affect the point we wish to make here.)

We'll look at three ways in which this anointing resembles the sacrifice of Jesus himself.

First, Mary was motivated to do this out of love. Nobody told her to do it. It was not commanded. It was just something Mary took upon herself to do, and she did it out of love. Jesus also made his sacrifice out of love. He had no obligation to die for us, but he chose to do it, willingly, motivated by love. Even while we were sinners, he loved us with incredible intensity.

Mary may have known that Jesus was soon to die, but perhaps not. The disciples didn't understand that Jesus was going to die, and Mary probably didn't, either. Otherwise, she would have saved the perfume for the actual burial. She seems to have poured the perfume on Jesus simply because she had an incredibly intense devotion to Jesus. She was overwhelmed with love. Maybe it was a response to the resurrection of Lazarus.

Mary may have bought that perfume to anoint the dead body of her brother. Now that Lazarus was alive, Mary did not need the perfume for him — thanks to what Jesus had done. How could Mary thank Jesus for his wonderful gift of life? Why, she could use that same perfume to lavish it on Jesus, as a token of her thanks and love. Mary was praising Jesus, honoring Jesus—in effect, worshipping Jesus, sacrificing to Jesus.

Many people today are concerned with right beliefs. Right beliefs are good. We need them. Many people today are concerned with right behavior. Right behavior is good. We need it — but we need something else, too, and that is something that Mary demonstrates for us. Mary shows us right emotion, right feeling. The heart we need for God is an intensely personal devotion, a powerful dedication of ourselves to his service.

This intensity of emotion is unusual, and like most unusual things, this was criticized. This kind of devotion was not within the ordinary range of acceptable behavior. People would call Mary eccentric, maybe even out of her right mind. Society says, Don't get carried away with your emotions. Mary did. Her society criticized her, but Jesus praised her. Society says, Moderation in all things. Mary was not moderate. Her society criticized her, but Jesus praised her. The jury of 12 men said this is wrong, but Jesus said, she is better than you all.

Mary had an intense affection and devotion for Jesus. We can see it when she sat at Jesus' feet listening to him teach. She was a contemplative person who liked to think. Here, she is an expressive person — expressive not in words but in actions. Her quiet nature did not prevent her from making a powerful statement — more powerful than words could have possibly done.

An enormous sacrifice

The second way in which Mary's action was like the sacrifice of Jesus is that it was a sacrifice. This was some incredibly expensive perfume. Mary could have sold it for a large amount. Mark tells us it was worth about one year's wages — the amount of money that a working person would earn in an entire year. In today's economy, it would be worth several thousand dollars.

Can you imagine one bottle of perfume that costs several thousand dollars? Now, can you imagine just pouring it out? Thousands of dollars evaporating into thin air — gone forever. A year's worth of work, gone, just like that.

This shows us something of the intensity of Mary's love for Jesus. She must have known what she was doing, and how much it had cost her, but she did not care. Her love for Jesus was so great that she was not concerned about the cost. She was probably happy about it — she was getting a chance to demonstrate her devotion to Jesus. If she had sorrow, it was not about how much she was giving up, but that she had so little to give. Love often expresses itself in self-sacrifice, with little thought for self.

If an offering is to be meaningful, it should cost us something, and it should be done out of our own free will. We should give up something that is of value to us. Worship always involves sacrifice — sacrifice of money, time or pride, or all three. Maybe it requires everything we have, and everything we are. The disciples were concerned with self. They wanted to be great in the kingdom of God. But Mary was achieving greatness already, through her devotion to Jesus. She was not concerned for self and what she would get out of it. She was concerned for nothing but Jesus, and in that, she was already great.

Concern about the money

The disciples suggested that the money could be given to the poor. It wasn't just Judas who objected to this "waste" of money. All the disciples were indignant. It is good to give money to the poor. The traditional Jewish understanding of righteousness included giving money to the poor, and apparently the disciples sometimes did it. (When Judas went out from the last supper, the disciples thought that he might be going to give something to the poor. If Jesus had never given any money to the poor in the previous three years, the disciples probably would not guess that he would start right then. Charity seems to have been part of what they normally did.)

When someone has lots of money, it is appropriate to share some of it with those who need it. That is a good use of money. But in this case, Mary had picked an even better use of the money. She used it in an act of tremendous devotion, an act of worship. That is a legitimate use of money, too.

Some Christians make a religion out of social activism, and they do it very well. Social work can be part of the Christian faith. But some unfortunately see that as the only form of religion, and they have forgotten about devotion to Jesus. Social work is good, but it is not supreme. Jesus is supreme — and our devotion to him will cause us to help the people who need help. It's a question of priorities, and Jesus must always be first. For Christian service to really count, it must be done for Christ. We are serving him. Even when we are helping other people, we are serving Christ.

What Mary did, from an observer's perspective, was a big sacrifice. But because she was willing, it was for her a small price to pay, a token of her love. Jesus' crucifixion, from all perspectives, was a tremendous sacrifice, but he was willing to make it. For the joy set before him he endured the cross. He knew that glory was waiting not just for him, but for all who would be saved by what he did. He was willing to pay the price—and he was happy that he was able to pay the price, because he knew how valuable the result would be.

As we grasp the enormity of his sacrifice, we cannot help but respond in love and devotion — and there is no sacrifice too great. Nothing we do could ever compare to what he has done for us. Our love for him causes us to live for him, to give all that we are.

Extravagant sacrifice

The third way in which Mary's action was similar to Jesus' crucifixion is that it was extravagant. It was far more than what was necessary. It was outrageous! Mary was not a calculating person who thought, what is the least I can do? How much do I have to spend to be enough? What is my duty?

Nor was she tied down to tradition. Mary did not think, How do other women show respect for a rabbi? She was not afraid of public opinion. Her love freed her from that fear. She was not afraid to do something out of the ordinary. Mary did not ask the disciples if it was OK. No, Mary broke traditions. She broke the limits of what is public propriety. Mary didn't even ask Jesus if it was OK. She just seized the opportunity, and did it. She did what she could, because only that expressed her devotion to Jesus. Her love was so great that it called for an exceptional act of creative devotion.

The disciples didn't object to the anointing in itself. They didn't object to perfume, but they objected to the extravagance. This was too much of a good thing — way too much. This was ridiculous, wasteful, even sinful. No so, said Jesus. What she has done is a beautiful thing. It had an aesthetic value, like a beautiful work of art, a beautiful piece of music. It was a beautiful action — a beauty that defies cost analysis. It is impossible to put a price on such personal devotion.

Sometimes we are too concerned about the usefulness of something. I often think that way. But that may mean that I do only the ordinary things, never the unusual, never the beautiful, never anything heroic, never anything requiring faith.

The disciples wanted the money to be put to good use, for something practical, like food for the hungry. That is a very good use for money. It was the ordinary thing to do, the normal thing to do, even a respectable thing to do. But usefulness is not the most important thing in the universe. Usefulness is not our god. Efficiency is not our god. Public opinion is not our god. Traditional boundaries of politeness are not our god. Jesus is our God, and it is useful to use up our material resources to honor and glorify him.

Maybe there aren't any tangible results, but a sacrifice of love and devotion has a usefulness of its own. An act of great beauty has a usefulness of its own when it is done for Jesus Christ. Mary's act of extravagant waste was actually a picture of spiritual beauty — a heavenly fragrance. It pictured the sacrifice of Jesus Christ in a way that words could not. It was extravagant, and that is part of its beauty. God himself is extravagant.

When something is done out of the ordinary, someone is going to complain about it. Someone is not going to understand the motive, or understand the beauty, or they are going to say, "That's not right. We don't do things that way." To them, it seems that mediocrity is better than intense emotion. But Jesus praises extravagance, not mediocrity.

God gave us an extravagant gift in the person of

Jesus Christ. It was an outrageous gift, worth far more than what we deserve. Grace is extravagant. Jesus gave everything he had for us. He gave his life. He gave more than necessary — he died for the whole world, and yet the whole world does not accept him. He died even for the people who reject him.

What a waste!, some people might think, but it was really an act of love, of sacrifice, of extravagance. Some people said, "That can't be right. That's not the way God normally acts with us." But God does things out of the ordinary. Jesus shows us total commitment, total sacrifice, so that we might respond to him with all that we have.

An extravagant response

We need to respond to Jesus the way Mary did — with a supreme focus on him, a single-minded love that counts everything else loss for Jesus Christ, a love that does not ask how little we can do to get by, a love that is not worried about public opinion, a love that is no longer concerned about what is within the boundaries of normal devotion — a love that is willing to be extravagant.

When Mary poured perfume on Jesus, she was not only picturing some aspects of what Jesus did on the cross, she also pictured the way that we should respond to Jesus, with such complete devotion, such willingness to sacrifice, such willingness to go beyond the boundaries of normal and to have an extraordinary love for Jesus.

Have you ever done anything extravagant for Jesus Christ? Have you ever done anything so outrageous for him that other people thought you were foolish? Have you ever been so bold with love that other people have criticized what you did? Some of us have. Maybe it was a long time ago. Whenever it was, it was sweet-smelling aroma offered to God.

The example of Mary tells me that I am too reserved. I am too often concerned with what others think. I am not loving Jesus as much as I ought. I am too concerned with myself. I need to think more about actions of extraordinary beauty. God has been extravagant with me. He has lavished on me the riches of his grace. He has repeatedly given me things I did not deserve and things I did not appreciate the way I ought. His grace toward me abounds and abounds and abounds. How do I respond to him who gave his life for me?

Michael Morrison

Marketing the gospel?

In one of his earliest movies, John Wayne tells another cowboy, "I don't like branding—it hurts in the wrong place!" That comment made me chuckle, though it also got me thinking about how churches can hurt the gospel through an inappropriate use of marketing techniques like product branding. It happened in our history—seeking a marketing "hook," our founder branded us the one true church. This approach compromised biblical truth as the gospel was redefined in order to promote the brand.

Sharing with Jesus in advancing his gospel

Our calling as Christians is not to market a brand, but to join Jesus in what he is doing by the Spirit, through the church, to advance his gospel in the world. Jesus' gospel addresses several things: how forgiveness and reconciliation have been accomplished by Jesus' atonement; how the Spirit transforms us (and what the transformed life looks like); the nature of our vocation as followers of Jesus sent on mission with him into the world; and the ultimate hope we have of sharing forever in the communion that Jesus has with the Father and the Spirit.

There are some (though limited) ways in which marketing (including branding) can help us accomplish the gospel work to which Jesus has called us. For example, we can productively use logos, websites, social media, bulletins, newsletters, signs, mailers and other communication tools to help us spread Jesus' message, inviting people to respond in faith. But such tools must serve, not diminish our calling to be light and salt in our communities. I'm not against marketing rightly used, but I do want to offer a word of caution, along with some perspective.

A word of caution

According to George Barna (in *A Step by Step Guide to Church Marketing*), marketing is "a broad term that encompasses all the activities that lead up to an exchange of equally valued goods between consenting parties." Barna further defines marketing by saying that activities such as advertising, public relations, strategic planning, audience research, product distributions, fund raising, product pricing, developing a vision statement and customer service are all elements of marketing. He then says: "When these elements are combined in a transaction in which the parties involved exchange items of equivalent worth, the marketing act has been consummated." Let that idea of exchanging items of equivalent worth sink in for a moment.

Several years ago, several of our pastors read a book by the pastor of a Southern California megachurch. It promised, in essence, that if you will market your church in a particular manner, you cannot fail because everyone will be excited about what you are offering them and their community. Some of our pastors tried the recommended marketing techniques, but became discouraged when their congregations did not grow.

But should we be marketing the gospel (and our churches) the way Walmart markets t-shirts, or Sears markets tools—or even the way particular denominations and congregations use marketing to bring about numerical growth? We must not "peddle" the gospel as though it was a consumer good to be exchanged for something of seemingly equivalent value. That is not what Jesus had in mind in commissioning us to take his gospel to the world in order to make disciples of all people-groups.

As the apostle Paul noted, rather than being seen as attractive (like a desired consumer product), the gospel often is viewed as repulsive or foolish by those who, living according to the flesh, have a secular mindset (see 1 Corinthians 1:18-23). As those who follow Jesus, "We do not set our minds on what the flesh wants, but…on what the Spirit desires" (Romans 8:4-5). We're not perfect in that, but as we walk in step with the Spirit, our minds and actions are conformed to God's will (and thus his work). Given these understandings, it's no surprise Paul repudiated certain "fleshly" (secular) techniques for advancing the work of the gospel:

> Having this ministry by the mercy of God, we do not lose heart. But we have renounced disgraceful, underhanded ways. We refuse to practice cunning or to tamper with God's word, but by the open statement of the truth we would commend ourselves to everyone's conscience in the sight of God. (2 Corinthians 4:1-2 ESV)

Paul refused to use techniques that, though they might advance his ministry in the short-term, would ultimately compromise the message of the gospel. The only kind of "success" he wanted in life and ministry was being faithful to Christ and his gospel.

Some of the gospel-compromising, marketing-driven approaches used by some churches go like this: "Come to our church and your problems will be solved, you will achieve health and wealth, you will be richly blessed." The blessings being promised typically have to do with power, success, and getting what you want. The bait-and-switch occurs when those who come are told about the conditions they must meet to get the blessings—things like having a certain level of faith, or joining a small group, tithing one's income, actively serving in a ministry of the church, or spending a specific amount of time in prayer and Bible study. While some of these are helpful for growing as followers of Jesus, none are ways to get God to be favorable towards us—to obtain what we want in exchange for something God wants or needs from us.

False advertising and deceptive marketing

Attracting people to a church or a ministry by telling them how they can contract with God to get whatever they want is false advertising and deceptive marketing. It is nothing but paganism in a modern wrapper. Christ did not die to meet our selfish consumer needs. He did not come to guarantee us health and wealth. Instead, he came to bring us into a gracious relationship with the Father, Son and Spirit and the peace, joy and hope that is the fruit of that relationship. In and through that relationship, we are empowered to love and serve others with God's kind of costly, transforming love. That kind of love will, at times, be offensive to some (perhaps many), but it will always direct others to the very Source of that saving, redeeming and transforming love.

Should we market the gospel as an exchange of equally valued items between consenting parties? Certainly not! The gospel is, by grace, freely given to all. All we can do is receive this gift with empty, up-turned hands—thankfully receiving the blessing of belonging to God. That relationship of grace and love is lived out in a life of grateful worship—a response that is enabled by the Holy Spirit, who opens our eyes and sets aside our pride and rebellious demand for independence from God to live for his glory.

A glorious exchange

In the life we have in and with Christ, through the Spirit, there is an exchange of sorts, a glorious exchange. Note Paul's comment:

> I am crucified with Christ: nevertheless I live; yet not I, but Christ liveth in me: and the life which I now live in the flesh I live by the faith of the Son of God, who loved me, and gave himself for me. (Galatians 2:20 KJV)

We give Jesus our life of sin and he gives us his life of righteousness. When we give away our lives, we find his life at work in us. When we surrender our lives to Christ, we find real purpose for our lives so that we no longer live for ourselves but to advance the reputation of God our Creator and Redeemer. That exchange is not a marketing technique—it's grace. We get the whole God (Father, Son and Spirit), and he gets all of us: body and soul. We get the righteous character of Christ, and he takes away our sins, totally forgiving us. This is certainly not an exchange of equally valued goods!

If anyone believes in Christ, he or she is a new creation—a child of God. The Holy Spirit gives us this new life — the life of God living in us. As that new creation, the Spirit gracefully transforms us to share more and more in Christ's perfect love for God and for others. When our lives are placed in Christ, then we share in his life, in both his joy and in his long-suffering love. We share in his sufferings, in his death, in his righteousness, as well as in his resurrection, ascension and eventual glorification. As God's children we are co-heirs with Christ and we share in his perfect relationship with the Father. In that relationship we benefit from all that Christ has done for us to become God's beloved children, united with him — forever in glory!

Joseph Tkach

A Theological Look at Evangelism

Let's start with the Trinity as a doctrine, which says that God is best described as Father, Son, and Holy Spirit existing as one God. The early church formulated this doctrine because the Bible reveals that the Father is God, that Jesus Christ is God, and the Holy Spirit is God—yet the Bible also insists that there is only one God. The doctrine of the Trinity puts this complex idea into a shorter phrase. We do not want to teach a Trinity that is functionally unitarian, as if God is an undifferentiated singularity. Nor do we want to present a God that is functionally tri-theistic, as if the Persons of the Godhead are separate from one another and different in personality.

God is not a faceless, abstract principle existing in some distant place—God is love (1 John 4:8). Love is inherent to God—his essence and being—that's what makes him God. This God who is love by nature existed before he created anything, before there was anything else to love. Can love be expressed by a solitary person? It cannot. The doctrine of the Trinity explains that God not a solitary person, but three persons. The Father loves the Son and the Spirit, the Son loves the Father and the Spirit, the Holy Spirit loves the Father and the Son, in a criss-crossing interchange. This love relationship is part of the inner life of the Godhead. Not only do they love one another, they also live in one another—the Father in the Son, the Son in the Father, etc.

God intends to share this life with us. He created human beings "in the image of God," and he wants us to love, because that is what he designed us for. The Father, Son, and Holy Spirit want us to enjoy the same love that exists in the Godhead. Salvation does not consist in a change of location ("going to heaven"), as if that would solve all our problems. Nor is it better enforcement of the rules in a kingdom. Rather, it involves entry into the life of God—or we should say, the entry of his life into us. God's plan is for us to join in his life of love for all eternity.

Humans have fallen short of what God wants, and we are incapable of attaining what God wants to give us. We do not live in love because we are sinful. Humanity's "fall" into sinfulness was no surprise to God, because he had already planned the solution to our problem. He created us knowing in advance that he would have to rescue us from our own foolishness. God the Father sent the Son to become a human to redeem humanity, to re-connect humanity to the Creator in whom we all live and have our being.

There is no Father-Son separation here. This is not a case of the Father being angry at humanity and wanting to punish us, and the Son doing something to change the Father's mind. No, the New Testament says that the Father sent the Son—the Father wants to save us just as much as the Son does. The Father is love just as much as the Son is. He wants to share his life and love with us.

The first step was our physical creation: humanity was made from elements of earth, and made to breathe oxygen. But love cannot be manufactured out of physical elements—it is a spiritual quality, and God continues his creative work in us spiritually. This takes time.

So Jesus became a human in order to save us, to rescue us from our physical and spiritual weakness. In doing so, Jesus revealed to us what the Father is like. He told Philip, "Anyone who has seen me has seen the Father" (John 14:9). Jesus has the essential divine characteristic: love. Our concept of God is formed not by philosophical reasoning about what "the perfect" is—we form our concept of God based on what Jesus is and what he has done. That brings us back to love, which is serving others instead of ourselves.

Jesus became human and took our sins upon himself, and he experienced the results of our sins (including death) on the cross. This was not because God became angry at Jesus or punished him; that would suggest some separation within the Trinity. God loves his Son, just as he loves humanity. But this death, even the shame and pain of the cross, was part of what it meant for him to take our fallen condition upon himself. His resurrection demonstrated that death itself has been overcome.

Jesus has done all that is needed for our salvation. He died for our sins—past tense. He paid for them—past tense. The penalty has been paid—past tense. God does not count our sins against us. How could he? They've already been paid for. He has already forgiven us, and like the father of the prodigal son, he is eagerly waiting for us to return to him. He is not saying that we will be forgiven IF we repent or IF we believe in some particular doctrine. No, the gospel is that the penalty has already been paid in full, the sins are already forgiven, and God invites us to accept what he is offering in Christ.

In one popular evangelistic sketch, there is a great chasm between humanity and God—a gulf too wide for us to jump across, too deep for us to climb across. The gospel says that this chasm is an illusion—the truth is that in the incarnation, in his birth, life, death, and resurrection, Jesus has eliminated that chasm. He has come to us; it is not a matter of us having to go to him. Our sins made us feel like we are separated from God, but because of Jesus Christ, they do not separate us. God is not unreachable – he is with us in Jesus Christ. God does not want us to live in sin, but those sins do not constitute a barrier between him and us.

However, our sinfulness is a barrier between us and the life that God wants us to have—the life of love. Sin is anything that is contrary to love. God is offering us a life of love, not a life of sin and death. We cannot experience the joy of mutual acceptance, for example, at the same time as we harbor resentment against others. It is a contradiction. So ethical behavior goes hand-in-hand with a Trinitarian, love-based theology. Since none of us is perfect, we enter God's life imperfectly, but the gospel promises that perfection will eventually be given to us. Even now, through the Holy Spirit, God's love and righteousness are available to people.

What role does faith play? God can forgive us all he wants, but if we don't *think* we are forgiven, we will see our sins as a chasm we cannot cross. We will not experience the benefits of his forgiveness, even though it's there. To use a financial metaphor, it would be like we continue to make payments on our debt even though Jesus has already paid it in full. If we don't believe he paid for us, and we continue to make payments anyway, we are enslaved by our own mistaken idea, our unbelief. Our faith does not change the external circumstances, but our faith is essential for our experience of salvation. That's why we want people to believe the good news!

It is good news, but not everyone believes it. Why? The Bible explains that people, on their own, cannot believe it. God must intervene in their minds to call them or invite them to faith. We trust that he works in each person's life in the best possible way—and he has a far better understanding of those circumstances than we do. From our limited perspective, we do not always understand why God works in the way that he does, but we know that he loves each person, and can be trusted to carry out his work in the best possible way.

How does Christ give us salvation? The Bible describes it as a union between us and Christ: we died with him, we are raised with him, we are seated with him in heavenly places (Ephesians 2:1-6). He took our sinfulness, and he gives us his righteousness; we become partakers of the divine nature (2 Peter 1:4). There are different ways of saying it, but we become part of who he is, and he becomes part of what we are. He lives in us and our lives are hidden in him (Colossians 3:3). The goal is that we join the Trinitarian life and love of Father, Son and Spirit.

In our experience, there may be a specific point in time that we come to believe that our old self died with Christ and that we are forgiven. The Holy Spirit opened our minds to understand and believe what God has done for us. But in fact, the old self died when Christ died, which was before the foundation of the world. God's plan all along has been that the old self would be counted as dead and the new self be reconstructed in Christ. It is his idea, not ours, and we can't take any credit for catching on to what was his idea all along. We are time-bound creatures and cannot help but experience things as a succession of events, but from God's perspective it was a done deal all along.

The parable of the prodigal son (Luke 15:11-31) provides a useful outline. To put it concisely, Trinitarian theology says that the Father is eagerly awaiting for us to come to ourselves, to realize that we have been wasting our life, and to return to the Father—not as a servant or slave, but as the treasured child that he has always loved.

Key points

1) God created all humans in his image, and he wants everyone to share in the love that characterizes the Triune Godhead.

2) Christ became a human to redeem all humanity through his incarnation, life, death and resurrection. He atoned for the sins of all humanity.

3) Christ has already paid for our sins, and there is no further debt to pay. God has already forgiven us, does not want to punish us, and eagerly desires that we return to him.

4) We will not experience the blessing of receiving his love unless we believe that he loves us; we will not experience his forgiveness unless we believe he has forgiven us.

5) We will not experience the blessings of giving love while we continue living in sin. We will experience the joy of salvation only as we share in the life of Christ through the Holy Spirit.

The motive for evangelism

Some fear that this theology reduces the motive for evangelism. For some people, that may be true. If they were motivated by a misunderstanding, then it will weaken their motive if we explain the error in their thinking. One person might evangelize because he's afraid that people will go to hell if he doesn't tell them. Another might evangelize because she thinks it's the only way she can earn her salvation. A third person might think that God needs help. Hopefully each of these people will be given new and better motives for evangelism, but it may take a while before they are able to build on the new foundation.

God wants all people to be saved, and his plan includes everyone. We don't know how he will do it, but we trust that he (since he is fair and loving) will give everyone a decent opportunity. Not everyone will take what he gives, but he gives it anyway. However, if everyone will get an opportunity for salvation whether or not we tell them in this life, why should we risk our lives (or the risk of being embarrassed) to tell anyone?

Simply this: Jesus told his disciples to spread the gospel – our theology cannot change that – and doing so is an expression of love for God, of giving him glory for his astonishing generosity. The command of Jesus and the example of Paul show us that a willingness to share the gospel is part of the lifestyle of love that God wants us to participate in. These foundations for evangelism have not changed.

However, the way in which we explain the gospel may have to change—mainly that we don't want to imply that Jesus did something to change the Father's mind, and second, we don't want to imply that God holds people's sins against them when Jesus has already paid the debt for them. The debt has been paid, and from God's perspective, there is no huge chasm that people have to cross. Jesus has already crossed that chasm for them, and God is already on their side.

Some people prefer lifestyle evangelism, in which people are won to Christ by seeing an example of the way that Christ changes people from selfish to caring about others. Some of the people we meet can see our lifestyle; but others see us for only a few hours, and we may never see them again. Is there any way to share the gospel with them? Yes. For those who want some sort of outline, I'll give one, but I note in advance that many variations are possible, based on the personality of the presenter and the circumstances of the audience.

1) God created us because he wants to live with us. He loves us. Life is a gift from him to us.

2) Humans fall short of what we are supposed to be (Romans 3:23). We have all experienced pain from being let down or betrayed by a friend, and all of us have broken promises that we've made.

3) But God is not going to let our misdeeds thwart his plan. So he has acted to rescue us. Salvation is a free gift (Romans 6:23). If a friend gives us a gift, we do not pull out our wallet and offer to pay for it. It's a gift. In the same way, eternal life is a gift. We cannot earn it or deserve it, either before it is given or afterwards — God gives it to us as a gift. No one has earned their way into a perfect eternity. God knows we don't deserve it, but he gives it to us anyway.

4) It is made possible by Jesus Christ, who died for our sins, and was raised to life so that we might live again. The Bible says that we died with him, and we live with him (Romans 6:4; Colossians 2:12). The old self, with all its weaknesses and shortcomings, died with Christ. Some of the effects still linger with us, but in the next life, the old self will be gone, and only the new self will live — the new self that is created like Christ by the Holy Spirit. In the resurrection of Jesus, God has shown us that death has been defeated. He promises to raise us back to life, too. The problem of death has been overcome.

5) God will let us live forever, but he also wants to fix our other major problem: the quality of life. We were made for love, truth, kindness, and joy, not a life of betrayal and disappointment. We can't do this on our own, so God promises to live within us, to change us from the inside out, to create us anew.

6) God doesn't force himself on us. For this to work in our lives, we have to accept God's plan. We have to believe that it's true, and we have to trust him to let him do the work in us. We need faith to know that God has planned something better for us than what we see in this life, and we need faith to know that our failures don't disqualify us from this better eternity. We need faith to know that God has power over death, and he has power over our life. He will live within us and we will be his children.

7) Our new life is experienced in this age by faith in Christ. He died for our sins whether or not we believe — our faith can't change that reality one way or the other. But faith makes it a reality in our lives, that we see ourselves as new people, made by God and enabled by the Holy Spirit to be like Christ. We see that we were made for love — and with the guarantee of eternal life, we are given the courage to love. If we look to ourselves, we will always have doubts. But if our life depends on Christ, it depends on something that is 100 percent reliable. Our confidence is in him, not in what we do. When we see an eternity with God as the good life we've always wanted, we will also try to live the good life.

Will everyone be saved?

Some people think that Trinitarian theology leads to universalism, the idea that absolutely everybody will be saved. I do not know why this idea is repugnant to some people. I think it would be good if God turned the Hitlers of this world into kind and considerate people. However, I do not see anything in the Bible or in Trinitarian theology that requires this result.

Trinitarian theology teaches that God gives people freedom. He gives people a choice — love isn't really love unless it is freely given — and the Bible indicates that some people will insist on making the wrong choice, to live in self-imposed misery, in a world of selfishness rather than love. Jesus died for their sins, and they don't have to be trapped in them, but they choose to continue in them anyway.

Christ achieved reconciliation for all things and all people (Colossians 1:20), so we can speak of universal reconciliation. However, this does not mean that everyone suddenly likes God — it means that God likes everyone. The reconciliation has been unilateral, but is not complete until it is bilateral.

"Salvation" is a word with several meanings. The Bible can say that we have been saved by the death of Christ, but it also says that we will be saved when Christ returns and our bodies are transformed from weakness into glory. One of the biggest problems humans have is that we are enslaved to sin—sin is like an alien power that causes us to make stupid choices in life. Salvation is not complete unless we are freed from the grip of sin, and so our salvation is not complete until we are liberated from our tendency to sin, which is at death, or our resurrection.

Salvation comes in steps. Christ, the creator of everyone, died for everyone, and God accepts his sacrifice as being effective for everyone. He forgives everyone, so everyone has been given that initial step in salvation. But when we say that everyone will be saved, we are speaking of salvation in the future and full meaning. This requires the acceptance of God's gift, the human response to God's unilateral action, and the cessation of all sin. We do not have biblical evidence that everyone will accept what God gives, so we cannot teach universalism.

Trinitarian theology helped me answer two questions that I had for a long time. First, what is the role of ethics, when we are judged on the basis of what Christ has done? If salvation merely consists of cancelling our sins, our debt, and our punishment, then why should we bother trying to be good? If the only thing bad about sin is that it is a violation of God's law, and that violation is stricken from the record, then what's the problem with sin? We should try to do right, but why? The answer is that we are anticipating the life of the age to come. If we really want this godly way of life, then we will try to live that way now. If we don't really want it, then God isn't going to force us to have it. We will get what we want, and that's a sobering thought.

The other puzzle I had was, How can God be so sure that nobody is ever going to sin in the age to come? That seems hard to believe, that I will sin until the day I die, and then suddenly at that point I will never sin, not even once, any more, ever. That's an amazing miracle. Trinitarian theology caused me to think more deeply about my union with Christ, what it means for my old self to die with him, and a new self to rise with him. My old self will stay dead; only what has been re-created in Christ will live, and that's why it's guaranteed to never sin again.

Michael Morrison

Do We Teach Universalism?

Some who criticize Trinitarian theology claim that it teaches universalism—the belief that everyone will be saved, regardless of whether they are good or bad, repentant or unrepentant, accepting or rejecting Jesus, and, consequently, there is no such thing as hell. This is not true. Trinitarian theology does not teach universalism. The noted Swiss theologian Karl Barth did not teach it. Neither theologians Thomas F. Torrance nor James B. Torrance taught it. Neither does Perichoresis Ministries director Baxter Kruger, author of *The Shack* William Paul Young, nor Grace Communion International.

GCI's website states our position on universalism:

> Universalism is a biblically unsound doctrine, which says that in the end all souls, whether human, angelic or demonic, will be saved by God's grace. Some Universalists argue that repentance toward God and faith in Jesus Christ are irrelevant. Universalists typically deny the doctrine of the Trinity, and many Universalists are Unitarians. Contrary to universalism, the Bible teaches that there is salvation only in Jesus Christ (Acts 4:12). In Jesus Christ, who is God's elect for our sakes, all humanity is elect, but that does not necessarily mean that all humans will ultimately accept God's free gift. God desires that all come to repentance, and he has created and redeemed humanity for true fellowship with him, but true fellowship can never constitute a forced relationship. We believe that in Christ, God makes gracious and just provision for all, even for those who at death appear not to have yet believed the gospel, but all who remain hostile to God remain unsaved by their own choice.

Those who claim that Trinitarian theology teaches universalism are either being dishonest or suffer from poor scholarship. Careful students of the Bible recognize that whereas we need not rule out the idea that God will save everyone, the scriptures are not conclusive. Therefore we should not be dogmatic about this issue.

The early church not dogmatic on hell

Why should the idea of the possibility of salvation for all arouse such hostility and accusations of "heresy"? The creeds of the early church were not dogmatic on the nature of hell. The metaphors are of flames, outer darkness and weeping and gnashing of teeth. They are meant to convey what it's like for people to be lost forever in a self-enclosed "world," with their own selfish heart, their own selfish desires, adamantly rejecting the source of all love, all goodness, all truth. These metaphors are, if taken literally, conflicting. But metaphors are not intended to be taken literally—they illustrate various aspects of the topic. What we gain from them is that hell, whatever it is, is not where we want to be.

However, to ardently desire for all humanity to be saved and for no one to suffer in hell does not make you a heretic. What Christian would not want every person who ever lived to repent, receive forgiveness and experience reconciliation with God? The idea of all humanity being transformed by the Spirit of Christ and in heaven together in relationship is something to be desired. That is exactly what God desires—that all come to repentance and not suffer the consequences of the rejection of his gracious provision for them. God wants this because he loves the world (Greek, *kosmos*), as we read in John 3:16. God tells us to love and forgive our enemies because he loves his enemies, as Jesus loved and served even his betrayer Judas Iscariot at his last supper (John 13:1, 26) and on the cross (Luke 23:34).

The biblical revelation does not offer any guarantee that all will necessarily accept God's forgiveness. It warns that there may be people who will refuse God's love and reject the redemption and the adoption he has for them. Nevertheless, it is difficult to believe that anyone would make such a choice. It is even more difficult to imagine that any would persist in rebellion against having a loving relationship with him. As C.S. Lewis described in *The Great Divorce,* "I willingly believe that the damned are, in one sense, successful, rebels to the end; that the doors of hell are locked on the inside."

God's desire for everyone

Universalism should not be confused with the universal or cosmic scope of the effectiveness of the saving work of Christ. In Jesus Christ, who is God's elect for our sakes, all humanity is elect. That does not mean we can say for certain that all humans will ultimately accept God's gift. But we can hope that is the case.

God desires that all come to repentance, as Peter expressed, "Not wishing for any to perish but for all to come to repentance" (2 Peter 3:9, NASB). Moreover, God has done everything possible to save us from the terrible and horrific situation that is hell. Yet, in the end, God will not violate the deliberate and persistent choice of those who willfully and deliberately reject his love and turn away from him. For God to override their minds, wills and hearts, he would have to undo their humanity and "un-create" them. But then there would be no human being to freely receive his costly gift of grace, life in Jesus Christ. He has created and redeemed humanity for true fellowship with him, but that true fellowship can never be constituted by a forced relationship.

The Bible does not blur the difference between believer and unbeliever, and neither should we. When we say that all people are forgiven, saved and reconciled in Christ, we mean that while we all belong to Christ, not all are in communion with him. While God has reconciled all to himself, not all are yet trusting and living in that reconciliation. So the apostle Paul says: "God was reconciling the world [*kosmos*] in Christ…We implore you on Christ's behalf: Be reconciled" (2 Corinthians 5:19-20). That is why ours is a ministry, not of condemnation, but of the announcement of Christ's finished work of reconciliation, just as Paul exhorts us.

That is why we do not agree with or teach any of the various forms of universalism. Rather, we bear witness to the biblical revelation and orthodox teaching on God's own character, mind, heart, purpose and attitude towards all manifested in Jesus Christ. We preach the universal or cosmic lordship of Jesus Christ, and we hope in the cosmic reconciliation of all those created according to his image. Since the Bible communicates that it is God's desire for all to come to him in repentance to receive his gracious and costly forgiveness, why would that not also be the desire for all followers of Jesus? Should we desire for others something less than God desires?

Joseph Tkach

Why Would Anyone Want to Be a Christian?

In several nations, it is illegal to become a Christian. But people become Christians anyway — despite penalties and even threats of death. Thousands of believers are killed each year, yet more people become Christians. Christianity can spread even when it is persecuted. That is the way Christianity started — Jesus was killed as a political criminal. In the first 200 years after his death, thousands of Christians were killed as the Roman Empire tried to exterminate this new faith.

Millions of people become Christians each year. Scientists, farmers, historians, and clerks — people from all walks of life — become Christians. Why? This article gives several reasons. You can see whether any of them make sense to you.

1. The teachings of Jesus

Christianity wouldn't make any sense without Jesus at its center. Jesus began his ministry as a teacher. He emphasized love, mercy, faith, forgiveness and honesty. He taught gentleness rather than violence, generosity rather than selfishness, doing good rather than evil. Jesus had respect for all people, even people others looked down on. Jesus touched lepers, welcomed children, and treated women and foreigners with respect.

But Jesus said some harsh things about religious leaders. He hated hypocrisy and the attitude of looking down on others. Jesus spent time with the "sinners" that the leaders despised. He was tolerant. He spent time with the tax collectors that many people hated. Prostitutes found forgiveness, not condemnation.

Jesus kept on teaching even when he knew the religious leaders were trying to kill him. He was sincere, and it cost him his life. People worldwide respect Jesus for his teachings. Many have tried to apply these teachings in their own lives. They have become followers of Jesus.

But sometimes the people who like Jesus' teachings are surprised to learn what he really taught. He said he had a unique relationship with God and that no one could get to God except through him. "No one knows the Son except the Father, and no one knows the Father except the Son and those to whom the Son chooses to reveal him" (Matthew 11:27). Some people accept this; others do not.

2. The resurrection of Jesus

Roman soldiers crucified thousands of people, but only one of them has a following today. Why? Perhaps because only one of them is alive today. The resurrection of Jesus was the main message of the early church, according to the book of Acts. This is what the early disciples testified about and preached about. "God has raised this Jesus to life, and we are all witnesses of the fact" (Acts 2:32). With this simple message, Christianity grew rapidly. Paul said there were hundreds of people who had seen Jesus alive (1 Corinthians 15:6). The early apostles risked their lives to tell what they believed, and thousands were convinced.

No other explanation makes sense. If Jesus' body had remained in the tomb, the religious leaders would have used it to stop the message. Nor would it make any sense for the disciples to steal the body, then risk their lives for the next 30 years preaching that he was alive, without any of them ever betraying the secret. Ordinary fishermen do not risk their lives to preach something they know to be false. Nor does it make sense that the disciples had hallucinations. Dozens of people do not have identical dreams, all substantiated by an empty tomb. The disciples were not deceived, nor were they deceivers. They preached that Jesus had been raised from the dead and had gone into heaven to be at the right hand of God.

On this testimony, preached by ordinary people with an extraordinary boldness, thousands more believed. Even by first-century standards, it was a strange story, but they accepted it. If God raised this man from the dead, then God must have approved of what he taught — even his claims to be our route to salvation.

3. The death of Jesus

If Jesus was such a good man, if God really approved his teachings, why did God allow him to die? What was the purpose of his hideous death? Early Christians were not long in trying to explain the purpose of his death, and more people found reason to believe the story.

It started with Jesus himself, who taught that he "did not come to be served, but to serve, and to give his life as a ransom for many" (Matthew 20:28). Jesus said he was giving his life for a reason. His death had a purpose — it was to serve other people, to pay a price to rescue them. The disciples said that Jesus "died for our sins" — he died so that our sins, the things we have done wrong, would be forgiven. First-century Jews and Greeks were used to thinking about religion in terms of sacrifices. Jesus was a sacrifice, a payment of some kind, dying on behalf of other people to rescue them.

Scholars debate the reasons why Jesus had to die so others could be forgiven. But the bottom line is that he did it. He willingly gave his life to save us. It shows his great love for us — "God demonstrates his own love for us in this: While we were still sinners, Christ died for us" (Romans 5:8).

For some people, this makes tremendous sense. Evil is serious, and it cannot be waived aside as if it did not matter. It matters a great deal, and the death of Jesus shows that it does. A huge cost was involved in paying for the consequences of sin. Jesus' death shows not only the seriousness of sin, but also the depth of God's love for us. Because of Jesus' death, people believe that God loves them.

4. The disciples of Jesus

One reason that Christianity spread so quickly is the believers. They set an example of sincerity, faith, love and mercy. They were letting Christ live in them. They, like their Master, were willing to give their lives to serve others. They changed their ways from selfishness to helpfulness, from violence to peace, from greed to generosity. It was an astonishing transformation, and their friends wondered why they no longer lived in debauchery, lust and drunkenness (1 Peter 4:3-4). These Christians had a change of life that spoke well of Jesus Christ. Some people were convinced of the truth of Christianity simply by seeing the results in their lives (1 Peter 3:1).

Yet, the example set by Christians today is a reason some people do *not* believe! The church is supposedly full of hypocrites. There is some truth in this objection. The church does have people who are less than Christ-like in their attitudes and behavior. But the church is exactly where such people need to be! The church is not a showcase for perfect people — it is a hospital for sinners. People with flaws are invited in, so it should be no surprise that problems are inside it. Sinners need to be in church to hear the message of forgiveness, to hear the teachings of Jesus, and to be exhorted to be more like Jesus.

There are some hypocrites in the church. Some people like the social advantages of the church, but do not follow Jesus. But there are also people remarkably changed by Christ. Former prostitutes, former alcoholics, former white-collar criminals, and even former hypocrites give their testimony that Jesus has changed them. This evidence convinces some people believe that Christianity is true.

5. Good and evil

Some people reject God because there is evil in the world. "If God is all good, loving, and powerful, then he would eliminate evil." But they do not consider the possibility that this is what God is actually in the process of doing. Selfishness is evil, and love is good. God has demonstrated his love by sending Jesus to rescue us from our selfishness. Jesus shows us that love triumphs over evil — evil does not have the last word in his life or in ours. Evil is not eliminated yet, but it will be.

The concept of "evil" requires that there be a God to define what "good" is. Atheism cannot define good — it even implies that aggression is just as good as kindness, as long as it helps the species survive. But is it good for the species to survive? Atheism cannot say. Good and evil become matters of opinion, and that changes from time to time. There have been times in history when most people in a particular culture thought that slavery was good, or genocide was good. If we are to label anything as evil, we need a standard that transcends public opinion. Many believe that this standard is given to us most clearly in the Christian faith.

6. The return of Christ

This life, with all its pains and problems, is not all there is. There will come a time when injustices will be set right, and goodness will be rewarded. The apostle Paul, preaching to philosophers in Athens, ended his speech with this claim: "God commands all people everywhere to repent. For he has set a day when he will judge the world with justice by the man he has appointed. He has given proof of this to everyone by raising him from the dead" (Acts 17:30-31). Only a person who has been through death and come out the other side can credibly claim to give eternal life.

There will come a day of judgment, a day on which everyone will be called into account in front of the Judge who died for us. How can we stand before him? Not through our own wisdom, strength or goodness. We can stand only through the mercy of Jesus Christ, the only way of salvation. The Judge loved us so much that he gave his life to save us.

Christianity teaches the good news that eternal life is given through faith in Christ. We can live forever with God in great joy and peace! There is tremendous purpose in our lives, purpose in our experiences, even in our pains and sorrows. Just as Jesus was raised from the dead, we will be, too, if we believe in him. If this life is all there is, it has no lasting value. But if eternity is possible, it is worth everything in the world. In Christianity, there is everything to gain, and nothing to lose. Some people choose to believe.

Conclusion

Christians believe for many different reasons. Do any of these reasons make sense to you? We'd love to talk about it. Jesus means a lot to us.

For further reading:
Michael Green. *Who Is This Jesus?* Nelson, 1994.
Tim Keller, *The Reason for God: Belief in an Age of Skepticism.* Dutton, 2008.
C.S. Lewis. *Mere Christianity.* Touchstone, 1996.
Paul Little. *Know Why You Believe.* InterVarsity Press, 1988.
John Stott. *Basic Christianity.* InterVarsity Press, 1986.
Lee Strobel. *The Case for Christ.* Zondervan, 1998.

Michael Morrison

Grace and Obedience

Even after centuries of debate, Christians still have not settled on how best to speak about the connection between faith in God's grace and obedience. Biblically grounded Christian teachers recognize that salvation is God's work and that it is received by faith. They also recognize that the resulting life with Christ involves obedience. The problem arises in how to affirm the one without denying (or severely qualifying) the other. The challenge is avoiding either lawlessness (antinomianism) or legalism (works-righteousness).

Both-and?

Most recognize the validity of both grace and obedience (faith and works). Rather than going the "either-or" route, most embrace some form of the "both-and" approach. However, this approach typically has little to say about the "and"—about how grace and obedience are actually connected. The result is that grace and obedience are artificially laminated together or stacked on top of one another. It is as if they are put into a room together and told to "get along."

Following this approach, efforts to correct perceived errors on one side typically involve emphasizing the other. If the perceived problem is too much works, then grace is emphasized. If it's too much grace, then obedience is emphasized. In similar fashion, various ministries emphasize one or the other, depending on which they think is more dangerous or prevalent. The result of this approach is a "seesaw theology" where the connection between law (works) and grace (faith) remains vague if not altogether absent.

In contrast, the Bible deeply relates and integrates grace and obedience as fundamental to Christian faith and life. For example, in Romans 1:5 and 16:26 the apostle Paul says that bringing about this integration was the goal of his ministry. In 14:23 he says that any obedience that does not spring from faith is sin! Hebrews 11 offers illustrations of people who obeyed God "by faith." In 1 John 5 we are told that God's commands are not burdensome because of the victory of faith in God's grace (verses 3-4). Jesus reminds us that his burden is easy and his yoke light (Matthew 11:29-30) and that we are God's "friends," not his slaves. In Galatians, Paul tells us that "faith is made effective through love" (5:6 NRSV, footnote).

The nature of "AND"

There are dozens of places in the New Testament that clearly establish this connection between grace (faith) and obedience (love for God and for others). But how does the connection work? What is the nature of AND? It is found in the person of Jesus, who alone embodies fully the character, mind, attitude and purpose of God. The object of our faith is Jesus Christ, and the essence of that faith is trusting in Jesus as God in person according to who he is and what he has done. Faith is our response to who Jesus is in person, word and deed. We put our trust in God because of who Jesus Christ is. He himself is the grace of God towards us.

Jesus is the gospel. He is our salvation. We receive all the benefits of who he is as we trust in him and cast aside (repent of) all rival objects of trust. We then enjoy union and communion with Jesus as our Lord and God. Our lives are united to him and we share in his life, participating with him in all he is doing and will do in our relationship of trust (faith).

We have our being by being in fellowship and communion with Jesus, receiving from him all that he has for us, and he taking from us all that we give him. In that union and communion we are transformed, bit by bit (2 Corinthians 3:18) to share more of Christ's glorified human nature, his character. We can count on this on-going gracious work of Christ by the Spirit even if much remains hidden (Colossians 3:3) and we remain mere earthen vessels (2 Corinthians 4:7).

Our view of Jesus

The problem is that people have too small a view of Jesus and thus a restricted faith in him. Though they may trust him for future salvation (getting into heaven), that's pretty much it. However, when we look closely at Scripture, we see that Jesus is both Savior and Commander. Jesus saves us by grace and also commands things of us.

Our obedience to his commands does not earn us salvation, so why is obedience important? Perhaps we think that we must obey simply because our Commander says so—because he is big and powerful and we had better obey or else! Approached in this way, obedience becomes an act of will in response to the might and seemingly arbitrary will of God. This is the obedience of a slave.

The problem with this approach to obedience is that it reflects a shrunken conception of Jesus and what he offers. We need to see all of who Jesus is and all of what he offers if we are to grasp all of what we can trust him for. We begin by understanding that Jesus is Lord of the whole cosmos, the entire universe; Lord of all reality, and he has a good and loving purpose for it all. He is redeeming all things and will renew heaven and earth. He is Lord and Savior over every aspect of human life and has a purpose for every dimension of our existence. It is all to be a channel of his blessing to us and through us to others. All of it, every relationship, is meant to lead to life and life abundantly. Even our eating and drinking is to reflect the glory of our life-giving God (1 Corinthians 10:31). Every relationship is to be a fruitful gift exchange that contributes to a fullness of life and a fullness of love.

Jesus' authority extends into every aspect of created existence, into every dimension of life at every level: mathematical, physical, chemical, biological, animal, human, social, cultural, linguistic, artistic, judicial, economic, psychological, philosophical, religious and spiritual. All this has its origin in fellowship and communion with God through Christ. This relationship with God through Christ works its way into every avenue of life under his redeeming lordship. God's grace has to do with everything. That's the foundation of a Christian worldview.

Everything we receive from God we pass on to others to contribute to God's universe-wide purposes. This is especially true in our relationships. We receive forgiveness of sins—renewing grace to start again with hope. We receive God's generosity, providing us all the fruit of the Spirit. We receive comfort, love, transforming power, purpose and direction in life to be a sign and witness to the grace and goodness of God. We become witnesses to the truth and holy loving character of God. All these things point to eternal life—life with God as his beloved children in holy, loving unity.

Trust and obey

Our faith is a trust in God through Christ for all these things, not just for "going to heaven" or "being in the kingdom" someday. Every command of God and every act of obedience is keyed to some aspect of what we can trust God for:

- We forgive because we have been and will be forgiven.
- We love, because we are first loved by God.
- We love our enemies because God first loved us and also loves (wants his best) for his and our enemies.
- We can be generous because God is generous with us.
- We can be truthful and honest because God is truthful and honest and will bring out the truth in the end.
- We can be creative and helpful because God is creative and helpful to us.
- We comfort others in their grief because God comforts us in our grief.
- We can be patient because God is patient with us.
- We can be peacemakers because God is a peacemaker.
- We can pursue justice and right relationships at every level, because God is just and righteous.

- We can be reconcilers because God is a reconciler.

All our doing by faith is participating in what God is doing through Christ and in the Spirit. That means everything we do is fellowship and communion with Christ. We never act alone—because we are never alone but are united to Christ as his brothers and sisters and members of the family of God.

Imperatives flow from indicatives

We obey by faith when we see all of who Jesus is in any given situation, trust him to be faithful in that situation and then act as if he will be faithful. That is, we act on our faith in who he is. Connected to every command in Scripture is some kind of reference to who God is and what he can be trusted for. Seeing the connection between what God can be trusted for and what he then directs us to do generates the obedience of faith.

James Torrance said that every imperative of grace is built on a foundation of an indicative of grace.[1] There is always a connection, because all of God's commands to us (the imperatives) arise out of his own character, heart, nature and purpose, including everything he has done for us in Jesus Christ (the indicatives). God is not arbitrary—his will for us always is informed and controlled by his nature and character as the Triune God who came to us in Jesus Christ so that we might have fellowship and communion with him in holy love.

Faith in God's grace arises out of a trust in God because of Jesus Christ, and obedience to the God of grace arises out of a trust in God because of Jesus Christ. Faith and obedience have the same source—the faithfulness of God in Christ. They both are a response to who Christ is. They have the same Trinitarian, Incarnational theological source. Both are the fruit of a trusting relationship with God through Christ in the Spirit.

Guidelines for preaching/teaching

Here are guidelines that I've developed to help keep grace and obedience together in Jesus:
- Never call for an act of obedience without first showing how that call to action corresponds to something we can trust God for. Always look for the indicatives of grace that are the foundation for the imperatives (commands) of grace in every biblical passage.
- Always indicate the character of the gracious, saving, redeeming Commander. Never present God as merely a commander with a strong will disconnected from his heart, mind, character and purpose, which we see in Jesus Christ. Always begin by answering the foundational question, Who are you, Lord? Doing so makes our preaching and teaching truly Trinitarian and Incarnational.
- Never simply preach to a person's will or power of choice. Behind every act of will and choice is a desire, a hope, a love, a fear, a trust or distrust. That is, behind every act there is belief or unbelief, trust or distrust in God. Preach to persons' hearts, their affections, their yearnings concerning the character, purpose and heart of God and his desire for our fellowship and communion with him. Preach what God can be trusted for. He can be counted on to keep his promises. Feed people's faith, hope and love for God. Obedience will flow out of that.
- Do not preach: "If you…then God." Doing so tempts people into legal obedience and works-righteousness. Instead, preach: "Since God in Christ by the Spirit…then you ____." Or, "As you do x, y or z out of trust, you will be receiving what God offers us in Christ." For example, say, "As we confess our sins, we experience the forgiveness that God has already given us in Christ."
- Present obedience as "going to work with God"—as an act of fellowship with God that involves us in what the Spirit of God is doing.
- Preach obedience as a "get to," not a "have to." Preach it as the privilege of a child of

---

[1] These are grammatical terms for Greek verbs. Commands are in the imperative mood; statements of fact are in the indicative mood.

God, not the grit-your-teeth duty of the slave of a God who imposes his will on others.
- Do not seek to motivate others on the basis of trying to close a supposed "credibility gap" between the "reality" of this fallen world and an ideal that we suppose God hopes for. It is not our calling to build the kingdom or to make God's ideal actual. Rather, preach the reality of who God is and what he does (and has done), and the calling we have to participate with God in making visible a bit of that reality. With this approach, our only choice is either to affirm and participate in the reality that God has established in Christ by the Spirit, or to deny and to refuse to participate. We have no power to change that reality, but only to choose whether we will participate.
- Preach and teach the grace of God as a finished work—a reality that we can count on even if it is hidden for now. Do not teach it as a potential that God has made possible if we do x, y or z—God is not dependent on our actions. Rather, he invites our participation in what he has done, is doing and will do. Preach like Jesus: "The kingdom of God has come near, so repent and believe in that good news." Preach like Peter: "Since God has made Jesus Lord and Savior, therefore repent and believe." The desired action is presented as a response to who God is and what he has done.
- Never preach as if God cannot be more faithful than we are—as if God is limited by what we do or don't do. Paul says, "If we are faithless, he [God] remains faithful" (2 Timothy 2:13). We may miss out on being involved, but God will still accomplish his good purposes. God does not need us, but he delights in having his children involved in what he is doing. We were created for fellowship (communion, partnership) with God.
- Do not grant reality-making power to human actions, as if what we do makes "all the difference." Christ alone gets that credit. Our actions, whether they be great or small (as small as a cup of water, or a mustard seed of faith), amount only to a few loaves and fish to feed 5000. They are signs pointing to the coming kingdom of God. We are mere witnesses, and our sign-acts are partial, imperfect, temporary and only provisional. But by God's grace, the Spirit uses these meager things to point people to Christ so that they may put their entire trust in him according to who he really is.
- Realize that you will have to trust mightily—trust in the unconditional grace of God to bring about the obedience of faith—in order to preach and teach this way and not succumb to the temptation to revert back to making it sound like God's grace depends on our response (and thus conditional upon our action).
- Know that you, like Paul, will not be able to prevent some people from trying to take advantage of grace (even though taking advantage of it is not receiving it, but rejecting it!). You will be accused by some, just like Paul was, of encouraging sin and disobedience (antinomianism)! But Paul did not change his message of grace under the pressure of such accusations. We must not attempt to prevent this rejection and abuse of grace by changing our message to a conditioned grace or an arbitrary obedience, as happened in Galatia. Making that switch would be a denial of the gospel of God in Jesus Christ.

I hope you can see how this biblical orientation brings together grace and obedience in an organic, personal and integrated way so that there is no "either-or" separation, nor a simplistic seesaw "both-and" juxtaposition of two different things. Those who love and trust God through Christ in the Spirit as Lord of the universe will desire to be faithful to him and with him in every dimension of life here and now, even in our current fallen condition.

Gary W. Deddo

Relationship With Christ
A Bible Study

Various words are used to illustrate different truths of the gospel. The word *justification* comes from a law-court setting, and *redemption* comes from a financial setting. But salvation involves much more than those words can convey. Scripture also uses several other terms. In this study we will examine some of the other words that describe our relationship with God and Christ.

1. Before we had faith in Jesus Christ, we were alienated from God, cut off from him. Whether we thought of ourselves in this way or not, we were his enemies (Colossians 1:21). But now, as a result of Jesus Christ, what are we? Verse 22. How has this peace been achieved? Verse 20.

Comment: *Reconciliation* is a relationship term. It is another word-picture for the gospel, since reconciliation means to make peace between people who used to be enemies. The gospel tells us that we, who were once enemies of God, are now on good terms with him. We are more than friends—we are loved as children and heirs. The word reconciliation helps make the point that we used to be God's enemies, and have now been set right through Jesus Christ.

2. How was our reconciliation achieved? Romans 5:8, 10-11. Does this reconciliation mean that our sins are not counted against us? 2 Corinthians 5:18-19. Does the gospel message, the good news that we preach, include this concept? Verses 19-20. How is reconciliation possible? Verse 21; Ephesians 2:16.

Comment: God made Jesus, who was sinless, to be sin on our behalf. As Paul explains elsewhere, Jesus died for us. He was the perfect sin offering, and the result is that in him, "we might become the righteousness of God." This is astonishing news: Sinners can become God's righteousness through Jesus Christ. Jesus' death on the cross enabled our sins to be forgiven, for us to have peace with God, for us to be counted righteous with him, and in right relationship with him.

3. What family metaphor does Paul use to describe our new relationship with God? Romans 8:15; Galatians 4:5-6. What are the implications of this status? Romans 8:17; Galatians 3:29; 4:7.

Comment: In Romans 8:15, the Greek word for "sonship," seen in some translations, means adoption. The picture is that God has chosen us to be in his family, even though we had no right to be there. There are two thoughts here: 1) God has chosen us and 2) we will be given an inheritance from him. In the ancient world, wealthy people who had no children of their own would adopt people (sometimes adults) to be their heirs. Paul is saying that God has chosen us as his children for the purpose of being his heirs, so that we will share with him in all the goodness of the universe.

When we are in Christ, when we identify ourselves with him, when our life is hidden in him, then we share in his rights as Son. We have all the legal rights of children, and we are heirs with Christ of all things (Hebrews 2:6-11). Normally, children do not inherit property until the parent dies. But this is not possible with God, so the analogy falls short at this point. In salvation, the truth is the other way around: it is the children who must die before they can inherit the property! The old self must die, and the new person must be created in Christ. Through faith, we are united to Christ. We share in his death (Romans 6:3-4) and will also share in his resurrection to eternal life (Romans 6:5; Ephesians 2:5-6; 2 Timothy 2:11).

The word adoption points us to the fact that we have a great inheritance. It also reminds us that God has chosen us, selected us, elected us for his purpose. We are "set apart for holy use" — the meaning of the word *sanctified*. We are "holy ones" — the meaning of the word saints. Because of what Jesus Christ has done for us and is doing in us, our lives are different, described in new ways. Paul says, "If anyone is in Christ, the new creation has come; the old has gone, the new is here!" (2 Corinthians 5:17).

Now let's look at one more word-picture of how new our lives are in Christ.

4. Another biblical image of our relationship to God is not as adopted children, but as direct descendants, children born in the household of God. Did Jesus describe our need for a new birth? John 3:3-8. Has God now given us that new birth? 1 Peter 1:3. How does God give us this new start in life? 1 Peter 1:23; James 1:18; Titus 3:5.

5. Do those who accept Christ become born of God? John 1:12-13; 1 John 5:1. Are we his children? 1 John 3:1-2. Does John stress that someone who is born of God should forsake sin, and live a new way of life? 1 John 2:29; 3:9-10; 4:7; 5:4, 18.

Comment: These verses use the Greek word *gennao*, which usually refers to the birth of a child. In a few verses, it has the more general meaning of "produce." Here are some verses where the word clearly means the birth of a baby: Matthew 2:1, 4; Luke 1:57; John 16:21; Romans 9:11; Hebrews 11:23.

In James 1:18, a different Greek word is used, *apokueo*, which comes from *apo*, meaning "from," and *kueo*, meaning "to be swollen" or "to be pregnant." *Apokueo* means to get something from a pregnancy — to give birth, to bring forth. James 1:18 says that God "chose to give us birth through the word of truth." Through the gospel, God has given us a second birth, a spiritual birth.

Jesus, John, Peter and James are using the same analogy: that Christians are born again, with a new start in life, with a family-like relationship with God, in which we call God the affectionate term Abba. Scripture describes Christians as babies and children (1 Corinthians 3:1-2; Hebrews 5:12-14).

Shortly after Peter tells us that we have been born again (1 Peter 1:23), he tells us to desire milk as eagerly as a newborn baby does (1 Peter 2:2).

We are to have a new source of life and a new way of life. The stress is on newness — our new nature as children of God. Our new life is energized and guided by the Holy Spirit.

We have examined several biblical words that describe our relationship with God. But physical things can only partially describe spiritual truths. The spiritual meaning of salvation is more profound than can be captured in legal terminology, financial ideas, or friendship or family terms. All the terms describe something true about the good news we have in Jesus Christ, but the complete truth is better than any of these terms can convey. Eternal life with a perfectly good God will be better than we can currently describe.

It is sometimes said that Christianity is not a religion — it is a relationship. In sociology, Christianity is correctly classified as a religion. When people say that Christianity is not a religion, they are making the point that our faith is not just a list of things we do for God, not a series of rituals, not a set of behaviors — it is an interactive relationship with God. He has a relationship not just with humanity as a whole, but with each person.

God wants us to do certain things and have certain behaviors, but the greatest commandment of all is to love God with all our being (Matthew 22:37-38). *Love* is a relationship word; our relationship with God is to be characterized by love. He has already shown us his love for us; we are to respond with love for him. Our obedience and behavior should be motivated by love. We are to seek God and desire him; we are to be eager to do his will. God does not want a reluctant obedience (motivated perhaps by fear), but a willing desire to be more and more like his Son. An eternity with God, in his kingdom and family, will be a blessing only if we enjoy being with God.

Scripture describes an interactive relationship with God. He has a personal concern for each of his children, tells them of his love, and leads them in what he wants them to do. In response to God, we love and speak to him in prayer, and in gratitude, we want to please him. He responds to us, and we respond to him. It is a personal and interactive relationship for each of us.

The intimacy of this relationship is shown further by the fact that God lives within us (sometimes expressed as the Father living in us, sometimes as the Son living in us and sometimes as the Holy Spirit living in us). When we accept Christ as our Savior, his Spirit lives within us. Whether we put it in these words or not, we are inviting God to be Lord of our lives, to build a relationship that will last forever.

Eternal life involves knowing God and knowing Jesus Christ (John 17:3). To "know" a person means more than knowing about them—it is a relationship term. Faith is also a relationship term, since it involves not only belief but also trust. Our relationship with Christ is not just a servant-master relationship, but a friendship (John 15:15). God is our Father, and Jesus Christ is our Brother. Christ's love for his people is compared to a husband's love for his wife (2 Corinthians 11:2; Ephesians 5:21-33). These analogies show that God wants a close relationship with us—a companionship closer than the best marriage, closer than the best friendship, closer than the best parent-child relationship.

Everyone, Christian or not, has some sort of relationship with God. Some people are like slaves who have run away from the master, some are like children who have run away from home. Some try to act as if God did not exist; others openly resent him. For them, the relationship is characterized by the word enemies. The good news is that God does not want us to remain as enemies—he wants us to be his children, his friends, who love him dearly. He wants this so much that he sent his Son to die for us, to reconcile us to himself and give us a new start in life, in which we have invited God to lead us and reshape what we are, so that we become more and more like him, better prepared to live with him in his kingdom with joy forever and ever. This is the good news of the kingdom of God, the gospel of Jesus Christ, the message of salvation.

Michael Morrison

A New Look at the Good Samaritan

The Good Samaritan is one of Jesus' most popular parables. Preachers often use it to encourage people to be unselfish, to think ahead and help others. But there is more to the story than that. Jesus was doing far more than putting hypocritical religious leaders in their place. Let's take a closer look.

> A man was going down from Jerusalem to Jericho, when he fell into the hands of robbers. They stripped him of his clothes, beat him and went away, leaving him half dead.
>
> A priest happened to be going down the same road, and when he saw the man, he passed by on the other side. So too, a Levite, when he came to the place and saw him, passed by on the other side.
>
> But a Samaritan, as he traveled, came where the man was; and when he saw him, he took pity on him. He went to him and bandaged his wounds, pouring on oil and wine. Then he put the man on his own donkey, took him to an inn and took care of him. The next day he took out two silver coins and gave them to the innkeeper. "Look after him," he said, "and when I return, I will reimburse you for any extra expense you may have."
>
> Which of these three do you think was a neighbor to the man who fell into the hands of robbers? (Luke 10:30-37)

The answer to Jesus' question was obvious. But Jesus was teaching much more than a lesson in social responsibility. Let's consider the context. Jesus was answering a lawyer who had asked, "What must I do to inherit eternal life?" (verse 25). This man was a religious lawyer, priding himself in his understanding of all 613 points of the Torah. The religious leaders of Jesus' day had inherited a system that had turned obedience to God into an obstacle course, so strewn with picky dos and don'ts that it left the average person on a permanent guilt trip.

This approach contradicted what Jesus taught, and confrontation became inevitable. The lawyers, along with the Pharisees, Sadducees, scribes and others in religious leadership, were constantly trying to discredit Jesus. There was a motive behind the lawyer's apparently innocent question. So Jesus let the expert speak first: "What is written in the law?... How do you read it?" (verse 26).

The lawyer knew the answer: "'Love the Lord your God with all your heart and with all your soul and with all your strength and with all your mind'; and, 'Love your neighbor as yourself'" (verse 27).

"You have answered correctly," Jesus replied. "Do this and you will live" (verse 28).

It was a good answer, as far as it went. But you know what lawyers are like. They are trained to look for some extenuating circumstance that might in some way limit the extent of the law. The lawyer knew that the command to "love your neighbor as yourself" was impossible to fulfill. So he thought he had found a loophole. "Who is my neighbor?" he asked Jesus. That is when Jesus gave his famous parable.

Cast and location

Jesus set his story on the road from Jerusalem to Jericho, a distance of about 17 miles. Jerusalem was where the Temple was, the center of the Levitical priesthood. The priests were the highest class of the Levites. They were supported by thousands of other Levites who served at lower levels, doing such tasks as keeping the altar fire going, lighting the incense, singing in the Temple chorus and playing musical instruments. When they were not on duty, many of these priests and temple workers lived in Jericho. They often traveled this road between Jerusalem and Jericho.

Travel in those days could be hazardous. One stretch of the Jericho road was known as the "Way of Blood," because so many people were robbed and killed there. This was where Jesus set the scene for his parable. People knew exactly where he was talking about.

In Jesus' story, the first person to see the victim is a priest, but rather than get involved, he passes by on the other side of the road. He is followed by a Levite, a temple-worker. The Levite does the same—he passes by. Then along comes a Samaritan.

A what? Jesus would have caused a stir with that. The Samaritans were a mix of Jew and Gentile, and the Jews did not like them. They had names for Samaritans like "half breeds" and "heathen dogs," and considered them to be spiritually defiled. The Jews of that time did not often hear the words "good" and "Samaritan" used in the same sentence.

But in Jesus' story, it is this outcast who stops to help. Not only does this Samaritan help, but he goes far beyond what most people do. He cleans the victim's wounds with oil and wine, then bandages them. People didn't carry first-aid kits back then. He likely would have had to tear up some of his own clothing to make a bandage. Next, he puts the injured man on his donkey and takes him to an inn. He takes two silver coins, a considerable amount in those days, and promises to reimburse the innkeeper for any further expense. This is an exceptional level of assistance, especially for a total stranger and someone who is supposed to be a social enemy. But the Samaritan did not let that stand in the way.

With this deceptively simple little story, Jesus impales the lawyer on his own hook. He asks him, "Which of these three do you think was a neighbor to the man who fell into the hands of robbers?" (verse 36). Jesus has turned the question around. He is not asking, "Which people should I help?" He is saying: To answer the question, you need to put yourself into the shoes (or lack thereof) of the man who was beaten and left to die. The better question is: "When I need help, who do I want to help me?" Don't you hope that the Samaritan will be a neighbor to you?

Who was a good neighbor? The answer is obvious, but the expert in the law didn't want to say the word Samaritan, so he said, "The one who had mercy on him." Then Jesus delivers the knockout blow: "Go and do likewise" (verse 37).

Remember, this "teacher of the law" was from a class of people who prided themselves on how carefully they obeyed God. For example, they would not pronounce God's name, considering it too holy to utter. They would even take a ritual bath to ensure purity before writing God's name. Along with the Pharisees, they were fastidious about observing the law in every detail. The lawyer had asked what he needed to do in order to inherit eternal life. Jesus' answer was, in effect, "You have to do the impossible." Your love for others needs to extend far beyond what humans are capable of doing.

A story of salvation

How could anyone be expected to live up to the standard of the Samaritan in this story? If that is what God expects, even the meticulous lawyer was doomed. Jesus was showing that humans cannot meet the perfect requirements of the law. Even those who dedicate themselves to it fall short. Jesus is the only one to fulfill the law in its deepest intent. Jesus is the Good Samaritan.

Jesus knew that there is nothing we can "do" to earn an eternity with a holy God. So he crafted his answer-story at two levels of meaning. On the surface, it made the point that people ought to love and do good to their enemies. But on a deeper level, it addressed the question of eternal life. To answer the question, we need to put ourselves in the place of the man who was beaten and left to die. He represents us—all humanity. The robbers correspond to sin and the forces of evil, the devil and his dominion. We do not have enough strength to combat these forces, and if we are left to ourselves, we will die.

The priest and the Levite represent the laws and sacrifices of the old covenant. They can't help us. The Good Samaritan is the only one who can help. The wine and the oil correspond, roughly, to the blood Jesus shed for us and the Holy Spirit who dwells in us. That is what heals us. The inn could then represent the church, where God puts his people to be spiritually nurtured until he returns for them. Jesus pays for this ongoing need in our life, too.

Jesus used the lawyer's question to show how inadequate for salvation even the best human effort is, and how wonderful and sure is his work of redemption for humanity. Jesus, and only Jesus, can rescue us from the "Way of Blood" — and he did it by way of his own blood.

Joseph Tkach

Grace From First to Last

Grace is the first word in the name of our denomination. We chose it, but not because it sounds "religious." Each word in our name identifies our experience as a fellowship, and grace is an integral part of our identity — especially our identity in Christ. As a denomination, we have always understood grace to be God's unconditional and unmerited pardon. But we tended to think of it as a component of salvation that needed to be "stirred into the mix" because of our inability to keep the law. We now see God's grace as much more than that.

Grace is not some sort of passive concept of forgiveness. It is not a principle, a proposition, or a product. Grace is the love and freedom-producing action of God to reconstitute humanity into what the apostles Peter and Paul refer to as being made into God's own people (2 Corinthians 5:17-20; Galatians 6:15; 1 Peter 2:9-10).

Grace is not just a spiritual supplement that God provides because we can't keep his law, like a whiff of oxygen to help a sick person breathe a bit easier. Grace is an entirely new atmosphere that transforms us and gives us a new kind of life — life that no amount of law keeping could sustain. Note Paul's explanation:

> I through the law am dead to the law, that I might live unto God. I am crucified with Christ: nevertheless I live; yet not I, but Christ liveth in me: and the life which I now live in the flesh I live by the faith of the Son of God, who loved me, and gave himself for me. (Galatians 2:19-20, KJV)

Grace is the environment that allows us, God's new creation, to not just survive, but to grow and flourish. At the risk of over-simplification (a danger inherent in all analogies) we might think of grace as God's "operating system." The Father, Son and Holy Spirit have been giving, receiving and sharing love for all eternity. When they extend that sharing of love to us, it is their gift of grace. This grace of God is not the exception to a rule — his rule is a gracious one, all the time, to give us life and to bless us, even if obstacles to our receiving it have to be removed at his own cost.

We see God's grace most clearly in the person of Jesus, who as Paul said, loved us and gave himself for us. As the early church leader Irenaeus taught, the Son and the Spirit are the "two arms" of the Father lovingly embracing us back to himself. The Gospel of John gives us Jesus' own encouraging words:

> The glory that you have given me I have given them, so that they may be one, as we are one. I in them and you in me, that they may become completely one, so that the world may know that you have sent me and have loved them even as you have loved me. (John 17:22-23, NRSV).

As recipients of the grace of God in Christ, we not only share in the love and life of the Father through his Son in the Spirit, but we also share in the mission of God to the world. That mission is the complete restoration and renewal of all creation in Christ Jesus, through the Spirit, into a state of perfect glory. God's grace in the person of Jesus

Christ is for all humanity without distinction to race, status or gender. That is why the vision of Grace Communion International is for "all kinds of churches for all kinds of people in all kinds of places."

Joseph Tkach

Responding to the Church With Teamwork

Sometimes Christians assume that full-time pastors serve the Lord more than other members do. Although that may be true in some cases, it is not true in all cases. Paul tells us, "Whatever you do, do it all for the glory of God" (1 Corinthians 10:31). Whenever Christians work in a bank, they do it for the glory of God. A Christian who teaches school does it to glorify God. A Christian who takes care of children at home glorifies God in changing diapers and cleaning floors. They are all serving the Lord—full-time, perhaps 100 hours a week!

Every member lives to the glory and honor of Jesus Christ (2 Corinthians 5:15). Every member serves him as circumstances and abilities allow. Every member is a witness of Jesus Christ working in this world—and that includes secular occupations as well as religious jobs. Jesus served God by working as a carpenter for many years. Even today, Christian carpenters serve God in the work they do.

Members have a mission

The church is not a building, social club or a self-benefit society. The church is the people of God. That means both ministers and lay members (or perhaps we should say lay ministers, since all members have a ministry). The church has a mission to the world. The people of God have a mission to the world. All members have a mission to the world.

Ordinary members have a prominent role in the church's mission—partly because there are many more of them than there are ordained elders. Another reason for the importance of members is that they are more often "in the world." Due to the nature of their role, full-time elders often interact mostly with people who are already Christians. It is the other members who are mixing with non-Christians on a daily basis—on the job, in the neighborhoods, in hobbies and sports. They set examples of Christ-like life, hopefully a life that evidences hope and joy despite the troubles of this world. Non-Christians need that kind of example.

The church meets for worship and fellowship a few hours each week. What is the church doing during the rest of the week? Much of our time is spent interacting with the world, in our jobs, in our neighborhoods, even in our families. Most of the time, the church is dispersed, setting an example in the world. This is part of our Christian calling, part of our mission, even part of our worship as we seek to make God look good in all that we do.

Our weekly worship services should fill us with the joy of salvation and strengthen and instruct us in living in Christ throughout the week. They remind us of what life is for. They also give us opportunity to come together into the presence of God and express thanks to him for what he has done in our lives the preceding week. They give us opportunity to join the angelic choir in praising him in collective song and prayer. They help us seek guidance from his Word regarding how we serve him in the coming week.

Similarly, small group meetings give us opportunity to reflect on the Word of God and share with one another the work God is doing in our lives, so that we might encourage one another and pray for one another, that our service might be all the more effective.

All members are ministers of Jesus Christ. Some serve God primarily in prayer, some in helping the poor, some in their family and neighborhood responsibilities, etc.—each according to our circumstances, each according to our abilities. Pastors serve him in pastoring his flock; members serve him in contributing to the spiritual health and unity of the flock, and we all serve him throughout the week in our homes, schools, jobs, and community activities.

When Christ said "take up your cross and follow me," he was not referring to pastors only!

We cannot hire someone to do Christian service for us. Pastors are to lead, to teach, to equip members for service. But each of us must do our own part, as we have been called and gifted by the Holy Spirit. All Christians follow Christ in denying the self and in serving others. The Lord served others, and service is not beneath the dignity of anyone who accepts Jesus' death as being payment for his or her sins. He served us, and calls on us to serve others, to do good to all.

The question is not whether we serve Christ throughout the week—it is how we serve him. Whether we want to or not, we represent Jesus Christ in the office, on the highway, in our homes. What we do throughout the week is important—this is where doctrine comes to life to illustrate the fact that we are being transformed into the likeness of Jesus Christ. He is living in us, Paul says, and the effect he can have in our lives is limited only by the vitality of our faith in him.

Most of us are responsive to the will of our Lord. But many of us are not used to thinking of ourselves as ministers of Jesus Christ. Every member is ministering, being led by Christ to work and serve in the world. This fact magnifies the importance of what we do in the name of Jesus throughout the week—not just in the work we do, but also in our relationships with the people we work with.

The fact that our work is a ministry magnifies the importance of community service. Works of service are of value in themselves, but they are also opportunities to show what Christ is doing in our lives. Some people are better at sharing the gospel in words; some are better at sharing it through their work. When Christians work together, they can often be more effective than either one would be alone.

Mutual support

Throughout the week, members are at the "front line" of the church's work. We can support each other in prayer in this work. We need to be aware of how we are serving, and how others are serving, so that we might better encourage them. We can share our experiences and opportunities whenever we meet. Worship services can also strengthen and equip us for this work. Our success as a church is measured in large part by what we do during the week. When members are doing good in Jesus' name throughout the week, and when they are being energized and encouraged by what they do and hear at worship services and in their small group meetings, then the gospel is being spread.

When members realize that they are ministers of Jesus Christ, they have a realistic view of who they are, what they have been called for, and how to live. Their identity is in Christ. They come to worship services not only to give worship, but also to receive instruction that will help them serve better during the week. That attitude generates fewer complaints of "I'm not getting fed" and more thoughts of "How can I glorify God in what I am doing?"

Pastors are to provide leadership as they equip members for their ministries. For one thing, this means helping people connect to God, from whom all ministry should originate. They want to inspire, encourage, comfort, exhort and challenge people. It includes preaching and administration, and it also includes training leaders for small groups and developing and mentoring leaders for other ministries.

The church, from the pulpit and in small groups, can provide moral support for the work that is being done, reminding one another that our activities are serving Jesus Christ, and that he gives us the power and courage to carry out his will. In small groups and other activities, the church also provides practical opportunities for skills to be developed, spiritual gifts to be discovered, and ministries to be encouraged.

How to help pastors

Pastors have a difficult job. How can members help their pastors? For one, pray for them. The pastors' job cannot be done without supernatural help. Second, *ask* pastors what to do to help. Be a volunteer—don't wait for an assignment. Third, help create an environment of love in the congregation. This will give "weak" members comfort and time to work through some of their needs. Strong members need to assist in the ministry of reconciliation, of soothing hurts within the body of Christ, of encouraging, comforting and edifying one another.

Fourth, many members have some pastoral skills. They can help equip other members for works of ministry. They can invite other members to join them in their ministries during the week. They can mentor and set examples of service. In small groups and one-on-one, they can share their faith in Christ with other members, to strengthen their faith. They can pray for other members. In all these ways, members can assist the pastor. Every member is a minister.

Joseph Tkach

The Three-Fold Meaning of the Lord's Supper

The Lord's Supper is a reminder of what Jesus did in the past, a symbol of our present relationship with him, and a promise of what he will do in the future. Let's survey these three aspects.

Memorials of Jesus' death on the cross

On the evening he was betrayed, while Jesus was eating a meal with his disciples, he took some bread and said, "This is my body given for you; do this in remembrance of me" (Luke 22:19). When we participate in the Lord's Supper, we each eat a small piece of bread in remembrance of Jesus.

"In the same way, after the supper he took the cup, saying, 'This cup is the new covenant in my blood, which is poured out for you'" (verse 20). When we drink a small amount of wine (or grape juice) at the Lord's Supper, we remember that Jesus' blood was shed for us, and that his blood inaugurated the new covenant. Just as the old covenant was sealed by the sprinkling of blood, the new covenant was established by Jesus' blood (Hebrews 9:18-28).

Paul said, "Whenever you eat this bread and drink this cup, you proclaim the Lord's death until he comes" (1 Corinthians 11:26). The Lord's Supper looks back to the death of Jesus Christ on the cross.

Is Jesus' death a good thing, or a bad thing? There are some very sorrowful aspects to his death, but the bigger picture is that his death is wonderful news for all of us. Jesus is glad that he did it. It shows how much God loves us—so much that he sent his Son to die for us, so that our sins would be forgiven and we may live forever with him.

The death of Jesus is a tremendous gift to us. It is precious. When we are given a gift of great value, a gift that involved personal sacrifice for us, how should we receive it? With mourning and regret at the sacrifice? No, that is not what the giver wants. Rather, we should receive it with great gratitude, as an expression of great love. If we have tears, they should be tears of joy.

So the Lord's Supper, although a memorial of a death, is not a funeral, as if Jesus were still dead. Rather, we observe this memorial knowing that death held Jesus only three days—knowing that death will not hold us forever, either. We rejoice that Jesus has conquered death, and has set free all who were enslaved by a fear of death (Hebrews 2:14-15). We can remember Jesus' death with the happy knowledge that he has triumphed over sin and death! As Jesus predicted, our mourning has turned into joy (John 16:20). Coming to the Lord's table and having communion should be a celebration, not a funeral.

The ancient Israelites looked back to the Passover events as the defining moment in their history, when their identity as a nation began. That was when they escaped death and slavery through the intervention of God and they were freed to serve the Lord. In the church, we look back to the events surrounding the crucifixion and resurrection of Jesus as the defining moment in our history. That is how we escape death and the slavery of sin, and that is how we are freed to serve the Lord. The Lord's Supper is a memorial of this defining moment in our history.

Our present relationship with Jesus Christ

The crucifixion of Jesus has a continuing significance to all who have taken up a cross to follow him. We continue to participate in his death and in the new covenant because we participate in his life. Paul wrote, "Is not the cup of thanksgiving for which we give thanks a participation in the blood of Christ? And is not the bread that we break a participation in the body of Christ?" (1 Corinthians 10:16). In the Lord's Supper, we show that we share in Jesus Christ. We commune with him. We are united in him.

The New Testament speaks of our sharing with Jesus in several ways. We share in his crucifixion (Galatians 2:20; Colossians 2:20), death (Romans 6:4), resurrection (Ephesians 2:6; Colossians 2:13; 3:1) and life (Galatians 2:20). Our lives are in him, and he is in us. The Lord's Supper pictures this spiritual reality.

John 6 conveys a similar idea. After Jesus proclaimed himself to be the "bread of life," he said, "Whoever eats my flesh and drinks my blood has eternal life, and I will raise him up at the last day" (verse 54). Our spiritual food is in Jesus Christ. The Lord's Supper pictures this ongoing truth. "Whoever eats my flesh and drinks my blood remains in me, and I in him" (verse 56). We show that we live in Christ, and he lives in us.

So the Lord's Supper helps us look upward, to Christ, and be mindful that true life can only be in him and with him. When we are aware that Jesus lives in us, we also pause to think what kind of home we are giving him. Before he came into our lives, we were habitations of sin. Jesus knew that before he even knocked on the door of our lives. He wants to get in so he can start cleaning things up. But when Jesus knocks, many people try to do a quick tidy-up before they open the door. However, we are humanly unable to cleanse our sins—the most we can do is hide them in the closet.

So we hide our sins in the closet, and invite Jesus into the living room. Eventually we let him into the kitchen, and then the hallway, and then a bedroom. It is a gradual process. Eventually Jesus gets to the closet where our worst sins are hidden, and he cleans them, too. Year by year, as we grow in spiritual maturity, we surrender more of our lives to our Savior. We let him live in us.

It is a process, and the Lord's Supper plays a role in this process. Paul wrote, "Everyone should take a careful look at themselves before they eat the bread and drink from the cup" (1 Corinthians 11:28). Every time we participate, we should be mindful of the great meaning involved in this ceremony. When we examine ourselves, we often find sin. This is normal—it is not a reason to avoid the Lord's Supper. It is a reminder that we need Jesus in our lives. Only he can take our sins away.

Paul criticized the Corinthian Christians for their manner of observing the Lord's Supper. The wealthy members were coming first, eating a great meal and getting drunk. The poor members came last, still hungry. The wealthy were not sharing with the poor (verses 20-22). They were not really sharing in the life of Christ, for they were not doing what he would do. They did not understand what it means to be members of the body of Christ, and that members have responsibilities toward one another.

As we examine ourselves, we need to look around to see whether we are treating one another in the way that Jesus commanded. If you are united with Christ and I am united to Christ, then we are united to each other. So the Lord's Supper, by picturing our participation in Christ, also pictures our participation (other translations may say communion or sharing or fellowship) with each other. Paul wrote in 1 Corinthians 10:17, "Because there is one loaf, we, who are many, are one body, for we all share the one loaf." By participating together in the Lord's Supper, we picture the fact that we are one body in Christ, one with each other, with responsibilities toward one another.

At Jesus' last meal with his disciples, Jesus pictured the life of God's kingdom by washing the feet of his disciples (John 13:1-15). When Peter protested, Jesus said it was necessary that he wash his feet. The Christian life involves both serving and being served.

Reminds us of Jesus' return

Jesus said he would not drink the fruit of the vine again until he came in the fullness of the kingdom (Matthew 26:29; Luke 22:18; Mark 14:25). Whenever we participate, we are reminded of Jesus' promise. There will be a great messianic "banquet," a "wedding supper" of celebration. The bread and wine are miniature rehearsals of what will be the greatest victory celebration in all history. Paul wrote that "Whenever you eat this bread and drink this cup, you proclaim the Lord's death *until he comes*" (1 Corinthians 11:26). We know that he will come again.

The Lord's Supper is rich in meaning. That is why it has been a prominent part of the Christian tradition throughout the centuries. Sometimes it has been allowed to become a lifeless ritual, done more out of habit than with meaning. When a ritual loses meaning, some people overreact by stopping the ritual entirely. The better response is to restore the meaning. That's why it is helpful for us to review the meaning of our custom.

Joseph Tkach

Lay Members' Role in the Early Church

Acts 2 describes the setting: God-fearing Jews from various nations had gathered in Jerusalem for the Day of Pentecost. The Holy Spirit filled the apostles and other disciples, and they spoke in tongues. Although the pilgrims came from 15 territories — north, south, east and west — each traveler heard his or her own native language. After Peter spoke, 3,000 baptisms took place that day (Acts 2:41). The church continued to grow rapidly (verse 47).

What happened to these people? Where did they go? What is their legacy? We know of Peter, John and Paul. Stephen's strength in martyrdom inspires us; Philip's faith encourages us. What of the other members?

Every great work finds support in a group of people with a shared vision. The church is no different. Thousands of members supported Peter, John, Paul and other leaders. The mission of all these dedicated people was to preach redemption through Jesus Christ beginning in Jerusalem and extending to the whole world.

Heroic literature seldom mentions the commoner standing side-by-side with the hero. However, God's Word records the faith, courage, dedication and work of many members of the early church. Their lives are inspiring examples of personal evangelism. They helped spread the gospel. These faithful members of nearly 20 centuries ago inspire us in our work today. There were no fanfares, booklets or articles. But there was faith, the Holy Spirit, love for others and a vision of a new life. The ordinary members made a difference in their society for the kingdom of God. Let's look at what some of them did.

Examples of the earliest Christians

On the Day of Pentecost, people from many different lands became disciples of Jesus Christ. As the church grew, some of the Jewish leaders caused a persecution. After Stephen's martyrdom, members fled, but they did not remain silent. "Those who had been scattered preached the word wherever they went" (Acts 8:4). They were fruitful. In Acts 11:19-21, we see the result of their faithfulness:

> Those who had been scattered by the persecution in connection with Stephen traveled as far as Phoenicia, Cyprus and Antioch, telling the message only to Jews. Some of them, however, men from Cyprus and Cyrene, went to Antioch and began to speak to Greeks also, telling them the good news about the Lord Jesus. The Lord's hand was with them, and a great number of people believed and turned to the Lord.

Despite persecution, these believers — perhaps thousands of them — bravely and faithfully taught the word given them. In the deep conviction of their faith and inspired by the Holy Spirit, they preached the gospel (the Greek word in verse 20 is *euangelizomai*). Many people responded to their teaching and believed in Jesus Christ. Some of these believers may have been the 70 or 72 that Christ had commissioned earlier (Luke 10:1), but most were probably lay members. That's why the Jerusalem church needed to send Barnabas to minister to the new believers (Acts 11:22-23).

One man in the Decapolis

In at least one instance, Jesus instructed someone other than the apostles to tell people what Jesus had done. After casting a legion of demons out of a man who lived on the southeast side of the Sea of Galilee (Luke 8:26-37), the man asked for permission to travel with Jesus (verse 38). Jesus replied, "Return home and tell how much God has done for you."

The man did more than Jesus had asked: "The man went away and told all over town how much Jesus had done for him" (verse 39). "All the people were amazed" (Mark 5:20). Later, Christ toured the area of the Decapolis. People brought a man to him for healing (Mark 7:31-32). Perhaps the witness of the healed demoniac helped the people respond to Jesus.

Similarly, the Samaritan woman told her people about Jesus (John 4:28-29). "Many of the Samaritans from that town believed in him because of the woman's testimony" (verse 39).

Paul refers to the staying power of some early converts in Romans 16:7. He says Andronicus and Junia "were in Christ before I was." They were probably some of the Roman Jews converted on the Day of Pentecost. Paul also mentions Epenetus, "who was the first convert to Christ in the province of Asia" (verse 5). Acts 2:9 mentions people from Asia in Jerusalem for Pentecost.

Philip

As we follow the church's growth after Pentecost, many members of the earliest era of the church leave a remarkable legacy. Philip, a leader of the Greek-speaking Christians in Jerusalem (Acts 6:5-6), went to Samaria (Acts 8:5-8), perhaps fleeing Saul's persecutions (verses 3-4). There he preached the gospel, as other members did elsewhere. The intensity of his speaking and the power of the Holy Spirit were followed by miracles. "When they believed Philip as he preached the good news of the kingdom of God and the name of Jesus Christ, they were baptized, both men and women" (verse 12).

Later, Philip was led by the Holy Spirit to witness to an Ethiopian (verses 26-40). He explained "the good news about Jesus" (verse 35), and he baptized the Ethiopian. Was Philip ordained? The book of Acts doesn't say. Luke didn't think it important to indicate whether he was or not. Many years later, Philip was an evangelist in Caesarea, and his four daughters had the gift of prophecy (Acts 21:8).

Called to baptize an apostle

Acts 9 records the important role of another member, Ananias. All Judea and the surrounding regions knew of Saul's severe persecutions of the church. While on the way to Damascus, Saul lost his eyesight during a miraculous intervention. In response to a vision (Acts 9:10), Ananias sought for and baptized the chief persecutor, Saul of Tarsus.

We know little of Ananias except that he "was a devout observer of the law and highly respected by all the Jews" (Acts 22:12). Consider the faith and courage required of Ananias. Paul's reputation was so bad that even the Jerusalem disciples, veterans of many persecutions, feared to meet Paul when he later wanted to join them (Acts 9:26). Knowing Paul's reputation and authority to inflict terror, Ananias asked the Lord if this was the right person (verses 13-14). Assured by Jesus in vision that Paul was indeed the chosen individual, Ananias went into the house.

> Placing his hands on Saul, he said, "Brother Saul, the Lord — Jesus, who appeared to you on the road as you were coming here — has sent me so that you may see again and be filled with the Holy Spirit." Immediately, something like scales fell from Saul's eyes, and he could see again. He got up and was baptized. (verses 17-18)

In Damascus, in a little-known Christian community, Ananias, a member of whom we know little, baptized the New Testament figure of whom we know much, the apostle Paul. In spite of Saul's persecutions, Ananias acted, and God recorded his faith as an example for us. Faith and courage aren't confined to ministers; they are found in lay members, too.

Women

God also records the courage and faithful witness of many women. They bravely withstood not only religious persecution, but also risked social ostracism.

Cenchrea was a city east of Corinth. From there, Phoebe helped Paul minister to the Roman church. While Paul prepared for his journey to Jerusalem, Phoebe had business in Rome. Paul commends her to the Roman church (Romans 16:1-2) as one who showed generosity and hospitality to many. F.C. Conybeare postulates her as a widow (*The Life and Epistles of St. Paul,* page 497). Greek manners and customs would not normally allow a married or single woman to be so prominent. An ancient subscription to the book of Romans states that Phoebe carried the epistle by hand.

Philippi was a city of Macedonia north of Greece. Since no synagogue existed in this city (Conybeare, page 226), devout Jews would seek a "place of prayer" (Acts 16:13). Usually this was outside the city near running water, perhaps because it was peaceful. The group at Philippi was composed primarily of women. Among these women was Lydia, a businesswoman from Thyatira. God moved in her life, opening her heart (verse 14). Paul baptized not only her, but also her whole household (verse 15); she seems to have been the dominant individual in her home.

Her first work after baptism was an act of hospitality. She opened her home to Paul and his companions. Later, after his release from prison, Paul returned to her home to encourage the members before leaving the area (verse 40). The letter to the Philippians expresses thanks and joy for continued support by the believers in Philippi. Lydia, a founding member, set an excellent example for that church. She was a spiritual leader.

Paul mentions Lois and Eunice (2 Timothy 1:5), Timothy's grandmother and mother. Timothy, who had a non-Jewish father, lived in Lystra when he first met Paul (Acts 16:1). Paul referred to the sincere faith of the women (2 Timothy 1:5). They were spiritual leaders in their family.

Paul had first-hand knowledge of their faith. He came to Lystra, in Galatia, on his first journey. There, after a miraculous healing (Acts 14:8-10), the residents declared Paul and Barnabas to be gods. But Paul was eventually stoned and left for dead. "After the disciples had gathered around him, he got up and went back into the city" (verses 19-20). The disciples probably included Timothy and his family (2 Timothy 3:10-11). Living in an area of persecution demands sincere faith. Lois and Eunice had that faith and instilled it in Timothy.

In Philippians 4:2-3, Paul acknowledges Euodia and Syntyche. Paul recalls "these women have contended at my side in the cause of the gospel, along with Clement and the rest of my fellow workers." Though Paul was greater in authority, he treated his spiritual brothers and sisters respectfully, as equals. They worked together to spread the gospel.

Priscilla and Aquila

One of the most significant couples mentioned is "a Jew named Aquila…with his wife Priscilla" (Acts 18:2). They lived in Corinth after being expelled from Rome by the Emperor Claudius. Paul went to see them and stayed and worked with them in Corinth. There is no mention of conversion; they were probably Christians when Paul met them.

Their contribution to the New Testament church is important. Not only were they in Corinth, but they were also in Ephesus (Acts 18:24-26; 2 Timothy 4:19) and in Rome (Romans 16:3). They were probably wealthy. The church in Corinth met in their house (1 Corinthians 16:19). So did a church in Rome (Romans 16:5).

Paul remarks that Priscilla and Aquila were his fellow-workers. "They risked their lives for me" (Romans 16:3-4). They went with Paul on his journey from Corinth to Ephesus (Acts 18:18-19). They helped Paul with physical and spiritual support. In Corinth, Priscilla and Aquila worked with Apollos, an eloquent and zealous man, and "they invited him to their home and explained to him the way of God more adequately" (Acts 18:26). Were they ordained, or were they lay members? Luke doesn't tell us. Service like this can be done by members whether or not they are ordained.

The work continues

Many other faithful members are mentioned in the New Testament. Throughout the centuries, many have dedicated their lives and wealth to proclaiming the name of Jesus Christ. The same Jesus Christ and the same Holy Spirit are guiding the church today. It is the same message: salvation through Jesus Christ. It is the same zeal. It is the same God who will not forget the sacrifices we may make. "God is not unjust; he will not forget your work and the love you have shown him as you have helped his people and continue to help them" (Hebrews 6:10).

The book of Acts shows us that various members were instrumental in spreading the gospel of salvation through Jesus Christ. Some of the people mentioned in this article may have been ordained, but others were probably not. All members can help spread the gospel. Lay members, as led by the Holy Spirit, continue to be a vital part of Christ's commission to the disciples.

Donald L. Jackson

Upward, Inward and Outward in Words and Deeds

People sometimes use the phrase "upward, inward, and outward" to describe our Christian lives. "Upward" refers to our relationship with God. "Inward" refers to our relationship with other believers. "Outward" refers to our relationship with nonbelievers. Let's look at some of the ways these three areas can be expressed in words and in actions.

Our upward relationship is the most important, and I will say more about it shortly. But I'd like to begin with our inward responsibilities – the relationships Christians have with one another.

Inward in words

There are two major ways in which we relate to fellow Christians. One is through fellowship, and the other is through ministry, or service. That is, our relationships are expressed in words and in deeds. Sometimes our words are "small talk" – chatting about the weather, sports, jobs, and other facts. Other times, as relationships develop, our conversations go beyond that, so that we are also discussing opinions, feelings and matters of the heart.

Christian fellowship includes spiritual matters, too – not just doctrinal facts, but the practical issues of the spiritual life. Small group fellowship is designed to bring out discussions on such a level, because sharing such things helps us grow spiritually. That's why I encourage members to find or form a small group in their congregation.

"Encourage one another daily," Hebrews 3:13 tells us. Encouragement is a two-way process. It involves both the giving and the receiving of encouragement from one another. Sometimes I am up and can encourage others, while other times I am down and need to be encouraged by others. Frequent fellowship with other believers gives us an opportunity to help and to be helped in this way. God designed the church to be like this, with people helping, strengthening and lifting up one another.

"Encourage" is a translation of the Greek word *parakaleo,* which comes from roots meaning to be called alongside. God has called us to be together, so that we might give hope, courage and support to one another. That is a major reason that we should meet together: "Let us consider how we may spur one another on toward love and good deeds. Let us not give up meeting together, as some are in the habit of doing, but let us encourage one another" (Hebrews 10:24-25).

How can we "spur one another on" in attitudes and in actions? In a variety of words and ways, all of which require that we meet together regularly. Otherwise, we will drift away (Hebrews 2:1), slowly and unconsciously getting further from Christ to the degree that we neglect Christian fellowship.

Inward in deeds

Our relationships need to involve more than words. We are exhorted to have brotherly love for one another, and that means more than lip-service. It means helping people who need help. The earliest disciples held their goods in common (Acts 2:44). Later, collections were taken to help the poor (Acts 11:29). Believers often ate together and helped one another in practical ways. Service can be person-to-person, or it can be toward a group or even toward the entire congregation. Setting up chairs for a meeting is one example. It serves the whole church and fills an important practical need. It is a type of ministry.

Each member is most "at home" in the body of Christ when he or she is involved in some type of ministry or service to others. Some serve by giving encouraging words. Some encourage by giving physical help. Some minister to individual needs, and some minister to the congregation as a whole. God takes joy in the wonderful variety of ways that we interact with one another.

Outward in words

Just as ministry applies to our relationships within the church, it also applies to our outward relationships. We minister to our neighbors, to our relatives and to the people we work with. On our jobs, we work not just for the money, but also to be able to help others. In our families and neighborhoods, we do not just do the minimum, but we try to make a positive contribution. Because we are God's children in the world, we want every place we live, and every place we go, to be better because we have been there. This is not because we are so great, but because God has given us his love and called us to do the kinds of things he would do if he were one of us. We do this as individuals, and sometimes we do it as congregations. Working together, we can make a positive difference in our neighborhoods.

Our outward relationship also includes words. Words can be a powerful force – not in a magical sense, but in their potential to influence people. Words can give strength, or they can destroy. They can honor, or they can debase. "The tongue has the power of life and death" (Proverbs 18:21). As God's people in the world, as ambassadors of Jesus Christ, our words should be wisely chosen to build up the people around us. Our words need to be truthful, filled with things of good report (Ephesians 5:4). We are to be good stewards of our tongues.

One way to be a good steward of words is through evangelism. The gospel is a powerful message that we have been given and told to share. This is the pearl of great price that we are to keep and give at the same time. This is the word of truth, the message of good report, the word of life we can give others. Paul says we have been "entrusted with the secret things of God" (1 Corinthians 4:1), the message of salvation.

Outward in deeds

By talking about words and deeds, I do not want to imply that everything we do can be neatly categorized. Our words and our actions work together. As we seek to encourage other Christians with our words, we also need to give them practical help when needed. The same is true for the words we say to non-Christians. If we are living like unbelievers, it is unlikely that the gospel will have any impact on their lives. If we lie and cheat, gossip and gripe, people won't tend to believe us when we share the gospel, no matter how convincingly we say the words. If we ignore their practical needs, they will be skeptical that we care about them.

There is also an overlapping of inward and outward activities. Small groups are not only inwardly nourishing, but they are also an excellent entry point for people interested in Christianity. Certain kinds of inward service can also open doors for evangelism. For example, children's ministry volunteers serve children by sharing the gospel, serve them physically in their needs, and at the same time, give parents a practical service so that the parents can take part in the worship service. Several types of ministry are being accomplished at once!

Children's ministry serves those within the church – but just by being there, it provides an avenue for evangelism, too. Children can invite their friends to join them for church, which in turn creates a relationship between the church and the friends' parents. Members can also feel free to invite friends and neighbors to church, knowing their children will be cared for, given good teaching and enjoy the service.

Upward in words

Our upward relationship may also be divided into words and actions. Our words with God may be further divided into two kinds: God's words to us, and our words to him.

How does God speak to us? Primarily through Scripture. These are the words he has inspired to be written and preserved for us today. These writings tell us how God has spoken in the past, and how he has been perfectly revealed in his Son, Jesus Christ. As we read these words again and again with spiritual openness, God speaks to us afresh, helping us apply the words to situations in our lives. Bible study is part of our worship response to God, who has revealed himself and his Word to us in the Scriptures.

God speaks to us in sermons, too. Anyone who speaks to the church should seek to speak "the very words of God" (1 Peter 4:11). It is appropriate for us to listen, then, with the expectation that words of God will be spoken. Not every sermon is a "thus saith the Lord," but we still need to listen attentively, for this is one of the ways God speaks to us. We evaluate the sermon by Scripture, our ultimate authority, but we still listen for what God may be saying through the imperfect speaker. "The others should weigh carefully what is said" (1 Corinthians 14:29).

Elders have the responsibility to speak "the very words of God." That is an intimidating challenge! It underscores the need we all have to pray constantly, and to prepare thoroughly. Speakers want their messages to be words that Jesus himself would approve. Teachers will be called into stricter judgment (James 3:1). That is another reason that we encourage exegetical sermons: messages that explain the written word of God. A message that conveys the sense of the text will be speaking the words of God.

God speaks through sermons; he may also speak through any member of the church. As we are called to exhort one another to good works, we are called to speak God's words of encouragement to one another. We often learn from one another what God wants us to do. Through fellowship, through small group discussions, we can come to know his will better.

These words from God to us are part of our upward relationship: our worship. When we listen attentively, willing to respond, we are worshipping God. The sermon is part of our worship service. Our worship does not stop when the "worship leader" sits down – rather, our worship changes from singing to listening. Our willingness to learn is part of our worship.

Our worship includes the words we speak to God, too. In prayer and in song, we speak to God. This is part of our upward relationship. We are telling him what we think about him, about ourselves, and about others. Praise is a form of worship, but even our requests are a form of worship when we recognize that God is the one who has the power to grant all our requests (and the wisdom and the love to not grant them all!). "In everything, by prayer and petition, with thanksgiving, present your requests to God" (Philippians 4:6).

The Psalms give us examples of worship songs filled with great emotion – fear, frustration, anxiety, even anger, as well as joy, hope, peace and love. In our relationship with God, we do not hide our true thoughts (it does no good, since he knows them, anyway).

Upward in deeds

Last, I want to comment on *actions* that we do in our upward relationship. The Old Testament stressed actions of worship: sacrifices, rituals, times and places. The New Testament has little of this. Our rituals include baptism and the Lord's Supper. Some Christian traditions have more rituals – they may follow a liturgical calendar, recite creeds and prayers in their weekly liturgies, have a more prominent place for communion, etc. Such rituals are not wrong, but neither are they commanded. Christian traditions vary, and each of them can be respected for the particular strength it brings to the fabric of the body of Christ.

What other actions form part of our worship? We offer our "bodies as living sacrifices" – that is a "spiritual act of worship" (Romans 12:1). Everything we do is part of our worship, our service toward God. God doesn't need anything from us, but we serve him by obeying him and by seeking to make a difference in this world for his kingdom. In our words and in our actions with other people, we want our lifestyle to be one of submission to the One who is all-wise, all-powerful and all-loving.

When our actions are done in obedience to God (at home, at work, in the marketplace, etc.), they are an expression of our worship of him. When we use our time for his glory, to advance his glory instead of ourselves, we have actions of worship, actions that strengthen our upward relationship. When we use money for his glory instead of for ourselves, we have actions of worship. In our words, in our time, in our finances, in our spiritual gifts, we want to use what God has given to serve him. Stewardship in all these areas is a life-style of worship.

As a denomination, we want to be good stewards of what God has given. We want to be good stewards of the gospel in our local churches. We want to encourage and edify our brothers and sisters in Christ. We want to be good stewards in our physical and financial assets, too.

"So, as the Holy Spirit says: 'Today, if you hear his voice, do not harden your hearts'" (Hebrews 3:7). Let us look to Jesus, our apostle, our high priest, the author and perfecter of our faith. Let us strengthen our arms and knees, and run with endurance the race set before us. For we have come to a kingdom that cannot be shaken, a kingdom of incomparable glory. Therefore, "let us be thankful, and so worship God acceptably with reverence and awe" (Hebrews 12:28).

Joseph Tkach

Leadership in the Church

Since every Christian has the Holy Spirit, and the Holy Spirit teaches each of us, is there any need for leadership within the church? Wouldn't it be better to view ourselves as a group of equals, as every person capable of every role? Various verses in the Bible, such as 1 John 2:27, may seem to support this idea—but only if they are taken out of context. For example, when John wrote that Christians did not need anyone to teach them, did he mean they didn't need to be taught by him? Did he say, don't pay any attention to what I write, because you don't need me or anyone else to teach you? This is not what he meant.

John wrote the letter because those people *did* need to be taught. He was warning his readers against the idea that salvation is found in secret teachings. He was saying that the truths of Christianity were already known in the church. Believers did not need any secret "knowledge" beyond what the Holy Spirit had already given the community. John was not saying that Christians do not need leaders and teachers.

Each Christian has individual responsibilities. Each person must decide what to believe and make decisions about how to live. But the New Testament is clear that we are not merely individuals—we are part of a body. The church is optional in the same sense that responsibility is optional—God lets us choose what to do, but that does not mean that all choices are equally helpful for us, or that all are equally within God's desire.

Do Christians need teachers? The New Testament is evidence that we do. The church at Antioch had "teachers" as one of their leadership roles (Acts 13:1). Teachers are one of the gifts the Holy Spirit gives to the church (1 Corinthians 12:28; Ephesians 4:11). Paul called himself a teacher (1 Timothy 2:7; Titus 1:11). Even after many years in the faith, believers needed teachers (Hebrews 5:12). James warned against the idea that everybody is a teacher (James 3:1); his comments indicate that the church normally had people assigned to teach.

Christians need sound teaching in the truths of the faith. We grow at different speeds and have strengths in different areas. God does not give the same gifts to everyone (1 Corinthians 12). Rather, he distributes them so that we will work together for the common good, helping each other, rather than each going off and doing our own thing (verse 7).

Some Christians are gifted with more ability for compassion, some for discernment, some for physical service, some for exhortation, some for coordination and some for teaching. All Christians are equal in value, but equality does not mean being identical or interchangeable. We are given different abilities, and although all are important, all are not the same. As children of God, as heirs of salvation, we are equal, but we do not all have the same role in the church. God puts people and distributes his gifts as he sees fit, not according to human expectations.

God puts teachers into the church—people who are able to help others learn. As a human organization, we do not always select the most gifted people, and teachers sometimes make mistakes. But this does not invalidate the clear witness of the New Testament that God's church has teachers, that this is a role that we should expect to see in communities of believers.

Although GCI does not have a specific office named "teacher," we do expect teachers to exist within the church, and we expect our pastors to be able to teach (1 Timothy 3:2; 2 Timothy 2:2). In Ephesians 4:11, Paul groups pastors and teachers together, structuring them grammatically as if this role were a dual responsibility, to shepherd and to teach.

A hierarchy?

The New Testament does not prescribe any particular hierarchy for the church. The Jerusalem church had apostles and elders. The church in Antioch had prophets and teachers (Acts 15:1; 13:1). Some New Testament passages call the leaders elders; others call them overseers or bishops; some just call them leaders (Acts 14:23; Titus 1:6-7; Philippians 1:1; 1 Timothy 3:2; Hebrews 13:17). These seem to be different words for overlapping roles.

The New Testament does not describe a hierarchy of apostles over prophets over evangelists over pastors over elders over deacons over lay members. "Over" may not be the best word to use, anyway, for all of these are service roles, designed to help the church. But the New Testament does tell people to obey the leaders in the church, to cooperate with their leadership (Hebrews 13:17). Blind obedience is not appropriate, nor is consistent skepticism or resistance.

Paul describes a simple hierarchy when he tells Timothy to appoint elders in churches. As apostle, church planter and mentor, Paul had authority over Timothy, and Timothy had authority to decide who would be elders and deacons. But this is a description of Ephesus, not a prescription for all future organization of the church. We do not see any attempt to tie every church to Jerusalem, or to Antioch, or to Rome. That would not have been practical in the first century, anyway.

What can we say for the church today? We can say that God expects the church to have leaders, but he does not specify what those leaders are to be called or how they are to be structured. He has left those details to be worked out in the changing circumstances that the church will find itself in. We should have leaders in local churches, but it does not matter so much what they are called: Pastor Jones, Elder Kim, Minister Lawson or Servant Chris might be equally acceptable.

In Grace Communion International, we use what might be called an episcopal model (the word episcopal is based on the Greek word for overseer—*episkopos,* sometimes translated as bishop) because of the circumstances we are in. We believe this is the best way for our churches to have doctrinal soundness and stability. Our episcopal model has its problems, but so do other models, for they all involve fallible humans. We believe that in our historical and geographical circumstances, our style of organization can serve our members better than a congregational or a presbyterian model can. (Keep in mind that all models of church government, whether congregational, presbyterian or episcopal, can take a variety of forms. Our form of the episcopal model is radically different from that of the Eastern Orthodox, Anglican, Episcopal, Roman Catholic or Lutheran churches.)

The head of the church is Jesus Christ, and all leaders within the church should seek his will in all things, in their own lives as well as in the functioning of the congregations. The leaders are to be Christlike in their leadership, which means that they must seek to help others, not to benefit themselves. The local church is not a work crew to help the pastor get his work done. Rather, the pastor is a facilitator, to help the members get *their* work done—the work of the gospel, the work Jesus Christ wants them to do.

Elders and ministry leaders

Paul compares the church to a body with many different parts. Its unity is not in uniformity, but in working together for a common Lord and for a common purpose. Different members have different strengths, and we are to use these for the common good (1 Corinthians 12:7).

Grace Communion International appoints through ordination elders to serve as pastoral leaders. It also appoints through commissioning ministry leaders (who may also be referred to as deacons or deaconesses). What is the difference between "ordination" and "commissioning"? In general, ordination is more public and more permanent; whereas commissioning may be done privately as well as in public, and may be revoked easily. Commissioning is less formal, and is not automatically renewable or transferable. An ordination may be revoked also, but this is done only in exceptional circumstances.

In Grace Communion International we do not have detailed descriptions of each church leadership role. Elders often serve in congregations as pastors (senior, associate or assistant pastors).

Most preach and teach, though not all. Some specialize in administration. Each serves according to ability, under the supervision of the lead pastor (the overseer, or *episkopos* of the congregation).

Ministry leaders come in even greater diversity, each serving (we hope) according to ability, each according to the needs of the congregation. The senior pastor may commission them for temporary assignments, or for indefinite periods. The roles of these leaders and the councils and committees that advise them are described in our Church Administration Manual. The policies in that manual allow for flexibility in organizing congregational leadership because our congregations exist in a variety of circumstances, having diverse gifts.

Senior pastors serve somewhat like orchestra conductors. They cannot force anyone to play on cue, but they can provide guidance and coordination, and the overall results will be much better when the players take the cues they are given. In our denomination, members cannot fire their lead pastor. Instead, lead pastors are chosen and dismissed at the regional level, which in the United States includes Church Administration & Development, in coordination with local leaders. What if a member believes a pastor is incompetent, or is leading the sheep astray? That's where our episcopal structure comes in. Problems of doctrine or leadership style should be discussed with the pastor first, and then with the overseer of the pastors in the area.

Just as congregations need local leaders and teachers, pastors also need leaders and teachers. That is why we believe that our denominational home office has an important role in serving our congregations. We strive to be a source of training, ideas, encouragement, supervision, and cooperation. We are not perfect, but that is the calling we see set before us, and that is what we will strive to do.

Our eyes need to be focused on Jesus. He has work for us to do, and much work is being done. Praise him for his patience, for his gifts, and for the work that helps us grow.

Joseph Tkach

The Pastor's Calling

Many people have no idea what pastors do, and it's not unusual for pastors to feel inadequate in their role. I've felt that way, as Paul apparently did in asking, "who is equal to such a task?" He then noted (speaking of the human body): "we have this treasure in jars of clay to show that this all-surpassing power is from God and not from us" (2 Corinthians 2:16; 4:7). Despite the times of doubt that pastors sometimes face, they find reassurance in remembering that God has called them and that they have his anointing to serve him in this way—an anointing confirmed by their ordination.

I am pleased that our elders approach their calling to pastoral ministry with humility and faith. Paul tells us that pastors, along with other ordained ministers, are called "to equip his people for works of service, so that the body of Christ may be built up until we all reach unity in the faith and in the knowledge of the Son of God and become mature, attaining to the whole measure of the fullness of Christ" (Ephesians 4:12-13). All Christians are called to share in the ministry of Jesus, through what Paul refers to here as "works of service." Ordained ministers, including pastors, are called to serve by equipping and then leading God's people in these works.

To be called by God to serve as a pastor is a privilege, blessing and responsibility. It's a calling that comes to different people in different ways—sometimes quietly, over a long period of time; at other times dramatically and suddenly—like Paul on the road to Damascus (Acts 26:12-14). I have been asked, "How do I know 'for sure' that I am called to be a pastor?" You will know "for sure" only in your spirit and through the confirmation of those you serve. We walk by faith, not by sight, and the opportunity to serve God is unlike any other life endeavor. The center of that service involves feeding others through sharing with them the living and written Word of God. This flows out of a desire that others come to know God through Jesus Christ and put their trust in him alone for life now and eternally. Signs that point to such a calling are love for studying and communicating the Word of God, desire to pray with and for people, desire to enable people to come to God in worship, and desire to help people become a fellowship of those gathered in the Holy Spirit around the Word of God both written and living.

Pastoral service brings with it the power of God moving through us in humility. Though that brings us joy, it can also bring disappointment. None of us are perfect, and neither are the ones we interact with in ministry. Sometimes God's leading is mysterious, beyond our comprehension.

Whether we are rich or poor, learned or uneducated, or anywhere in between, God has a job for us and he calls us to it. We must not confuse the form of that call with the substance of it. He usually calls people by dropping hints. Many have told me that they eventually realized that God was dropping such hints in their life for years, though they did not notice them right away. We humans can be dense at times. But when we look back on our lives and pray about God's will, the little hints he has placed in our lives are recognized as our call to pastoral ministry. It takes some time for us to hear, and it comes when we are ready to respond.

There are numerous ways we experience such affirmation. You might feel that you have fallen into this role because no one else was stepping up. But this may be a sign that God wants you to join others in his service. Some of us have been serving in pastoral ministry for years without perhaps even recognizing it. But others have seen the fruits of your service, and this could be God's affirmation. If you have been asked by others to serve in a pastoral leadership role, then this may also be a call on you to serve.

Pastoral ministry, regardless of the specific area of service, is extremely challenging. The stress level can be significant, rated by some to be second only to medical doctors. To function properly as a pastor requires that we resist the pull of our fallen human nature and maintain humility before God. We are all called to be his servants, using the gifts he has given us to direct others to him.

As we let our Lord serve us, we must then *grow* in our ability to shepherd and serve others. For that reason, we require our U.S. senior pastors to participate in a Continuing Education Program. Some pastors fulfill the requirement by taking classes at Grace Communion Seminary. Earning a degree takes considerable time, finances and other resources. If you are able to pursue a degree at GCS, or simply want to take a few classes there, I urge you to do so. GCS also offers several non-credit classes that are available online to anyone at no cost. You'll find them at www.gcs.edu/course/view.php?id=32.

Because many of our pastors cannot pursue a GCS degree, we offer other continuing education options, including classes at Ambassador College of Christian Ministry (www.ambascol.org).

Joseph Tkach

Sanctification

According to the *Concise Oxford Dictionary*, to sanctify is "to set apart or observe [something] as holy" or "to purify or free from sin."[1] These definitions reflect the fact that the Bible uses the word "holy" in two main ways: 1) a special status, that is, set apart for God's use, and 2) moral behavior—thoughts and actions appropriate to a holy status; thoughts and actions in keeping with what God wants.[2]

We cannot sanctify ourselves. God is the one who sanctifies his people. He sets them apart for his use, and he is the one who produces holy behavior in our lives. There is little controversy that God sets people apart for his use. But there is controversy regarding the divine-human interaction involved in sanctified behavior.

The questions include: How active a role should Christians take in sanctification? To what extent should Christians expect that their thoughts and actions will be conformed to the divine standard? How should pastors exhort their congregations?

We will present the following points:
- Sanctification is a result of the grace of God.
- Christians should try to bring their thoughts and actions into conformity with the will of God.
- Sanctification is a progressive growth in responsiveness to God's will.

Initial sanctification

From the beginning, God created humanity for a holy purpose: eternal fellowship with God. But humans rejected this purpose and became morally corrupt. Humans cannot of themselves choose God. Reconciliation must be initiated by God. God's gracious intervention is needed before a person can have faith and turn toward God. No one can understand the gospel except by the Holy Spirit (1 Corinthians 2:6-16). God chooses people and thereby sanctifies them or sets them apart for his purpose. Anciently, God chose the people of Israel, and within that nation he further sanctified the Levites (e.g., Leviticus 20:26; 21:6; Deuteronomy 7:6). He set them apart for his use.[3]

Christians are set apart in a different way: "sanctified in Christ Jesus" (1 Corinthians 1:2). "We have been made holy through the sacrifice of the body of Jesus Christ" (Hebrews 10:10).[4] Christians are made holy through the crucifixion of Jesus (Hebrews 10:29; 12:12). They have been declared holy (1 Peter 2:5, 9) and throughout the New Testament, believers are called "saints"—"holy ones." That is their status. This initial sanctification accompanies justification, a declaration of righteousness (1 Corinthians 6:11). "God chose you to be saved through the sanctifying work of the Spirit" (2 Thessalonians 2:13).

But God's purpose for his people goes beyond this declaration of a new status—it is a setting apart for his purpose, which is eternal life with God, and that involves a moral transformation in his people. People are "chosen…for obedience to Jesus Christ" (1 Peter 1:2). They are to be transformed into the image of Jesus Christ (2 Corinthians 3:18). They are not only declared to be holy and righteous, they are also regenerated. A new life begins to develop, a life that is exhorted to live in a holy and righteous way. The initial sanctification leads into behavioral sanctification.

Behavioral sanctification

In the Old Testament, God told his people that their holy status should be accompanied by a change in behavior. The Israelites were to avoid ceremonial uncleanness because God had chosen them (Deuteronomy 14:21). Their status depended on their obedience (Deuteronomy 28:9). The priests were to avoid certain behaviors because they were holy (Leviticus 21:6-7). Nazirites had to change their behavior while they were set apart (Numbers 6:5).

Our election in Christ has ethical implications. Since the Holy One has called us, Christians are exhorted to "be holy in all you do" (1 Peter 1:15-16). As God's chosen and holy people, we are to be compassionate, kind, humble, gentle and patient (Colossians 3:12). We are invited to share in the divine life not only in the future, but to participate in it now (2 Peter 1:4). If we do not want to live God's way in this life, the danger is that we will not want it in the future, either.

Sin and impurities "are improper for God's holy people" (Ephesians 5:3; cf. 1 Thessalonians 4:3). If people eliminate ignoble things from their lives, they will be "made holy" (2 Timothy 2:21). We should control our bodies in a way that is holy (1 Thessalonians 4:4). "Holy" is frequently linked to "blameless" (Ephesians 1:4; 5:27; 1 Thessalonians 2:10; 3:13; 5:23; cf. Titus 1:8); it is a life of righteousness.

Christians are "called to be holy" (1 Corinthians 1:2), "to live a holy life" (1 Thessalonians 4:7; 2 Timothy 1:9; 2 Peter 3:11). We are told to "make every effort...to be holy" (Hebrews 12:14). We are urged to be holy (Romans 12:1), told that we "are being made holy" (Hebrews 2:11; 10:14), and encouraged to continue being holy (Revelation 22:11). We are made holy by the work of Christ and the presence of the Holy Spirit in us. He changes us from the inside out.

This brief word study shows that holiness involves our behavior. God sets people apart as "holy" for the purpose that they live holy lives in Jesus Christ, both now and in eternity. We are saved so that we might produce good works and good fruit (Ephesians 2:8-10; Galatians 5:22-23). The good works are not a cause of salvation, but a result of it – when God declares us holy, we should respond by living in a holy way. Good works are evidence that a person's faith is genuine (James 2:18). Paul speaks of the "obedience of faith" and says that faith expresses itself in love (Romans 1:5; Galatians 5:6).

Lifelong growth

When people come to faith in Christ, they are not perfect in faith, love, good works, or behavior. Paul calls the Corinthians saints and members of God's family, but they have many sins in their lives. The numerous commands in the New Testament indicate that the readers need not only doctrinal instruction but also exhortations about behavior. The Holy Spirit changes us, but does not suppress the human will; holy living does not automatically flow without any guidance or effort. Each Christian must make decisions whether to do right or wrong, even as Christ is working in us to change our desires.

The "old self" may be dead, but Christians must also put it off (Romans 6:6-7; Ephesians 4:22). We must continue to kill the deeds of the flesh, the remnants of the old self (Romans 8:13; Colossians 3:5). Though we have died to sin, sin continues to be in us, and we should not let it reign (Romans 6:11-13). Thoughts and emotions and decisions must be consciously shaped after the divine pattern. Holiness is something that must be striven for (Hebrews 12:14).

We are commanded to be perfect and to love God with all of our being (Matthew 5:48; 22:37). Due to the limitations of the flesh and the remnants of the old self, we are unable to do this perfectly. John Wesley, who boldly talked about "perfection," explained that he did not mean complete absence of imperfections.[5] Growth is always possible and commanded. If a person has Christian love, he or she will strive to learn how to express it in better ways, with fewer mistakes.

The apostle Paul said that his behavior was "holy, righteous and blameless" (1 Thessalonians 2:10). But he did not claim to be perfect. Rather, he pressed on toward his goal, and he admonished others to not think that they had attained their goal (Philippians 3:12-15). All Christians need to grow in grace and knowledge (2 Peter 3:18). Sanctification should increase throughout life.

Our sanctification will not be completed in this life. Grudem explains: "When we appreciate that sanctification involves the whole person, including our bodies (see 2 Corinthians 7:1; 1 Thessalonians 5:23), then we realize that sanctification will not be entirely completed until the Lord returns and we receive new resurrection bodies."[6] It is then that we will be freed from all sin and be given a glorified body like Christ's (Philippians 3:21; 1 John 3:2). Because of this hope, we grow in sanctification by purifying ourselves, by putting away wrong behaviors (1 John 3:3).

Biblical exhortation to holiness

Wesley saw a pastoral need to exhort believers to practical obedience resulting from love. The New Testament contains many such exhortations, and it is right to preach these exhortations. However, these commands should not be isolated from God's grace and love, because it is only in the context of God's grace that we can obey them correctly. Behavior should be anchored in the motive of love, and more ultimately, in our union with Christ and the Holy Spirit, which is the source of love. God must initiate all holy behavior, and his grace is present in the heart of all believers, so we exhort them to respond to that grace.

McQuilken offers a practical rather than a dogmatic approach.[7] He does not insist that all believers must have similar experiences in sanctification. He advocates high ideals, but without implying perfection. His exhortation to service as a result of sanctification is good. He emphasizes the scriptural warnings about apostasy rather than get boxed in by theological conclusions about perseverance. His emphasis on faith is helpful, since faith is the basis of all Christianity, and faith has practical consequences in our lives. The means of growth are practical: prayer, Scripture, fellowship, and faith in trials. Robertson exhorts Christians to greater growth and witness without overstating the demands and expectations.

Christians are exhorted to become what they have been declared to be; the imperative (command) follows the indicative (statement of fact). Christians are to live holy lives because God has declared them to be holy, designated for a holy purpose: a never-ending life of love, joy and peace with the Father, Son, Holy Spirit, and each other.

Endnotes

[1] R.E. Allen, ed. *The Concise Oxford Dictionary of Current English,* 8th ed. (Oxford: Oxford, 1990), 1067.

[2] In the Old Testament, God is holy, his name is holy, and he is the Holy One (about 100 occurrences altogether). In the New Testament, "holy" is applied to Jesus more often than to the Father (about 14 times versus three times), but much more often to the Spirit (90 verses). The Old Testament refers to holy people (Nazirites, priests, and the nation) about 35 times, usually in reference to status; the New Testament refers to holy people about 50 times.

The Old Testament refers to holy places about 110 times; the New Testament only 17 times. The Old Testament refers to holy things about 70 times; the New Testament only three times, as metaphors for holy people. The Old Testament refers to holy times in 19 verses; the New Testament never calls time holy. In reference to places, things and time, holiness refers to a designated status, not a moral behavior. In both Testaments, God is holy, and holiness comes from him, but the way his holiness affects people is different. The New Testament emphasis on holiness concerns people and their behavior, not a special status for things and places and times.

[3] Especially in the Old Testament, sanctification does not imply salvation. This is obvious for things, places and times that were sanctified, and it applies to the nation of Israel, too. A non-salvific use of "sanctification" is also seen in 1 Corinthians 7:14—an unbeliever is in some way placed in a special category for God's use. Hebrews 9:13 uses the term "sanctify" to refer to a ceremonial status under the old covenant.

[4] Grudem notes that "sanctified" in several passages in Hebrews "is roughly equivalent to 'justified' in Paul's vocabulary" (Wayne Grudem, *Systematic Theology* [Zondervan, 1994], 748, note 3).

⁵ John Wesley, "A Plain Account of Christian Perfection," in Millard J. Erickson, ed. *Readings in Christian Theology, Volume 3: The New Life* (Baker, 1979), 159.

⁶ Grudem, 749.

⁷ J. Robertson McQuilken, "The Keswick Perspective," in *Five Views of Sanctification* (Zondervan, 1987), 149-183.

For more detailed studies of sanctification, you may want to consult:

Melvin Dieter et al., *Five Views on Sanctification*. Zondervan, 1987.

Donald Alexander, ed., *Christian Spirituality: Five Views of Sanctification*. InterVarsity, 1988.

Michael Morrison

Tell Peter

The life of Peter, Jesus' friend and leading disciple, is a lesson for all who are discouraged. He struggled with despair but, through the faithfulness of our Lord, he found acceptance and forgiveness.

Peter was a man of contradictions—impulsive and bold, yet affectionate and loyal. He responded eagerly to Jesus' call (Matthew 4:18). He left his net, his boat, his job and his familiar surroundings. He was the first of the disciples to recognize who Jesus was (Matthew 16:16). However, his strong and positive leadership qualities had a down side. He could be too assertive, and would sometimes have to be brought back into line. When Jesus was foretelling his suffering and death, Peter began to rebuke him, saying: "Never, Lord…this shall never happen to you!" Peter was firmly put in his place by the Lord's reply, "Get behind me, Satan! You are a stumbling block to me; you do not have in mind the concerns of God, but merely human concerns" (Matthew 16:21-23).

Only a few verses before, Peter had been praised by Jesus as blessed to have the revelation of the Father. He was now reprimanded for being used as a mouthpiece for Satan. Knowing that his dynamic friend was vulnerable, Jesus later told him, "Satan has asked to sift all of you as wheat. But I have prayed for you, Simon, that your faith may not fail. And when you have turned back, strengthen your brothers" (Luke 22:31-32). Peter answered Jesus with a bold pledge of loyalty: "Lord, I am ready to go with you to prison and to death" (verse 33). Brave words, but he was setting himself up for his greatest fall.

'Not me, Lord'

The night before his death, Jesus said to his disciples, "This very night you will all fall away on account of me, for it is written: 'I will strike the shepherd, and the sheep of the flock will be scattered.' But after I have risen, I will go ahead of you into Galilee" (Matthew 26:31-32).

Peter found that hard to accept. He may have said to himself, "Maybe the others, but not me!" Soon, however, he denied the Lord three times, fulfilling Jesus' prediction. Just as the rooster crowed and Jesus was led out by the soldiers, he turned his eyes to Peter. That gaze was too much for Peter to bear. He had betrayed his friend and his Lord in his hour of greatest need. Overcome with guilt, he wept bitterly.

During the next few hours, Jesus was beaten, crowned with thorns and killed by the soldiers. All the disciples were filled with grief, but perhaps none among them experienced the depths of Peter's discouragement and shame. How could he face the other disciples? Would they—would anybody—ever trust him again?

Mentioned by name

The resurrection of Jesus brought new hope—and fresh anxiety. The angel at the tomb that morning told the women who came to anoint Jesus body: "Don't be alarmed. You are looking for Jesus the Nazarene, who was crucified. He has risen! He is not here. See the place where they laid him. But go, tell his disciples and Peter, 'He is going ahead of you into Galilee. There you will see him, just as he told you'" (Mark 16:6-7). Not only had the Lord risen from the dead, but he mentioned Peter's name in particular. Imagine how that must have made Peter feel. Why had he been singled out? Was it because of the denials?

After Jesus' resurrection, Peter must have known for sure that Jesus was indeed the Christ, the Son of the living God! All Jesus' claims about giving his life as a ransom for many were true. But would he have anything to do with Peter, after Peter had denied him—not once, but three times over? Peter soon got his answer. Jesus still accepted him, trusted him and loved him, despite the way Peter had turned against him. Peter soon found out that the words, "tell Peter," were an expression of love, confidence and forgiveness from Jesus. The Lord was saying, "No matter what you have done, there is forgiveness, there is hope. I am alive. I am with you all the way. I offer you a new beginning."

The rest is history. Peter spent the rest of his days proclaiming boldly the good news of the Lord he once denied. He became a mighty witness to the gospel of Jesus, finally sealing his faith with his own blood in martyrdom. Peter left us a legacy of one who failed, but with the power of Jesus, one who had a new beginning and meaningful life for the glory of God.

Do you feel discouraged? Are you, like Peter, dismayed at the extent of your inadequacies, the pressure of living your faith, and those times when you may have also denied Jesus in your life? Jesus knows what Christians face in this life. Our faithfulness will be tested many times—through temptations, through rejection, opposition and discouragement. But in those words to Peter, we can see the will of our Lord that we will be able to bounce back and prevail. As those times come to us, we too can be a source of strength and inspiration for others.

Take heart! Be encouraged by the words of the Lord through the angel in the garden. His message is as much for you as it was for the apostle who felt he had gone too far to ever be accepted again. You can put your own name there: "Tell _____!" Jesus has risen from the dead – for you. He has been a ransom – for you!

Eugene Guzon

Our Relationship With Jesus Christ

Doctrine is only one portion of authentic Christianity. It is important — it is essential that the church teach right doctrines — but it is only part of what we must include in our worship of our Creator, Savior and Sanctifier. No matter how much we know, Paul says, it doesn't do us any good if we don't have love (1 Corinthians 13:2).

Jesus said the most important command in the Scriptures was to "love the Lord your God with all your heart and with all your soul and with all your mind" (Matthew 22:37). When we focus on the Word of God, we often focus on doctrines. That is because the Holy Spirit leads us to bring our minds and thoughts into conformity with God's will. But the Spirit does not stop there. Knowledge of God's purpose and will must be put to use, or it is worthless.

We are saved by faith alone, but not by a faith that is alone. The Holy Spirit leads us to combine right belief with right action. Faith in Jesus leads believers to obey the will of God. We do not want to have a dead orthodoxy, being correct in beliefs, but ineffective in life. Right doctrine, if held in true faith, will necessarily affect our behavior.

Let's get emotional

Likewise, right doctrine affects our emotions. It is not possible for us to love God with all our heart without getting emotional about it! When we understand the doctrine that God showed his love for us by sending his only Son to die for us, then it will have an effect on our emotions toward God. We love him because he first loved us. Our relationship with God is characterized by love. Love is more than emotion, but it includes emotion — a powerful affection and attraction. When we love him, we will adore him, seek him, yearn to spend time with him, desire to be like him and seek to please him.

The Psalms are very expressive emotionally. Psalm 69, for example, shows how David poured out his emotions to God. Psalm 63 is an example of David's yearning for God: "O God, you are my God, earnestly I seek you; my soul thirsts for you, my body longs for you, in a dry and weary land where there is no water." Psalm 42 gives a similar thought: "As the deer pants for streams of water, so my soul pants for you, O God."

The Holy Spirit leads believers to feel this way when they love the Lord with all their heart. After all, we are the "fiancée" of Jesus Christ (2 Corinthians 11:2). We are going to live with him forever and ever. The Spirit provides believers with true love, a love that transforms everything we do throughout the day. We can be happy and hopeful. We can have the peace that surpasses understanding. We can have a song on our heart. These are poetic ways of describing the love that surpasses our ability to describe in literal terms. We do not have words to describe how good we feel. That's how it is between us and our Savior.

It is often said that Christianity is a personal relationship with Jesus Christ. "Relationship" has many meanings. We must ask what kind of relationship we have. Some people ignore Jesus. Some are afraid, and some are angry. These are defective relationships. The Bible describes a good relationship with God in several ways. In a simple analogy, he is the Lord and Master, and we are his slaves. This analogy is correct — we should honor, revere, and obey our perfect and good Lord — but it is not the complete picture. Jesus said we could have more: "I no longer call you servants, because a servant does not know his master's business. Instead, I have called you friends, for everything that I learned from my Father I have made known to you" (John 15:15).

Is Jesus your friend? I hope so, but some people are not comfortable with that phrase. Some men are not comfortable expressing love for Jesus Christ. They may be able to say that they love their dad and love their children, but they are not comfortable saying, "I love Jesus." They find themselves embarrassed to express love for their Savior. Some people prefer more abstract titles, such as the Eternal, the Creator, the Almighty, the Messiah, the Christ. Those titles are good, and true, but they can make God seem aloof and far away. The name Jesus reminds us that the Word became flesh and lived among us as a human being.

Jesus Christ came to show us the Father. He showed us a personal being. He stressed that God is our Father, and the name Father shows a desire for love and companionship. Our Father in heaven wants to spend eternity with us, and he wants our relationship with him to be characterized by an emotion — love. He loves us, and he wants us to love him with intensity, with passion. He wants worship, but he also wants friendship. In this we follow in the footsteps of Abraham, our father in the faith, who walked with God and was called a friend of God (James 2:23).

Relationship terms

Faith is central to Christianity, and faith is a relationship term. We must have faith in Jesus Christ. This means that we believe that he is all he says he is, and he will do what he has promised. It means that we trust him. When we have faith in Jesus, it means more than simply believing that he exists, more than believing that he is the Son of God, more than believing that he died for our sins. Those are true, and they are essential, but faith also means trusting him day by day, walking with him, knowing that the love he has for us will never fail.

Jesus gave us this promise: "This is the will of him who sent me, that I shall lose none of all those he has given me, but raise them up at the last day. For my Father's will is that everyone who looks to the Son and believes in him shall have eternal life, and I will raise them up at the last day" (John 6:39-40). We can have confidence in him.

Paul described salvation as reconciliation between God and his people. Reconciliation is also a relationship word. Before we were called, we were hostile toward God, but we were reconciled through the death of Jesus Christ (Romans 5:10). This means that we are his friends rather than his enemies. This personal reconciliation is important. It is part of the message we have been called to proclaim: "He has committed to us the message of reconciliation" (2 Corinthians 5:19). We implore people on Christ's behalf that they be reconciled to God (verse 20). We urge them to accept the gift of friendship that has been made possible by the death of Jesus on the cross (Colossians 1:20).

By becoming friends of God, we also become friends of each other. Since we will each live with God eternally, we will also live with one another eternally, in a relationship characterized by love. We are reconciled not only with God, but also with each other. Paul described the reconciliation of Jews and Gentiles:

> In Christ Jesus you who once were far away have been brought near by the blood of Christ.... His purpose was to create in himself one new humanity out of the two, thus making peace, 16 and in one body to reconcile both of them to God through the cross.... You are no longer foreigners and strangers, but fellow citizens with God's people and also members of his household. (Ephesians 2:13-19)

We have citizenship rights in heaven — but not just citizenship — we are also part of the royal family. We are heirs of eternal life, heirs of a never-ending life with a Father who loves each of us individually and personally. He wants us to be with him, to enjoy him forever.

Invited in

To help convey some of this spiritual reality, let's imagine for a minute a throne room in heaven, larger than any we have ever seen, full of splendor and beauty. God the Father reigns supreme. Jesus is at his right hand. The Holy Spirit fills the room with tremendous brilliance. Do we come before his throne with fear and trembling, or also with joy and affection?

By his grace, through faith in Jesus, we can come to God with tremendous respect and awe, with never-ending worship. But we also come to God with joy, thanksgiving and confidence, with full assurance, knowing that the blood of Christ cleanses us from every sin (Hebrews 4:14-16). There is no condemnation for those who are in Christ Jesus (Romans 8:1). We come before God spotless and pure, clothed in the perfect righteousness of Jesus Christ.

We have an eager longing to enter the throne room of heaven, knowing that we are welcome. God wants us to be there. He loves us so much that he sent his only Son to die for us. We are his children, and we can enter his gates with praise. He wants us to come in, to feel the splendor, to experience the love and kindness, to know that the power is always used to help us.

Did you know that we are already in the heavenly throne room? Paul says:

> Because of his great love for us, God, who is rich in mercy, made us alive with Christ even when we were dead in transgressions — it is by grace you have been saved. And God raised us up with Christ and seated us with him in the heavenly realms in Christ Jesus, in order that in the coming ages he might show the incomparable riches of his grace, expressed in his kindness to us in Christ Jesus. (Ephesians 2:4-7)

Spiritually, we are already in heaven! God wants us to be in his presence. He wants us to be with him, to love him, to be friends of his Son — and even more than friends: to be part of the family. We can come boldly before his throne, knowing that he wants us to be there. We can ask ourselves, how is my friendship with the Lord? Am I comfortable in his presence? Do I welcome him in my life and heart? Is the gospel, grace and forgiveness making a difference in my life? The new covenant, sealed with the blood of our Savior, gives us forgiveness. It gives us reconciliation and confidence. It gives us personal friendship and brotherhood with Jesus Christ.

A good relationship with Jesus goes a long way in times of trial, in times of doctrinal uncertainty, and in times of blessing. It is a joy to know the Lord — not just know about him, but to know him, to have a friendship. It is a tremendous comfort to know that he values us, that he is like a father who gets up and runs toward us whenever we come back to him (Luke 15:20). He welcomes us as a beloved child, not as a servant (verses 22-23). He wants us to live in his house forever.

Jesus says you can have the joy of salvation. Faith and hope in him will transform your life. Do you need a better relationship with our Lord and Master? Yes, we all do. How can we have it? Let me suggest three things: prayer, study and fellowship.

Pray. Ask God to give you the joy of salvation. Ask him to help you know his love for you in the sacrifice and resurrection of his Son. Ask him to help you adore him, to know and feel his love for you. Ask him for faith in Jesus, and for his power to walk in his love.

Study. In this case, I suggest studying the four Gospels. Sometimes we study for doctrine and for commands regarding what we should do. This time, I suggest that we study simply to see what Jesus is like as a person. Get a feel for his love and compassion, his desire for friendship, his zeal for his Father's glory. Walk with him in the mountains, across the lake, into the city of his death. Meditate on it. Feel with him. Our life is hidden with Jesus Christ (Colossians 3:3) — discover what his life is like.

Fellowship. Our love for the Lord is expressed in part by our love for one another. Share with others the joy that you have in the Lord. Let it shine. In Christ, we will live forever with one another, with ever-growing love for one another. Let's express his love in us now! Encourage others, as often as we meet them (Hebrews 10:24-25). Treat others with the courtesy that Jesus would give them. Forgive them as he would forgive them, and as he has forgiven you.

Christianity is a way of life, changing our thoughts, our actions, and our emotions. It is Christ in us who makes it possible. May he live in us all.

Joseph Tkach

Trusting God With the Problem of Sin

"OK, I understand that the blood of Christ covers all sin. And I understand that there is nothing I can add to the equation. But here's my question: If God, for Christ's sake, has completely forgiven me for all my sins, past, present and future, then what is to stop me from just going out and sinning all I want? I mean, is the law meaningless for Christians? Does God now condone sin? Doesn't he want me to stop sinning?"

These questions are important. Let's go through them one at a time, and see if any more crop up along the way.

All sin forgiven

First, you said that you understand that the blood of Christ covers all sin. That's a great beginning. A lot of Christians don't understand that. They believe that the forgiveness of sins is a transaction, kind of a business deal, between a person and God. The idea is that you do the right thing for God, and God will give you forgiveness and salvation.

For example, you put your faith in Jesus, and God rewards you by applying Jesus' blood to your sins. Tit for tat. That would be good deal, but still a deal, a transaction, and not the pure grace proclaimed by the gospel. In this way of thinking, most people are damned because they didn't ante up in time, and God divvies out the blood of Jesus to only a few; it never actually redeemed the whole world.

But many churches don't even leave it there. Potential believers are lured in with the promise of being saved by grace alone, but once the believer enters the church, the list of rules comes out. If you don't toe the line, you might get kicked out, and under certain circumstances, not only out of the church, but out of the kingdom of God as well. So much for "saved by grace."

There are sometimes situations in which a person must be removed from the fellowship of the church (which does not remove a person from the kingdom), but that's another subject. For now, suffice it to say that organized religion tends to have a love affair with keeping sinners out of the church, whereas the gospel trumpets them an invitation to enter.

According to the gospel, Jesus Christ is the atoning sacrifice not only for our sins, but also for the sins *of the whole world* (1 John 2:2). That, contrary to what many Christians have been told by their preachers, means absolutely everybody. Jesus said, "I, when I am lifted up from the earth, will draw all people to myself" (John 12:32). Jesus is God the Son, by whom and through whom all things exist (Hebrews 1:2-3), and his blood redeems no less than everything he made (Colossians 1:20).

By grace alone

You also said that you understand that there is nothing you can bring to the table to sweeten the deal God has drawn up for you in Christ. There again, you are way ahead of the game. The world is full of sin-battling preachers who lay weekly guilt trips on their cowering flocks with a long list of specially selected commissions and omissions that reputedly ignite God's ever-shortening fuse and threaten to land the whole pathetic lot of spiritual low achievers in the fiery torments of hell.

The gospel, on the other hand, declares that God loves people. He is not out to get them. He is not against them. He is not waiting for them to trip up so he can squash them. Quite the contrary, he is on their side. He loves them so much that he has set free from sin and death all people everywhere by the atoning sacrifice of his Son (John 3:16).

In Christ, the door is open to the kingdom of God. People can believe God's word (faith), turn to him (repent) and claim their freely given inheritance—or they can continue to deny God as their Father and reject their part in the family of God. God honors our choice. If we disown him, he lets our decision stand. That is not the choice he wants us to make, but he does allow us the freedom to make it.

Response

God has done all that needed to be done for us. In Christ, he has said "Yes" to us. It is up to us to say "Yes" to his "Yes." But the Bible indicates that there are, amazingly, some who say "No." They are the wicked, the haters, the ones who oppose God and themselves. They have committed themselves to the proposition that they have a better way; they have no need of God. They regard not God or man. To them, God's offer of complete amnesty and eternal blessing is a meaningless and worthless insult. God, who gave his Son for them, ratifies their appalling decision to remain the children of the devil they have chosen over him.

God is the Redeemer, not the destroyer, and he has done this for no other reason than that he wants to, and he is free to do what he wants. He is bound by no outside rules, but he has freely chosen to be utterly faithful to his covenant love and promise. He is who he is, which is exactly who he wants to be, and he is our God, full of grace and truth and faithfulness. He forgives our sins because he loves us. That is how he wants it, so that is how it is.

No law could save

There is no law that could bring eternal life (Galatians 3:21). We humans simply don't keep laws. We can argue all day over whether it is theoretically possible for humans to keep the law, but the fact is, we don't keep it, never did and never will, and nobody ever has but Jesus.

There is only one way salvation comes, and that is through God's free gift apart from anything we do or don't do (Ephesians 2:8-10). Like any gift, we can take it or leave it. Either way, it is ours already by God's grace, but we can use it and enjoy it only if we actually take it. That is a simple matter of trust. We believe God and turn to him. If, on the other hand, we are foolish enough to reject it, we will, tragically, continue to live in our self-imposed darkness and death as though we never had light and life handed to us in a golden goblet.

Hell a choice

Such a choice, such contempt for God's free gift—a gift paid for by the blood of his Son through whom all things exist and consist—is nothing less than hell. But it is a choice made by people whose invitation to pre-paid life is just as real and valid as the invitation of those who accept theirs. Jesus' blood covers all sin, not just some sin (Colossians 1:20). His atonement is for all the creation, not just part of it.

Those who scorn such a gift are kicked out of the kingdom only because that is their own preference. They want no part of it, and God, though he never stops loving them, won't allow them to stick around and ruin the joy of the eternal celebration by stinking up the place with the pride and hate and unbelief they have made their gods. So they go to where they like it best—to hell, where there is nobody having fun to spoil their miserable self-absorption.

Free grace is good news! Even though we didn't earn it or deserve it, God decided to give us eternal life in his Son. Believe or scoff, it's our choice. Whatever we decide to do about it, this much is forever true: Through the death and resurrection of Jesus Christ, God has concretely demonstrated how much he loves us, and how far he has gone to forgive our sins and restore us to himself. He has freely poured out his mercy everywhere in abounding love on absolutely everybody. It is pure grace—God's free gift of salvation, and it is enjoyed by everybody who believes his word and accepts him on his terms.

What stops me?

That brings us to your questions. If God has

already forgiven my sins even before I commit them, what is to stop me from just going out and sinning my brains out?

First, let's clear some ground. Sin is primarily a condition of the heart, not merely individual acts of wrongdoing. The acts of wrongdoing don't come from nowhere; they spring naturally from our corrupt hearts. The solution to our sin problem therefore requires a repaired heart, getting at the source of sin, rather than merely treating its effects.

God is not interested in finely behaved robots. He wants a love relationship with us. He loves us. That is why Christ came to save us. Relationships are built on forgiveness and mercy, not on forced compliance. If I want my wife to love me, for example, do I force her to act as though she does? If I did, I might get compliance, but I certainly wouldn't get her to actually love me. You cannot force anybody to love. You can only force people to act.

Through self-sacrifice, God has shown us how much he loves us. Through forgiveness and mercy, he has proven his great love. By suffering for our sins in our place, he has demonstrated that there is nothing that can come between us and his love (Romans 8:38). God wants children, not slaves. He wants a love relationship with us, not a world of cowering whipped dogs. He made us free beings, with real choices to make that matter to him very much. The choice he wants us to make is him.

Real freedom

God gives us freedom to behave as we wish, and he forgives our failures. He does it because he wants to. He set things up that way, and he makes no apologies for it. If we have any sense, we will see his love for what it is and latch onto him like there's no tomorrow.

So what is there to stop us from sinning all we want? Absolutely nothing. There never has been. The law didn't stop anybody from sinning all they wanted (Galatians 3:21-22). We have always sinned all we want, and God has always permitted it. He's never stopped us. He doesn't like it. He doesn't condone it. He doesn't endorse it. In fact, it grieves him. But he has always permitted it. That's called freedom, and he gives us that freedom.

In Christ

The Bible says that we are righteous in Christ (1 Corinthians 1:30; Philippians 3:9). We are not righteous in ourselves; we are righteous in Christ. In ourselves, because of sin, we are dead, but we are also, at the same time, alive in Christ — our lives are hid in Christ (Colossians 3:3). Without Christ, we are in hopeless shape, sold under sin, with no future. But Christ saved us. That is the gospel — good news! His salvation, if we receive it, puts us on a new footing with God.

Because of what God has done in Christ for us, including his prompting, even urging, us to trust him, Christ is now in us. For Christ's sake (he intercedes for us), we are, in spite of our sin, acceptable — righteous — before God. The whole business, from start to finish, is done, not by us, but by God, who wins us not by force, but by the power of his self-sacrificial love.

Trusting God With the Problem of Sin
continued

The law meaningless?

Paul was plain about the purpose of the law. It shows us that we are sinners (Romans 7:7). It declares the fact of our slavery to sin so that we might be justified by faith when Christ came (Galatians 3:19-27).

Now, suppose for a moment that you enter the judgment believing you are righteous because you always tried hard to obey God. So, instead of taking the wedding garment provided at the door (the free, clean one that goes only to dirty people who know they need it), you go in by a side door wearing your striving-hard garment, reeking all the way, and sit down at your place at the table. The lord of the house will say to you, "Hey buddy, where did you get the brass to come in here and insult me in front of all my guests with your sewage-soaked rags?" Then he will say to the staff, "Handcuff this filthy imposter and dump him in the swamp."

We cannot clean our dirty faces with our own dirty water, our dirty soap and our dirty washcloths, and go happily on our way thinking our hopelessly filthy faces are clean. There is only one way to remedy sin, and it does not lie with us. Remember, we are dead in sin (Romans 8:10), and dead people, by definition, can't remedy their deadness. Rather, the acute knowledge of our sinfulness should lead us to trust Jesus to clean us (1 Peter 5:10-11).

God wants you sin-free

God has given us indescribably great mercy and salvation not so that we feel a license to sin, but to free us from sin. That freedom not only removes our guilt from sin, but it also empowers us to see sin stripped naked for what it really is, instead of dressed up in the pretty costume it wears to fool us, and to reject its fraudulent and pretentious power over us. Even so, when we sin, which we certainly do, Jesus remains no less our atoning sacrifice (1 John 2:1-2).

God not only does not condone sin, he condemns sin. He does not like or endorse our glazed-eyed rationalizations, our comatose suspension of good sense or our hair-trigger, dive-in responses to temptations of every sort, from anger to lust to scorn to pride. He rarely bails us out of the natural consequences of the things we choose to do. However, because our faith and trust are in him (which means we are wearing the clean wedding clothes he provides), neither does he kick us out (as some preachers seem to think) of his wedding feast because of the poor choices we make.

Confession

Have you ever noticed that when you become aware of sinfulness in your life, your conscience plagues you until you confess your sins to God? (Chances are, there are some forms of sinfulness that you find yourself confessing rather frequently.) Why do you do that? Because you have committed yourself to "go out and sin all you want"? Is it not, rather, because your heart rests in Christ, and you, in tune with the Spirit who dwells in you, are grieved until you re-establish a sense of right relationship with him?

The Spirit in us testifies with our spirit, we are told, to the truth that we are the children of God (Romans 8:15-17). Two things to remain keenly aware of here:

1) You, by the testimony of the Spirit of God, are, in Christ and with all the saints, a child of God.
2) The Spirit, as the inner witness to your real identity, does not neglect to rumble

your landscape when you choose to live as though you are still nothing but the dead meat you used to be before Jesus redeemed you.

Make no mistake. Sin is God's enemy and your enemy. We need to fight it tooth and nail. But we must never think that our salvation depends on the level of our success in overcoming sin. Salvation depends on Christ's success in overcoming sin, and that's already been done. Sin and the death that shadows it have already been defeated in Jesus' death and resurrection, and the power of that victory resounds through all the creation from the beginning of time and forever. The only overcomers in the world are those who trust in Christ to be their resurrection and life.

Good works

God takes joy in the good works of his children (Psalm 147:11; Revelation 8:4). He delights in our acts of kindness, our sacrifices of love, our devotion to justice, honesty and peace (Hebrews 6:10). These and every good work are the natural outgrowth of the Spirit's work in us, leading us to trust, love and honor God. They are part of the love relationship that he has built with us through the sacrificial death and resurrection of the Lord of life, Jesus Christ. Such deeds and such work are God's own work in us, his beloved children, and as such, they are never useless (1 Corinthians 15:53).

God's work in us

Our faithful devotion to do what pleases God reflects our Savior's love, but again, our works of righteousness in his name are not what saves us. The righteousness that finds expression in our words and deeds of obedience to God's commands is righteousness that God himself is behind, joyfully working in us to his glory to bring forth good fruit. For us to try to take credit for what he does in us would be silly.

It would also be silly to think that the blood of Jesus, which covers all sin, leaves any of our sinfulness uncovered. If we think that, then we still don't have a clue as to who this eternal and omnipotent triune God is—this Father, Son, and Holy Spirit, who created all things, redeems us freely and magnificently with the Son's own blood, dwells in us through the Holy Spirit, and renews the whole creation, and makes us into a new creation (2 Corinthians 5:17) along with the whole universe (Isaiah 65:17), because of his indescribable love.

True life

Though God commands us to do what is right and good, he does not determine salvation by keeping record books. That is good for us, because if he did, we would all turn up in the reject pile. God saves us by his grace, and we can walk in the joy of that salvation if we give up all our claims on life, turn to him, and trust him and him alone to raise us from the dead (Ephesians 2:4-10; James 4:10).

Salvation is determined by the One who writes names in the book of life, and he has already written everyone's name in that book with the Lamb's blood (1 John 2:2). It is a colossal tragedy that some refuse to believe it, because if they would trust the Lord of life they would find that the life they have been scratching to save is not really life at all, but death, and that their true life, waiting to be revealed, is hidden with Christ in God (Colossians 3:3). God loves even his enemies and wants them, along with all people, to turn to him and enter the joy of his kingdom (1 Timothy 2:4, 6).

Summing up

So let's summarize. You asked: "If God, for Christ's sake, has completely forgiven me for all my sins, past, present and future, then what is to stop me from just going out and sinning all I want? I mean, is the law meaningless for Christians? Does God now condone sin? Doesn't he want me to stop sinning?"

There is nothing to stop us from sinning all we want. There never has been. God has given us free will, and he values it. He loves us and desires a love relationship with us, and such a relationship comes only through free choice, rooted in trust and forgiveness, not through threats or forced compliance. We are not robots or videotaped characters in a predetermined play. We are created as real, free beings, made so by God in his own freedom, and the relationship God has with us is real.

The law is far from meaningless; it serves to make it abundantly plain that we are sinners, falling far short of God's perfect will for us. God permits us to sin, but he does not condone it. That is why he has gone to such astounding self-sacrificial lengths to save us from it. Sin hurts and destroys us and everyone around us. It springs from a corrupt heart of unbelief and selfish rebellion against the source of our life and being. It saps us of true life and being and imprisons us in the darkness of death and nothingness.

Sin hurts

In case you haven't noticed, sin hurts like hell—literally, since that is in essence what it is. It makes as much sense to "go out and sin all I want to" as it does to stick my hand into a running lawnmower. "Well, then," I heard one man say, "If we're already forgiven, we might as well just go out and commit adultery." Sure, if you want to live in constant fear of being caught while you risk unwanted pregnancy and some nasty diseases, breaking your family's hearts, discrediting yourself, losing your friends and paying alimony out the nose, not to mention a plagued conscience and the likelihood of having to deal with very angry husbands, boyfriends, brothers or fathers.

Sin has consequences, bad ones, which is why God is at work in you to conform you to the image of Christ. You can work on listening and cooperating, or you can keep feeding appendages to the law mower. We must not forget that the usual sins we think about when we say things like "go out and sin all I want" are only the tip of the iceberg. What about being greedy, or selfish or rude? What about being unthankful, or saying mean things, or not helping out when you ought? What about holding a grudge, envying someone's job, clothes, car or house, or harboring angry thoughts about someone? What about taking home your employer's office supplies, sharing in gossip, or belittling your spouse and children? On and on we could go.

These are sins, too, some big, some little, and guess what? We "go out" and do them all we want to. It's a good thing God saves us by grace and not by works, isn't it? Sin is not OK, but that does not stop us from sinning. God does not want us to sin, yet he knows better than we do that we are dead in sin, and that we will continue to be dogged by sin until our true life, redeemed and sinless, which is hidden in Christ, is revealed at his appearing (Colossians 3:4).

Sinners alive in Christ

Purely by the freely given grace and limitless power of our ever-living and ever-loving God, believers paradoxically have died to sin, yet are alive in Jesus Christ (Romans 5:12; 6:4-11). Despite our sins, we no longer walk in death because we have believed and accepted our resurrection in Christ (Romans 8:10-11; Ephesians 2:3-6), a resurrection that will find its consummation at the appearing of Christ, when even our mortal bodies put on immortality (1 Corinthians 15:52-53).

Nonbelievers continue to walk in death, unable to enjoy their life that is hidden in Christ (Colossians 3:3) until they come to faith, not because the blood of Christ does not cover their sin, but because they cannot trust Christ to raise them from the dead until they believe the good news that he is their Savior and turn to him. Nonbelievers are as redeemed as believers—Christ died for everybody (1 John 2:2)—only they don't know it yet. Since they don't believe what they don't know, they continue to live in the fear of death (Hebrews 2:14-15) and the futile pursuit of life in all the wrong places (Ephesians 2:3).

The Holy Spirit transforms believers into the image of Christ (Romans 8:29). In Christ, the power of sin is broken, and we are no longer its prisoners. Even so, we are still weak and sometimes give place to sin (Romans 7:14-29; Hebrews 12:1). Because he loves us, God cares very much about our sinful condition. He loves the world so much that he sent his eternal Son that whoever believes in him would not remain in the darkness of death that is the fruit of sin, but would have eternal life in him.

There is nothing that can separate you from his love, not even your sins. Trust him. He helps you walk in obedience, and he forgives your every sin. He is your Savior because he wants to be, and he is very good at what he does.

J. Michael Feazell

The Resurrection of the Body and Why It Matters

When Christ returns, the dead will be resurrected. "With what body do they come?" some ask. Will their atoms be re-assembled? Will there be male and female? Will we recognize one another? Will we look young, or old? Many other questions are asked.

It is understandable that we ask. But it is also understandable that we cannot understand what immortal life will be like, just as a fetus cannot understand what adult life is like, or a person born blind has difficulty in understanding color. Perhaps being glorified will be like entering new dimensions that we have never known before. We do not have the words to describe it because our words are based on our experiences in this age. Just as we cannot describe the aroma of coffee, we cannot describe our future life.

Scripture does not give us a detailed description of what life will be like when we have glorified bodies. It tells us 1) that we will be with God forever and 2) that all who trust in Christ will find it to be an immensely enjoyable life. We will enter our Master's happiness, and in his presence there are pleasures forevermore. We will never be bored, for we finite beings will always have new things to learn and enjoy about God's infinite goodness.

Scripture also tells us that when Christ returns, we will be like him (1 John 3:2). Paul tells us that our bodies will be changed when the final trumpet sounds (1 Corinthians 15:51-52). This brings us back to the question of what our bodies will be like. There are two approaches to this question. The first is to ask what kind of body Jesus had after his resurrection, and the second is to see what Paul wrote about our bodies in the resurrection. We have limited information about both, but we can see how they might fit together.

The resurrected Jesus

After his resurrection, Jesus could be recognized as Jesus. Special intervention was needed to prevent two disciples from recognizing him (Luke 24:16). Jesus had flesh and bones, and some (but not all) of the marks of crucifixion (verse 39). He could be touched, and he could eat. He could also appear in locked rooms, or ascend into heaven (John 20:19-20; Acts 1:9).

But is this the way Jesus now is? Is there a five-foot-six-inch body of flesh and bones somewhere in outer space? Is Jesus normally invisible, or does his body shine in glory, or does he look like a lamb that has been slain — with seven horns and seven eyes? (Revelation 5:6). Or are all of these merely appearances, not necessarily a permanent shape or form?

Here are some basic facts: First, the tomb was empty and the body of Jesus was gone. Second, the resurrected Jesus had a body, although that body had some extraordinary properties. One way to connect these two facts is to conclude that the body of Jesus was brought back to life and changed. The new Jesus had physical continuity with the old Jesus, but there were important differences.

Jesus does not have to remain visible. When he appeared, his body reflected photons; when he disappeared, it did not. Yet in both states, Jesus had a body. He inhabits eternity, and he does not have to conform to the finite electromagnetic quantum world that we are able to investigate. For that reason, I do not believe that Jesus' body has to conform to the dimensions that we know.

Our questions about "size" and "location" are

based on limits that probably do not apply to Jesus Christ. Such questions may make no more sense than asking what purple smells like — we are asking about a condition with terminology that is not suited for that condition.

Our resurrection

Paul tells us that we will be changed — metamorphosed (1 Corinthians 15:51). The body will then be imperishable, immortal, glorious, powerful and spiritual (verses 42-44, 53). But it will be a body, and it will have some continuity with the old body. Paul compares this change to the sprouting of a seed (verse 37). A tree does not look like an acorn, but it has physical continuity with the acorn. A butterfly looks nothing like a caterpillar, but it has physical continuity with it. Our metamorphosis may involve an even more dramatic change in what we are like. We cannot predict what it will be like any more than we can predict whether some unfamiliar seed will grow into a tree, or a flower.

There is continuity as well as change. The old body is not abandoned, nor is it totally kept. We do not worry about reassembling all the atoms that were once part of our bodies (that would be impossible, for bodies decompose after death and their atoms become incorporated into other things, sometimes of other people's bodies). But Paul still talks about the resurrection of the body.

He expects to find the tombs empty and the bones all gone. I do not know how this works, and it may involve realities I know nothing about. Lacking any further information, I simply have to accept what Paul was inspired to write: the body will be raised, and it will have new qualities.

Some may ask, What is a spiritual body? Isn't that a contradiction of terms? Paul is talking about a body that is different from the bodies we know, but he is not talking about a body that is "made" of spirit. In verse 44, when he says that our current bodies are "natural," he uses the Greek word *psychikos*, the adjective form of the word *psyche*, or soul. He is not talking about a body made out of soul, but a body that is characterized in some way by the soul.

Similarly, when he says the body will become a spiritual body, he uses the word *pneumatikos*, the adjective form of *pneuma*, or spirit. He is not talking about a body made out of spirit any more than he is talking about a body made out of soul. But the body will be characterized by spirit, perhaps in the same way that a spiritual person is (Galatians 6:1), with an ability to understand spiritual things. We will not understand what this body is like until it is given to us.

Why bother with the body?

Why does God bother with our bodies? Wouldn't it be simpler to take our spirits to heaven and live forever with the Lord without any need for a resurrection? I do not claim to have a complete answer. I do know that God created physical matter, and it is therefore good. God did not make it just to destroy it later. He will keep the physical world in a renewed form, in a new heavens and new earth.

The physical body is not some evil thing that we need to escape from (as many non-Christians have taught). Jesus had a physical body, and there was nothing wrong with that. Jesus was made flesh for the very purpose of redeeming all things (Colossians 1:19-20). God is not abandoning the physical world — he is rescuing it.

Romans 8:21 tells us that the physical creation will be liberated from its bondage when we are transformed into glory. This salvation involves the "redemption of our bodies" (verse 23). Our bodies will be redeemed, not discarded. Our bodies will be raised immortal and imperishable, freed from the decay that affects the physical world today. Christ has made it possible, as shown in his own resurrection with a body that transcends the limits of space and time.

The fact that the physical world will be redeemed, the fact that our bodies will be raised, means that we should value the physical world that God has placed us in and made us part of. We are to care for the creation and care for our bodies. We have environmental concerns and health concerns; we have interests in the biological and physical sciences. We are not to abandon the world we live in, but we are to improve it in whatever small ways we can.

Similarly, we are not to abandon the social world we live in, but are to improve it when we can, working against evil and promoting justice. The fact that our bodies will be redeemed and raised emphasizes our need to be involved in the world in a positive way. We are not escapists, merely passing time until time ends, but we are involved, letting Christ live in us and grow in us until we are raised with him in glory and we see him as he is and we share in his eternal joy.

Joseph Tkach

Hell

"If your right hand causes you to sin, cut it off and throw it away," said Jesus. "It is better for you to lose one part of your body than for your whole body to go into hell" (Matthew 5:30). Hell is serious. We need to take Jesus' warning seriously. On this subject, as with many others, we must listen to Jesus. If we take him seriously when he teaches about mercy, we should also take him seriously when he teaches about punishment. After all, mercy doesn't mean much unless we are escaping something.

Warnings about fire

In one parable, Jesus warned that wicked people will be thrown into a fiery furnace (Matthew 13:50). In this parable, he did not talk about annihilation, but about "weeping and gnashing of teeth." In another parable, Jesus describes the punishment of someone as "torture" (Matthew 18:34). Another parable describes the wicked person as tied up and thrown "into the darkness" (Matthew 22:13). This darkness is described as a place of weeping and grinding of teeth. Jesus does not explain whether people in the darkness weep from pain or from sorrow, and he does not explain whether they grind their teeth in remorse or in anger. That is not his purpose. In fact, he never explains in detail the fate of the wicked.

However, Jesus does warn people in vivid terms not to hang on to anything that would cause them to be thrown into eternal fire: "If your hand or your foot causes you to sin," Jesus warned, "cut it off and throw it away. It is better for you to enter life maimed or crippled than to have two hands or two feet and be thrown into eternal fire" (Matthew 18:7-8). It is better to deny yourself in this life than to be "thrown into the fire of hell" (verse 9).

Does the punishing of the wicked last forever? The Bible can be interpreted in different ways on that. Some verses suggest eternal suffering, while others suggest a limited duration. But either way, hell is to be avoided at all costs. This reminds me of a book on this subject: *Two Views of Hell*. Edward Fudge argues for annihilation; Robert Peterson argues for eternal suffering. On the cover of this book are two men, both with hand over face in an expression of dread or horror. The graphic suggests that even though there are two views of hell, no matter how you look at hell, it is ghastly. God is merciful, but the person who opposes God refuses his mercy and therefore suffers.

Epistles

Jesus used a variety of word-pictures for the punishment of those who refuse the mercy of God: fire, darkness, torture and destruction. The apostles also talked about judgment and punishment, but they described it in different ways. Paul wrote, "For those who are self-seeking and who reject the truth and follow evil, there will be wrath and anger. There will be trouble and distress for every human being who does evil"

(Romans 2:9). Regarding those who were persecuting the church at Thessalonica, Paul wrote, "They will be punished with everlasting destruction and shut out from the presence of the Lord and from the majesty of his power" (2 Thessalonians 1:9). So one definition of hell is "separation and alienation from God."

The Old Testament penalty for rejecting Moses was death, but anyone who deliberately rejects Jesus deserves a greater punishment, says Hebrews 10:28-29. God is merciful beyond imagination, but if people refuse his mercy, they will reap the consequences of their actions. God does not want anyone to suffer in hell — he wants everyone to come to repentance and salvation (2 Peter 2:9). But those who refuse his grace will suffer. That is their choice, not God's.

The final victory of God is also an important part of the picture. Everything will be brought under the control of Christ, for he has redeemed all creation (1 Corinthians 15:20-24; Colossians 1:20). Everything will be set right. Even death and Hades will be destroyed in the end (Revelation 20:14). The Bible does not tell us how hell fits into that picture. We trust that God, full of righteousness and mercy, will conclude it in the best possible way.

Of all that Jesus taught about hell, the most important thing is that Jesus is the solution to the problem. In him, there is no condemnation (Romans 8:1). He is the way, the truth and the life eternal.

Joseph Tkach

The justice and mercy of God

A God of love would not torture people forever and ever, say some people. The Bible reveals God to be compassionate. He would rather put people out of their misery than see them suffer eternally. The traditional doctrine of an ever-punishing hell, many believe, portrays God as a vengeful sadist who sets a terrible example. Moreover, it would not be right to punish people forever for a life that lasted only a few years or decades, say some.

But rebellion against God is infinitely terrible, say some theologians. We cannot measure evil by the time it takes to commit it, they explain. A murder may take only a few minutes, yet the consequences may extend over decades or centuries. Rebelling against God is the most serious crime in the universe, they contend, so it demands the worst punishment.

Unfortunately, humans don't have a very good handle on either justice or mercy. Humans are not qualified to judge, but Jesus Christ is. He will judge the world righteously (Psalm 9:8; John 5:22; Romans 2:6-11). We can trust his judgment, knowing he will be both righteous and merciful. When it comes to hell, some parts of the Bible stress anguish and punishment and others use images of destruction and cessation. Rather than trying to make one description conform to the other, we let them both speak. When it comes to hell, we must trust God, not our imagination.

Revelation: Book of Cosmic Symbols

To understand Revelation it is helpful to think of this writing as first and foremost a book of symbols. For example, we see the victorious Christ, riding on a horse (Revelation 19:11-16). He smites the nations with a sword. But what good is a sword in an age of nuclear weapons? Does Christ need a physical weapon at all? The sword is a picture, a symbol, of an event and divine power — the return of the Messiah, who destroys the forces of evil.

Contrast of good and evil

Revelation's symbols are often juxtaposed one against another. This use of comparison and contrast is seen throughout the book. In the middle chapters of Revelation, Satan's forces — the beast and false prophet — are pitted against God's earthly representative, the church. The book describes two ages of human existence, each contrary to the other. Satan, the dragon, the adversary of God, dominates this present world. Jesus Christ, the Lamb of God, rules a world of peace, popularly known as the millennium.

Revelation portrays and compares two opposing ways of life. Two symbols embody these conflicting lifestyles. A harlot pictures the deceived group, deluded by what's called her "spiritual fornication." This refers to her illicit spiritual liaisons with political rulers. Another group of people follows the Lamb, who is Jesus. These are called the spiritually pure Bride of Christ.

The image of an enormous city — Babylon the Great — stands for the corrupt system that seduces the world. Revelation contrasts this wicked city with the purity and perfection of the New Jerusalem. Ultimately, the latter stands for the ideal and eternal congregation of those who are faithful to Christ.

Even the promise to share in salvation is represented by this-worldly symbols. Symbols are used in the seven letters to Christian congregations in the province of Asia. For example, the church in Ephesus is promised salvation by being told it will have "the right to eat from the tree of life" (2:7). That is a metaphor for salvation and eternal life.

Norman Perrin outlined this dualistic and symbolic structure of Revelation in which the spiritual realm, the church, and the world system are given their parts to play. He wrote:

> At the pinnacle of power on one side is God, the Pantocrator, ruler of all (1:8). On the other is Satan, the Dragon, who has power, a throne, and great authority (13:2). Allied with God is the Lamb who was slain (5:6).... Allied with Satan is the beast from the sea (13:1-2).... All the people on the earth are divided into two groups; those who have the seal of God on their foreheads and whose names are in the book of life (3:5, 12; 7:3; 20:4; 21:27; 22:4) and those who bear the mark of the beast and worship it (9:4; 13:8; 17:14:9-11; 16:2; 20:15). There is also a sharp contrast between the luxurious and voluptuous harlot, who represents Babylon, the earthly city of abominations (ch.17) and the pure bride of the Lamb, who symbolizes Jerusalem, the heavenly city of salvation (19:7-8; 21: 2, 9-11). This literary tension reflects the political tension between the adherents of the kingdom of God and those of the kingdom of Caesar (11:15; 12:10; 16:10; 17:18) (*Jesus and the Language of the Kingdom*, p. 142).

Symbolism

To the modern western world, Revelation's symbols seem weird and alien. They include a multi-headed dragon; two strange beasts; a city shaped like a cube 1,500 miles high, wide and long;

marks on heads and right hands; a figure's mouth with a sword emerging from it, and so on.

These symbols were not strange to John's original audience for whom the book was written. Revelation drew on commonly known pagan myths, Old Testament and Jewish typologies, as well as New Testament Christian traditions and beliefs. These symbols were generally understood to refer to spiritual truths and historical realities. For example, in the Roman world of John's time there were various stories about a god of heaven slaying a sea monster.

Some of Revelation's symbols played off of such myths circulating in the pagan world. However, the book's symbols are heavily based on Old Testament themes, which in turn had been reinterpreted by Jewish apocalyptic literature. In Revelation, the meanings of symbols existing in the Jewish and pagan world were again reinterpreted in the light of the Christian's experience in Christ. The symbols were not strange codes that one had to have special knowledge to understand. John's readers knew what he meant. In the words of G. B. Caird:

> The first readers were almost certainly well versed in the sort of symbolic language and imagery in which the book is written. Whether they had formerly been Jews or pagans, they would read the language of myth as fluently as any modern reader of the daily papers reads the conventional symbols of a political cartoon. Much of this language we can reconstruct for ourselves from the Old Testament and Jewish apocalyptic writings on the one hand and from Greek and Roman literature, inscriptions, and coinage on the other (*A Commentary on the Revelation of St. John the Divine*, 2nd edition, page 6).

This makes sense if we consider a modern graphic genre, the political cartoon. G. R. Beasley-Murray calls the political cartoon "the closest modern parallel" to Revelation's symbols (*Revelation*, page 17). Political cartoons use stereotyped images. Beasley-Murray gives some examples of modern cartoon symbols. Two examples are John Bull, who represents Britain, and Uncle Sam, the United States. The lion also represents Britain and the eagle the United States. Two other symbols are the bear for Russia and the dragon for China.

Often these and other political figures are drawn as caricatures. Says Beasley-Murray, "Frequently the situations depicted are deliberately exaggerated, and even made grotesque, in order that the message may be made plain" (*Revelation*, 17). The symbols of Revelation were plain, simple and quickly understood by the original readers. Beasley-Murray explains the point further:

> The symbols by which the contemporary political forces and the spiritual powers of heaven and hell are portrayed [in Revelation] were as traditional as Britannia and the British lion, the Russian bear, and the Chinese dragon…. What to the uninitiated modern reader appears grotesque imagery, spoke with power to John's fellow Christians (17).

Many people are familiar with George Orwell's *Animal Farm*, in which animals speak. The book is a political-social statement about the excesses of political leadership and the subjugation of the weak. We do not think the book bizarre because animals talk in it. We know it is symbolic. We also readily understand the meaning of Orwell's symbols — and enjoy them. It was precisely because of the form in which *Animal Farm* was written that has made it a timeless piece of literature.

Symbols have meaning

There are several lessons in this. First, we should not consider Revelation strange or bizarre. The book was probably easy to understand, extremely interesting and thoroughly meaningful to the original readers. If we can put ourselves in their place, this biblical writing can be all these things to us as well.

Second, we should not force Revelation's symbols into a literal mode. If the book is a kind of painting of God's purpose, it is much more expressionistic or impressionistic than realistic. In the words of George Eldon Ladd: "Apocalyptic language does not convey its message in precise photographic style, but more in the style of modern surrealistic art with great fluidity and imagination" (*A Commentary on the Revelation of John*, p. 111). Ladd explains that Revelation's symbols are "not meant to be photographs of objective facts; they are often symbolic representations of almost unimaginable spiritual realities" (p. 102).

M. Eugene Boring explains it this way:

> Many of the scenes John describes simply cannot be imaged. Not only can they not be placed on a canvas or movie screen, they cannot be placed on the screen of the mind. The vision of the exalted Christ in 1:12-16, for example, simply becomes grotesque if one attempts to understand it as a reporter's account of what John actually saw in the objective world (*Revelation*, 54).

Here Christ is pictured as speaking through a mouth out of which a sharp double-edged sword protrudes. If an attempt is made to understand the anthropomorphic picture of Christ in Revelation 1 as a literal representation of what he looks like, this part of the portrait is bizarre. The portrait becomes meaningful only if we understand John's portrayal of the sword as a symbol of the sharpness and power of God's word (Hebrews 4:12; Ephesians 6:17).

We need to be careful about overly allegorizing Revelation, just as we also need to avoid a strict literalism. This was probably not a difficulty John's original readers faced. They knew the situation in which they lived and the meaning of the symbols. But we are removed from both. In the words of G. B. Caird:

> Our difficulties begin when we try to decide how far to take this picture language literally and how far to take it figuratively. When John echoes the Roman legend that the dead Nero was about to return, how literally does he mean it? Does he believe that Nero was not in fact dead, or that he would be resurrected, or that another paranoiac would come to fill his empty shoes? (*A Commentary on the Revelation of St. John the Divine,* 2nd edition, 7).

In one sense, these issues are only of historical importance, vital only to John's original readers. But if that was all that Revelation's symbols pictured — that is, events, situations and people in John's day — they would have little meaning for us. However, since Revelation uses symbols to represent spiritual realities, the book has universal meaning for all times and generations.

Another caution is in order. We should not dismiss the historical context and meaning of the symbols, nor their possible application to specific situations and individuals. These, however, are not the primary meanings. Symbols can have different kinds of meaning. The symbol "bear" can have a simple meaning when referring to Russia. That is, bear = Russia. On another level, the bear says something about the kind of political power the nation embodies. On a third level, "bear," already known to be symbolic of a lumbering political giant, can stand for all such empires — including perhaps the massive ancient Persian empire.

The American flag can be described as 13 stripes and 50 stars. That's what the flag is, literally. It is also a symbol representing 13 original colonies and 50 states. The American flag also represents the nation. When we see the flag, we think "United States." But the American flag waving in the breeze during a patriotic parade represents something much more. It symbolizes a concept — a big idea — the pride of being an American.

In the same way, Revelation's symbols can have various kinds and levels of meanings. Its symbols are not what are called "steno-symbols," those with only a single reference point. For example, if the symbol "bear" were such a symbol, it could only be a nickname for the nation. But as we saw, the "bear" symbol has meanings on several levels.

Revelation's symbols are often what are called "tensive" symbols. They are open-ended to some degree in that they can represent several conceptions or ideas. For example, if the first beast of Revelation 13 can be identified with the city of Rome in John's day, this does not exhaust its meaning. The tensive symbol "beast" may also represent the Roman Empire, or refer to a specific individual such as the emperor Nero or Domitian. "Beast" may also stand for all human empires that oppress Christians.

G. B. Caird is correct when he says that it is "misleading to say that in Revelation the monster is Rome, and still more misleading to say that it is ruler worship. The monster is both an older and a newer phenomenon than Caesar, and the great city is more ancient and more modern than Rome" (*A Commentary on the Revelation of St. John the Divine,* 2nd edition, p. xii).

Revelation speaks of concepts that deal with an ultimate reality about which we have no direct experience or knowledge. That's why it uses symbols and why the book can indicate earthly and heavenly realities only in rough outline. To cite an example, God is pictured as sitting on a heavenly throne in Revelation. The throne represents, in symbol, to us who are limited to this physical world, the glory, the lordship and universal authority of God. The throne symbol is a poor reflection of God's real supremacy. But those are the limitations of human language and our experiential knowledge of God.

Common knowledge

Some commentators suggest that the symbols in Revelation were not readily understood by those of John's time. This idea claims John used coded language so that the criticism it contained of the Roman government would be kept secret from outsiders. However, the average reader would have quite easily picked out the possible references to Rome.

Jews typically equated Rome with Babylon in apocalyptic writings. It was also common knowledge that Rome was the city built on seven hills. Both images are used in Revelation. Assuming the Roman authorities were of at least average intelligence and could read, it hardly seems they would have missed this. M. Eugene Boring points out that the mere reference to God or Christ as king (11:15) would have appeared subversive to Roman authorities.

On the other hand, only a small portion of Revelation's material could be construed as applying to Rome. If John's use of symbolic material was meant to confound the Roman secret police, why is virtually *all* the book written in symbolic, apocalyptic form? Whatever the answer, John's purpose is clearly stated: it is to reveal, not conceal. M. Eugene Boring points out: "With reference to the Roman government, John does not veil whom he means; he writes to reveal the essential nature of Roman power, which was not at all obvious to many members of John's churches" (*Revelation,* p. 55).

Revelation is not written as an attack against the outside world. It is written to be read in the church — the worshipful community of the saints. The book would not be very concerned with outsiders' reactions. But the book is not simply a straightforward letter such as a Colossians or 1 Peter. Revelation seeks to create a symbolic world for its readers and to put them into it. The book attempts to create for them the same wonder and awe that John experienced. In modern language, we might call Revelation a "virtual reality" experience. In the words of G. B. Caird:

> John uses his allusions not as a code in which each symbol requires separate and exact translation, but rather for their evocative and emotive power. This is not photographic art. His aim is to set the echoes of memory and association ringing (*A Commentary on the Revelation of St. John the Divine,* 2nd edition, p. 26).

Revelation does not have as its primary purpose the aim of providing the curiosity seeker with information to bolster speculations about an apocalyptic "end-time." The symbols in the book are meant to bring forth a response on the part of God's people of continued faith in Jesus Christ as Lord of creation, the world and the church.

Paul Kroll

The Rewards of Following Christ

Peter once asked Jesus, "We have left everything to follow you! What then will there be for us?" (Matthew 19:27). We might paraphrase it like this: "We've given up a lot to be here. Is it really worth it?" Some people today might ask the same thing. We have given up a lot — careers, families, jobs, status, pride — in our spiritual journey. Is it worth it? Is there some sort of reward in store for us?

Our labors and sacrifices are not in vain. Our efforts will be rewarded — even if they were based on a misunderstanding. Whenever our motive is right — when our labor and sacrifice are for Jesus — we will be rewarded. Scripture has something to say about rewards. God knows that we ask the question and, in this case, we need an answer. He inspired Scripture writers to talk about rewards, and I am confident that when God promises a reward, we will find it extremely rewarding — far above what we could even think to ask (Ephesians 3:20).

Rewards both now and forever

Let's begin by noting the way that Jesus answered Peter's question:

> At the renewal of all things, when the Son of Man sits on his glorious throne, you who have followed me will also sit on twelve thrones, judging the twelve tribes of Israel. And everyone who has left houses or brothers or sisters or father or mother or children or fields for my sake will receive a hundred times as much and will inherit eternal life. (verses 28-29)

The Gospel of Mark shows that Jesus is talking about two time periods:

> No one who has left home or brothers or sisters or mother or father or children or fields for me and the gospel will fail to receive a hundred times as much in this present age (homes, brothers, sisters, mothers, children and fields — and with them, persecutions) and in the age to come, eternal life. (Mark 10:29-30)

God will reward us generously — but Jesus also warns us that this life is not a life of physical luxury. We will have persecutions, trials and sufferings in this life. But the blessings outweigh the difficulties by a hundred-to-one margin! Whatever sacrifices we make will be richly compensated. The Christian life is certainly "worth it."

Jesus is not promising to give 100 fields to everyone who gave up a farm to follow him. He is not promising to give 100 mothers. He is not promising to make everyone wealthy. He is not talking in literal terms. He means that the things we receive in the next life will be 100 times as valuable as the things we give up in this life — as measured by real value, eternal value, not by temporary fads about physical things.

Even our trials have spiritual value to our benefit (Romans 5:3-4; James 1:2-4), and this is of greater value than gold (1 Peter 1:7). God sometimes gives us gold and other temporary rewards (perhaps as an indication of better things to come), but the rewards that count most are those that last forever.

I doubt that the disciples understood what Jesus was saying. They were still thinking in terms of a physical kingdom that would soon bring earthly freedom and power to the people of Israel (Acts 1:6). The martyrdom of Stephen and James (Acts 7:57-60; 12:2) may have come as a surprise. Where were the hundredfold rewards for them?

Parables of reward

In several parables, Jesus indicated that faithful disciples would receive great rewards. Sometimes the reward is described as authority over other people, but Jesus also used other ways to describe our reward. In the parable of the vineyard workers, the gift of salvation is symbolized by one day's wage (Matthew 20:9-16). In the parable of the virgins, the reward is a marriage banquet (Matthew 25:10). In the parable of talents, the reward is described in general terms: being put "in charge of many things" and being able to "share your master's happiness" (verses 20-23).

In the parable of sheep and goats, the faithful are allowed to inherit a kingdom (verse 34). In the parable of the servants, the faithful servant is rewarded by being put in charge of all the master's possessions (Luke 12:42-44). In the parables of the pounds, the trustworthy servants were given authority over cities (Luke 19:16-19). Jesus promised the 12 disciples authority over the tribes of Israel (Matthew 19:28; Luke 22:30). Members of the church in Thyatira were promised authority over the nations (Revelation 2:26-27).

Jesus advised his disciples to "store up for yourselves treasures in heaven" (Matthew 6:19-21). By this, he implied that what we do in this life will be rewarded in the future — but what sort of reward is it? What good is a treasure when there is nothing to buy? When streets are made of gold, what will be the value of gold?

In the resurrection, we will not need physical things. When we think of eternal rewards, we should think primarily about spiritual rewards, not physical things that will pass away. But the problem is that we do not have the vocabulary to describe details of an existence we have never experienced. So we need to use words based on the physical world when we attempt to describe what the spiritual is like.

Our eternal reward will be like a treasure. In some respects, it will be like inheriting a kingdom. In some way, it will be like being given all our master's possessions. It will be similar to having a vineyard to take care of on behalf of the master. It will be like having responsibility over cities. It will be like a wedding banquet when we share in our master's happiness. It is like all of these things, and much more.

Our spiritual blessings will be far better than the physical things we know in this life. Our eternity in God's presence will be much more glorious and joyful than physical rewards. All physical things, no matter how beautiful, enjoyable or valuable, are only weak shadows of infinitely better heavenly rewards.

Eternal joy with God

The Psalmist put it this way: "You will fill me with joy in your presence, with eternal pleasures at your right hand" (Psalm 16:11). John described it as a time when "there will be no more death or mourning or crying or pain" (Revelation 21:4). Everyone will be fully happy. There will be no dissatisfaction. No one will be able to think of even a tiny way in which things could be better. We will have reached the purpose for which God has made us.

Isaiah described some of this joy when he predicted a nation returning to its land: "The ransomed of the Lord will return. They will enter Zion with singing; everlasting joy will crown their heads. Gladness and joy will overtake them, and sorrow and sighing will flee away" (Isaiah 35:10). We will be in the presence of God, and we will be happier than we have ever been. This is what Christianity has traditionally tried to convey by the concept of "going to heaven."

Is it wrong to want a reward?

Some critics of Christianity have ridiculed the concept of heaven as "pie in the sky" — but ridicule is not a logical argument. The real question is, Is there a reward, or not? If there is a reward in heaven, then it is not ridiculous to hope to enjoy it. If we will be rewarded, it is ridiculous not to want it.

"Anyone who comes to him [God] must believe that he exists and that he rewards those who earnestly seek him" (Hebrews 11:6). Belief in rewards is part of the Christian faith. Nevertheless, some people think that it is somehow demeaning or less than honorable for Christians to want to be rewarded for their labors. They think that Christians should serve with a motive of love, expecting no reward for their labors. But that is not the complete message of the Bible. In addition to the free gift of salvation by grace through faith, the Bible does promise rewards for God's people, and it is not wrong to desire the promises of God.

Yes, we are to serve God from the motivation of love and not as hirelings who work only to be paid. However, Scripture does speak of rewards, and assures us that we will be rewarded. It is honorable for us to believe in God's promises and to find them motivating. Rewards are not the only motive of the redeemed children of God, but it is part of the package God has given us.

When life becomes difficult, it is helpful for us to remember that there is another life, in which we will be rewarded. "If only for this life we have hope in Christ, we are to be pitied more than all people" (1 Corinthians 15:19). Paul knew that the future life would make his sacrifices worthwhile. He gave up temporary pleasures to seek better, longer-lasting pleasures in Christ (Philippians 3:8).

Paul used the language of "gain" (Philippians 1:21; 1 Timothy 3:13; 6:6; cf. Hebrews 11:35). He knew that his future life would be much better than the persecutions of this life. Jesus was also mindful of the benefits of his own sacrifice, and he was willing to endure the cross because he saw great joy on the other side (Hebrews 12:2).

When Jesus counseled us to lay up for ourselves treasures in heaven (Matthew 6:19-20), he was not against investing — he was against bad investments. Do not invest in temporary rewards, but invest in heavenly rewards that will last forever. "Great is your reward in heaven" (Matthew 5:12). "The kingdom of heaven is like treasure hidden in a field" (Matthew 13:44).

God has prepared something wonderfully good for us, and we will find it to be extremely enjoyable. It is right for us to eagerly look forward to these great blessings, and when we count the cost of following Jesus, it is also right for us to count the blessings and rewards promised for us.

"The Lord will reward everyone for whatever good he does" (Ephesians 6:8). "Whatever you do, work at it with all your heart, as working for the Lord, not for men, since you know that you will receive an inheritance from the Lord as a reward" (Colossians 3:23-24). "Watch out that you do not lose what you have worked for, but that you may be rewarded fully" (2 John 8).

Exceedingly great rewards

What God has in store for us is beyond our ability to imagine. Even in this life, the love of God is beyond our ability to understand (Ephesians 3:19). The peace of God is beyond our comprehension (Philippians 4:7), and his joy is beyond our ability to put into words (1 Peter 1:8). How much more, then, is it impossible to describe how good it will be to live with God forever?

The biblical writers didn't give us many details. But one thing we know for certain — it is going to be the most wonderful experience we have ever had. It is better than the most beautiful paintings, better than the most delicious food, better than the most exciting sport, better than the best feelings and experiences we have ever had. It is better than anything on earth. It is going to be a tremendous reward!

God is generous! We have been given exceedingly great and precious promises — and the privilege of sharing this wonderful news with others. What joy should fill our hearts! In the words of 1 Peter 1:3-9:

> Praise be to the God and Father of our Lord Jesus Christ! In his great mercy he has given us new birth into a living hope through the resurrection of Jesus Christ from the dead, and into an inheritance that can never perish, spoil or fade — kept in heaven for you, who through faith are shielded by God's power until the coming of the salvation that is ready to be revealed in the last time.
>
> In this you greatly rejoice, though now for a little while you may have had to suffer grief in all kinds of trials. These have come so that your faith — of greater worth than gold, which perishes even though refined by fire — may be proved genuine and may result in praise, glory and honor when Jesus Christ is revealed. Though you have not seen him, you love him; and even though you do not see him now, you believe in him and are filled with an inexpressible and glorious joy, for you are receiving the goal of your faith, the salvation of your souls.

We have much to be thankful for, much to rejoice about, much to celebrate!

Joseph Tkach

The Millennium of Revelation 20

The idea of a thousand-year reign of Christ – a millennium – is found in only two verses in the Bible — Revelation 20:4, 6. The length of the martyrs' or saints' reign is here said to be a thousand years. This number has produced the term "millennium," which is derived from the Latin *mille* (thousand) and *annus* (year).

Jewish apocalyptic writings of the first century speculated about the length of the Messiah's reign, when it was assumed that the nation of Israel would be restored to glory by God. The time spans were as little as 40 to as many as 7,000 years. The author of 4 Ezra thought the Messiah's reign would last 400 years (7:28). The original audience of Revelation probably would have been familiar with the idea of a limited reign of the Messiah.

The writer of Revelation may have mentioned the "millennium" to counter the idea that the "kingdom of God" was to be based around a Jewish nation. An important point of Revelation is to reinterpret Old Testament prophecies in terms of Jesus' redemptive work and the church. Revelation was written to point out that the church was the recipient of God's grace, made possible by Jesus' saving work. The book's message to the church contradicted the Jewish idea that salvation would come to the Jewish people alone. Given this context, it's not surprising that Revelation would make a comment about Jewish millennial speculations and expectations, and reinterpret them in terms of God's real purpose in the church.

However, we also have to distinguish between some Jewish ideas about God's ideal kingdom and what the Old Testament says about it. The Old Testament says nothing about the Messiah's rule as being a thousand years in length, or that it would last for a limited time. It seems to speak of the kingdom of God on earth as being open-ended, continuing without end once it begins. Even the kingdom of the "new heavens and new earth" in Isaiah 65:17-25 and 66:22-24 appears to be an extension of the earthly and seemingly eternal reign of God.

Neither does the New Testament speak of Christ's kingdom as existing for any limited time. The only passage that might indicate a time-limited kingdom as existing between Christ's coming and the beginning of a more glorious kingdom is 1 Corinthians 15:22-24. Paul here may speak of "the end" as being in some way distinct in time from Christ's return. If that is so, Paul gives no specifics. In none of his writings does he express any interest in or undertake any discussion of a limited "millennium." Neither do the other New Testament writings. We should also note that the concept of "the end" is understood in the New Testament as beginning with the completion of Jesus' work of redemption – that is, his crucifixion and resurrection.

The only mention of 1,000 years is in the book of Revelation – a book of symbolic numbers. This prompts us to ask whether this period of time is literally 1,000 years, or whether it is to be taken as a limited period of time at all. Any attempt to answer this question must rely on the context of Revelation 20, for no other Bible verse clearly discusses such a period of time. But if we attempt to use a single passage in a highly symbolic book as the basis of a dogmatic conclusion about a theological doctrine, we are violating one of the most important rules of biblical interpretation.

Despite those limitations, some commentators nevertheless believe that the figure given in Revelation 20 represents a literal 1,000 years. Other biblical commentators feel that while the "millennium" is a period of substantial length, its actual time is undetermined. In the same way that "one hour" means a very short time (Revelation 17:12), 1,000 years would mean a very long time.

One thousand is the cube of ten — ten times ten times ten. Ten is another number of completeness — as in the ten commandments. John uses the number several times in Revelation. The ten horns is one example. Perhaps what Revelation means to say is that God's kingdom will last for whatever complete time God has determined it should last.

Those who feel the number "thousand" refers to an indefinite though long time cite examples of similar usage from the Old Testament. In Psalm 50:10 God speaks of himself as owner of all that exists. He says, "Every animal of the forest is mine, and the cattle on a thousand hills." The expression is not to be taken literally, as if God owned cattle only on 1,000 specific hills.

Job 9:3 speaks of a human's inability to box God in with arguments by saying, "Though they wished to dispute with him [God], they could not answer him one time out of a thousand." In any dispute with God, we humans lose the argument because his wisdom and understanding is infinite and ours is very limited.

In the New Testament, Peter says that with God one day might just as well be a thousand years and a thousand years a day (2 Peter 3:8). That is, what we think of as a long time, to God is but a very short time. It is a metaphorical way of expressing the idea that time has no meaning for God, so we need to understand the significance and timing of events from his perspective, and not ours.

The "millennium," as a time of limited duration, is mentioned only in Revelation, a highly symbolic book. Because of the uncertainties of symbolic numbers in this book, we do not want to build a doctrine on this idea. The millennium is a doctrine the Bible does not speak about with a clear and loud voice.

But don't the Old Testament prophets speak of a physical kingdom on earth, and can't we bring those pictures of a universal Promised Land into the concept of a millennium? Many people do shape their understanding of the millennium by the Old Testament Scriptures. How are we to understand these prophecies of God's kingdom? One way is to see that the kingdom was described in terms ancient Israel could understand.

In the Hebrew Scriptures, the focus of the salvation was on the deliverance of Israel out of Egypt and the nation's entrance into the Promised Land. It was a physical deliverance, and that is what Israel expected for the future — another physical deliverance, and a restoration within the Promised Land. Thus, the prophecies of the kingdom used physical terms, too — as restoring people into a perfect land of beauty and physical plenty where God's law reigned supreme. These descriptions of God's kingdom can be seen as "shadows" in the same way that the sacrificial system, the priesthood, the temple with its holy of holies, physical circumcision, the annual festivals and the weekly Sabbath were shadows of the salvation we have in Jesus Christ. The Christians' Garden of Eden, Paradise of God and Promised Land would represent the joy of eternal life in the presence of God.

The New Testament doesn't describe the characteristics of the kingdom of God. When the kingdom is mentioned, the emphasis is on the church age, on the return of Jesus, and/or the judgment, as in Matthew 25:31-46. The book of Revelation, which spends much time describing the time immediately before Jesus' return and the establishment of God's kingdom in glory, gives only a brief description of events that come after his return. In what little detail it offers regarding the kingdom of God to come, it concentrates on the judgment.

The book of Revelation treats the physical events and situations described in the Hebrew Scriptures as symbols of salvation. Revelation is a good example of a work that takes Old Testament physical typologies and gives them a spiritual meaning. For example, the seven churches are told they will have a right to eat from the tree of life in the paradise or garden of God. They are also told that they will be part of the temple of God in a new Jerusalem and sit on the Father's throne. In Revelation 22, readers are told they will have access to the river of the water of life, and the leaves from the trees on either side will heal the nations. The river of life metaphor is taken from Ezekiel's description of a new temple.

These physical types are to be taken symbolically, as the eternal life we will have in the presence of the Father. When we have imperishable life, we do not need to look for leaves and waters, for we have the reality that those things only pictured. The Old Testament details need not be taken in a physical or literal sense. They can refer to spiritual realities. Today, that is how we may see the physical descriptions of God's kingdom in the Old Testament prophecies.

Perhaps there will be a future kingdom of God on earth with human beings and human society under the loving government of a returned Christ. But the Scriptures are not that clear as to the specifics of such a future kingdom of God. Some people take too literal a view of such things — and often carry the Scriptures beyond meanings they can support. We should be more cautious, particularly in view of the fact that the New Testament interprets Old Testament prophecies as metaphors of salvation.

Paul Kroll

A Balanced Approach to the Millennium

The amillennialist says that we are already in the last days and that it is wrong to expect another major phase of God's kingdom either before or after Christ's return. There is only one "last days."

The premillennialist says that everything will be restored *after* Christ's return, not before. Satan is not gradually bound and restricted — the picture in Revelation is a sudden and complete containment.

The postmillennialist responds with the belief that God has promised victory for the gospel, and it is right to be optimistic about what God will do even in this age.

What can we say? We can safely say that "the Millennium is the time span described in the book of Revelation during which Christian martyrs reign with Jesus Christ." We do not need to say whether they are in heaven or on earth, whether they are reigning right now or in the future. We can leave those interpretive options open. We can also say, "after the millennium, when all enemies have been put under Christ's feet, and all things made subject to him, Christ will deliver the kingdom to God the Father, and heaven and earth will be made new." This repeats ideas from 1 Corinthians 15 — and this statement is acceptable to all views.

We can also safely acknowledge that there are various views — that "some Christian traditions interpret the Millennium as a literal 1,000 years to precede or follow the return of Jesus, while others believe that the scriptural evidence points to a figurative interpretation: an indeterminate time span commencing with Jesus' resurrection and concluding with his return." In saying this, we accept others as Christian without any need to promote one view over the others. We may personally prefer a view that is different, but we do not have to make it an obstacle between us.

The millennium is not a defining doctrine of who is a true Christian and who is not. We do not want to divide Christians by their interpretive choices on this matter. Equally sincere, equally educated and equally faithful Christians can come to different conclusions on this doctrine. Some members of our denomination are premillennial, some are amillennial, and some are postmillennial. But we have much to agree on:

- God has all power and will do all that he purposes and will fulfill all his prophecies.
- Jesus Christ has all power and authority, and

he has brought us into his kingdom even in this age.
- Christ has given us life when we were dead in trespasses and sins, we go to be with him when we die, and we will be resurrected.
- Jesus has defeated Satan and Satan still exercises some influence in this world.
- Satan's influence will be completely and permanently stopped in the future.
- All humans will be resurrected and judged by our merciful and loving and righteous God.
- Christ will return, and will triumph over all enemies, and will lead us all into an eternity with God.
- There will be a new heavens and new earth in which righteousness dwells, and this wonderful world tomorrow will last forever.
- Eternity will be better than the millennium (no matter how we define the millennium).

We have much to agree on; we do not need to get upset about differences in the *sequence* in which God will complete his plan. The chronology of the last days is not part of our commission. The gospel is how we can *enter* the kingdom, not about the chronology of when things happen. Jesus did not stress the chronology; he did not emphasize a kingdom that would last for a finite period of time. Paul did not preach about a temporary kingdom. Peter did not write about this time span. The book of Revelation has something about it, but John gave it less space than he did the new heavens and new earth. He gave the worship of Jesus more space than he did the millennium. Out of the 260 chapters in the New Testament, only part of one is about the millennium.

The millennium *is* part of Scripture, and we should study it, just as we do any other chapter in Scripture. But we do not make the interpretation of Revelation 20 an article of faith. We have more important things to preach, and we have better news to preach. We preach that through Jesus Christ, we can live with God not just in this age, not just for 1,000 years, but forever and ever in joy and peace and prosperity that never ends.

Michael Morrison

Perspective on the Millennium

1) Christians have had, and now have, various beliefs about the millennium. Proponents of each theory believe that the Bible supports their view.
2) Proponents of each view agree that Christ will return and that there will be a judgment. For the faithful, there will be an eternity of perfection and glory with God.
3) The eternal age is much more glorious than the millennial age, no matter how the millennium is understood. At best, the millennium is second-best.
4) When Jesus Christ returns, everyone will rejoice. Premillennialists will rejoice even if a millennial reign is not set up. Amillennialists will rejoice even if one is. Postmillennialism will rejoice even if a golden age did not precede his return. No one will be disappointed, and everyone will have better things to do than to gloat about getting the chronological details right.
5) Christians who have an equally high view of the authority of Scripture may nevertheless have different opinions about the millennium. Christians who hold one view about the millennium should acknowledge that other Christians sincerely believe that the Bible teaches something else.
6) Millennialism is not a doctrinal point on which we must seek conformity. Christian authenticity does not depend, for example, on the belief that Christ will set up a temporary kingdom after he returns. We should not condemn or ridicule people who hold different views.
7) People can be saved without any particular belief about the millennium. The gospel is about how to enter the kingdom, not the chronological or physical details of particular phases of that kingdom. Since

the New Testament books do not emphasize the nature of the millennium, we conclude that it is not a central plank in the church's message. Millennial positions should not dominate our messages. Rather, we should focus on the bigger picture that we all hold in common. See points 2 and 3.

8) In any study of the millennium, one should be aware of how others view the scriptures and how they come to differing conclusions. The following books may help:

- Darrell Bock, editor. *Three Views on the Millennium and Beyond*. Zondervan, 1999.
- Robert Clouse, editor. *The Meaning of the Millennium: Four Views*. InterVarsity, 1977.
- Millard Erickson. *A Basic Guide to Eschatology: Making Sense of the Millennium*. Second edition, Baker, 1999.
- Stanley Grenz. *The Millennial Maze: Sorting Out Evangelical Options*. InterVarsity, 1992.
- Michael Morrison. "Three Views of the Millennium." https://www.gcs.edu/mod/page/view.php?id=4275

Appendix
A Theology of the Holy Spirit
Part 6

The Spirit and sovereign grace

There are two words I like to use to powerfully remind us about the personal nature and dynamic relationship we have with God the Spirit, and they apply equally to the Father and the Son. Those words are sovereign grace. How do these words help us faithfully grasp the character of the Spirit's working towards us? Sovereign means that the Holy Spirit works as he wills according to his own nature. We're talking about God the Spirit. He is just as personal as God the Father and God the Son—not less personal and not an abstract machine, magic, electricity or some impersonal force. The Spirit is sovereign.

The Holy Spirit is a personal agent. He has a will. We could say "he has a brain." He acts as the sovereign God. We can't forget the sovereignty of God and start thinking that we're moving the levers connected to the Holy Spirit who is under our control like a vending machine or electricity or a genie. Thinking and acting in that way amounts to denying the Spirit's sovereignty. It makes me sovereign over an impersonal power. In that mode, I simply want to know: How can I get control of this power and make good use of it? What steps, what techniques, what conditions do I need to fulfill to get it to work?

The error of Simon

Those who foster such an approach to the Spirit would do well to remember a story from the book of Acts. Simon the sorcerer became a convert, but as soon as he found out about this awesome power of the Holy Spirit, he wanted to purchase it from Peter. Buy it! Why did he approach the Spirit in that way? He was formerly a magician. Apparently, his magician mind hadn't been sanctified yet. He didn't know the nature and character of this Holy Spirit. He thought like a magician: "What power! Power for good. If only I could get hold of it like the power I had as a magician. Then, I could do miracles for the glory of God!"

Simon was still thinking like a magician, looking to possess and control the power of the Spirit. He had changed, in that he desired a different power, but he hadn't yet changed his approach to power. He switched loyalty to the Holy Spirit, but he approached the Holy Spirit in the same way he did evil power. His mind had not yet been converted. He was repudiated by Peter with some very sharp words: "May your silver perish with you, because you thought you could obtain God's gift with money!" He was told to repent immediately because God's power cannot be used or controlled by us (Acts 8:14-24).

This is one of the first heresies reported in the New Testament besides denying the divinity of Jesus and his being raised from the dead. This heresy is the desire to control the Holy Spirit as if he were an impersonal power and not sovereign Holy God. Such a view does not regard the Spirit as free to blow where he wills, as one who works according to sovereign grace.

When the character and mind of the Holy Spirit is not taken into account, the door is left open for us to think we can shape the Spirit into our own image and use him/it for our own purposes.

However, when known in relationship to the Son and the Father, that door is closed. Simon needed to see, "This is the Spirit of the Father and the Son," not just an impersonal power. The Spirit shares God's sovereign and freely-given grace. There is nothing impersonal about the power of the Spirit. We could say the Spirit is the most personal and the most sovereign working of God, not only around us but in us!

The problem with Simon Magus was he wanted to *use* the Spirit. It wasn't that he wanted to use it for evil things. He saw the apostles healing people. He said, "I want to have that power." What was wrong was his approach to the Spirit, his understanding of who the Spirit is. He wanted to use the power to serve like the apostles, but his desire was to possess and control, to manipulate or to think that the Spirit needed to be conditioned or appeased to bless. That was to think of the Holy Spirit as if he were really an evil spirit.

Thinking he needed to or even could buy the Spirit misrepresents the nature and the character of the Holy Spirit who is at work with the apostles. The apostles received the Spirit as a gift of sovereign grace. You could not buy the Spirit any more than you could purchase God's grace. They had a different kind of relationship with the Holy Spirit than Simon was imagining. They must have been shocked when he came to them and asked, "Can I buy some of that power?" They realized that he was thinking like he used to—thinking of the Spirit in the same way as his former magical powers. They recognized that Simon was entirely wrong. The Holy Spirit is not just another magical power. This was a huge lesson the church needed to learn at the beginning. It still is a lesson we need to learn!

For us to take to heart that lesson is important, since the desire to control the Spirit never completely disappears. The story reminds us of who the Holy Spirit is in relationship to the Father and the Son. The Holy Spirit is sovereign and not under our control. The Holy Spirit is also gracious, because he doesn't need to be cajoled, conditioned or manipulated into working. Nor does he need to be persuaded. He's not locked up in some kind of transcendent bottle, waiting for us to get him out. The grace of the Spirit is moving before we even ask or think of it. His ministry is one of sovereign grace, as are those of the Son and the Father—the Father, Son and Spirit are one in being and one in action. If we have to condition or persuade or somehow exert some influence on the Spirit to get him to work, then the Spirit no longer is operating out of sovereign grace.

It's possible to be just as legalistic and contractual towards the Spirit as towards the Father or the Sabbath or salvation. It's possible for some to claim that the blessings of the Spirit are conditioned by us, are dependent on us. A magical or impersonal view of the Spirit is a form of law- or rule-based relationship. But the gracious work of the Holy Spirit is a continuation of the gracious working of the Father and the Son. The Spirit always works graciously.

How should we approach the Spirit?

That brings up the question as to whether it makes any difference how we approach the Spirit. The answer is yes! But whatever difference is made cannot amount to changing the sovereign grace of the Spirit into its opposite! The difference is in our reception, awareness and participation in what the Spirit is graciously and sovereignly doing. We can resist the Spirit. We can participate or not. We can be more or less ready to recognize and receive the full benefits of the Spirit. But the Spirit is not dependent on us to initiate and make the first move. The Spirit ministers to enable us to do things, even overcoming our resistance as he shares with us Christ's own responses to the Spirit in our place and on our behalf. The Spirit moves us, frees us, guides us, and we can then respond.

We can describe ways we can participate and ways to grow in our understanding and in our recognition of the ministry of the Spirit. When we recognize the ways of the Spirit, we'll respond: "That was the work of the Holy Spirit. It is amazing. Praise God, Father, Son and the Holy Spirit! That was a marvel of sovereign grace we just saw manifested among us."

We can participate more fully and be filled with the Holy Spirit's glory, or we can resist or avoid it. If we resist, we are resisting a gracious work—one that is freely-given, like Christ's gracious work. We shouldn't think about participating in the life of the Spirit as if it's not freely-given grace that comes from God's sovereignty. When we seek to participate more fully, and through prayer seek to be filled with the Spirit, we are not conditioning the Spirit's working. We're not earning his blessing and presence. We're especially not "channeling it"—not manipulating, controlling or determining the Spirit's working or manifestations.

These are important things to remember, since we ought always to affirm the gracious sovereignty of the Spirit. This understanding will prevent us from committing heresy, from flipping over into that false view, since there will always be temptations to go in that direction. We like techniques and we like to make God predictable. When we're in big trouble, we often feel a need to bring some kind of pressure on God to act in this situation. Perhaps we're desperate. Or maybe we're curious to discover some technique or formula or to identify some pattern or secret where we hold the key.

Especially in times of desperation, we want God to be more like a magical and impersonal power. Sometimes God's sovereignty doesn't align with our will, our speed or our immediate needs. At such times, we're tempted to be like Simon Magus, saying to ourselves, "I just want to know the formula, God, because something needs to happen here and you're not doing it!" At that point, evil temptation can enter our minds and suggest: "God didn't show up! You know why? Because it's up to you and you're missing it. If only you knew the formula. If only you were holy enough. If only you were sincere enough. If only your expectations were high enough. If only your church was more united. If only you read the Bible more. If only…if only…if only x, y or z had been done, then God would show up!" But every "if only" makes *us* the key – it says that grace isn't grace after all. Each "if only" throws us back on ourselves and undermine our trust, our faith in God. Each is a method to purchase blessings, not participation in the sovereign grace of God.

Working in the Spirit is of the same character as the saving work of Christ. We receive it in the same way, by trusting God to freely give it to us. There are ways to participate with what the Spirit is doing, but the Spirit will never relinquish his sovereignty nor cease to be gracious and somehow become conditional and set up a legal relationship with us. But we can be tempted, and certain teachings tend to push us in that direction.

What's it like to participate with the Spirit?

Who the Spirit is carries a number of implications we can draw out with the help of other insights from the biblical revelation. Let's explore our participation in this gracious ministry of the Holy Spirit.

Sanctification. The first thing is that the primary ministry of the Holy Spirit is transforming us, sanctifying us and enabling us to share in that new nature Christ shares with us. This is primarily a work in us. Transformation into Christ-likeness is key. Christian maturity is of central concern in New Testament teaching. The Christian life is presented there as one of continual growth in faith, in hope and in love for God and life lived out towards others. There are many obstacles to be overcome or avoided in taking that journey of spiritual maturity and health.

These obstacles are not just internal temptations but also external pressures, ways of living, habits, even mindsets that are not engendered by the Spirit but by "the world, the flesh and the devil." It's an uphill battle. It is a fight of faith. It is not easy, but it can be joyful and peaceful. It involves dying to the old self over and over again and being raised up in newness of life, being restored. The Christian life involves repentance and renewed faith, hope and love. It involves forgiving and asking forgiveness. The Spirit enables us to share more and more in the new life we have in Christ, so that we live in daily union and communion with him, dying and being raised up every day. He, our crucified and risen Lord, is the center of our life.

Fruit and gifts. There is a good amount of information on the Holy Spirit involving both the gifts of the Spirit and the fruit of the Spirit. These indicate something of the shape of the Spirit's ministry. The Spirit is a "Giving Gift," as one theologian put it. When we hear of gifts, we often think of abilities or capacities to do something, to serve in certain ways. But the fruit of the Spirit is also given by the Spirit! The fruit points to the qualities of the life of Jesus that the Holy Spirit is building into us. The ultimate definition of the fruit and the gifts is demonstrated for us in the life of Jesus lived out in the power of the Spirit.

Part of the fruit of the Spirit is the gift of "self-control," which is essential to sharing in the life of Christ by the Spirit. It's often said that the Spirit is all spontaneity, "letting go—going with the flow," aligned with our feelings or with love. These characteristics are then put in contrast with our thoughts, mind or truth or with any kind of intentional process or self-discipline. But the fruit of self-control serves as a reminder that Christian freedom involves self-discipline. The Spirit should never be used as an excuse for irresponsibility. The Spirit always joins truth with love, freedom with self-discipline, feelings with order or structure, especially with the moral order of right and good relationships. The Holy Spirit brings wholeness to life, not compartmentalization.

The gifts of the Spirit mentioned by Paul refer to the variety of ways members of the body of Christ are enabled to serve one another. We will not take time to explore the individual gifts. But let me point out a problem that often arises when there is a strong focus on these serving gifts of the Spirit. The problem arises when the serving-gifts of the Spirit are separated from the fruit of the Spirit, or the two are not seen to be in vital connection. Any such disjunction is a huge mistake—it amounts to dividing up the ministry of the Spirit into separate parts and pieces. What often happens in that case is that the gifts of the Spirit are exercised in ways that don't exhibit the fruit of the Spirit. Serving-gifts used without love, joy, peace, patience, self-control, etc. are being misused! It seems that it has often been assumed that if the gifts come from the Spirit, they can't be misused. But that is wrong. Even gifts given by the Spirit can be misused, and they often are when they are not joined with an equal emphasis on the fruit-gifts of the Spirit.

Jesus: fruit and gifts. The primary work of the Spirit is to deliver all the benefits of Christ to us and in us. That includes both the fruit and the gifts. The Spirit doesn't give us the option of choosing one kind over the other, placing an emphasis on one and neglecting the other. If we look to the life of Jesus, we see in him no disconnect between the fruit of his character and the quality of his ministry of service to others. These are perfectly joined in his humanity, lived out in perfect communion with the Holy Spirit. So when we talk about Christ's likeness, we're talking about the fruit of the Spirit, which then shapes all his ministry service. Jesus lived by the Spirit. He's one of us. In his life, we see the use of the gifts of the Spirit through the fruit of the Spirit.

Fruit primary, gifts secondary. The fruit is primary, is foundational to the gifts of service. Paul indicates this by teaching that love is the primary thing when he's talking about the gifts. What went wrong in Corinth is they went ahead with the gifts but exercised them without love. The result was damage to the body. We cannot separate the fruit from the gifts. Fruit is essential to who we are. The gifts are the manifestations of who we are and who we're becoming in Christ, filled with his likeness or his sanctification, that is, with his fruits.

Perhaps unexpectedly, the Holy Spirit doesn't give us his own sanctification. Rather, he gives us Christ's sanctification, which was worked out in his human nature. The holiness of the Spirit, if offered to us apart from what Christ accomplished for us in his incarnate life, wouldn't fit us directly as human beings. But the sanctification that Christ worked out for us in his humanity, by the Spirit, has become in him suited to us, and that is what the Holy Spirit shares with us.

Love. That's why, as the Holy Spirit works, we become like Christ, exhibiting the spiritual fruit of his perfected humanity. The primary center of that fruit, as Paul describes it, is love. In his letter to the Corinthian church, he makes clear that love manifests itself through a desire for unity, peace, harmony and upbuilding. The Spirit generates no sense of superiority or competition, possessiveness or even self-sufficiency. Paul's image of our being differing members of a united body holds these elements together well.

Paul surrounds his discussion of the gifts of the Spirit with the fruit of the Spirit even though he doesn't use that term but names love as the central aspect of the fruit. The gifts and fruit cannot be disconnected. Any working of the gifts should be a form of loving and serving others. If the gifts do not serve the unity, peace, harmony and upbuilding of one another, then they're not gifts of the Spirit. Just as Christ is, love is a proper test of the Spirit's working.

Since the Spirit works distinctly with individuals and also with groups to promote unity and harmony, we would not expect the movement of the Spirit to set up a hierarchy of super-spiritual over less spiritual persons. The Spirit wouldn't foster envy and jealousy, moving some to think or say that "They're less spiritual than we are" or "Their fellowship is more spiritual than ours." Nor would anyone be moved to say "I'm less spiritual than they are" or "My gift is more important than yours" or "My gift is less important than yours." That's not where the Spirit is going to take us. That's not what the Spirit is about. For in that case, the fruit and the gifts would be falling apart rather than being brought together by the Spirit. But they can never come apart, because the Spirit is one in his ministry and Person. The Spirit will not foster competitiveness of one trying to be more spiritual than another. Unfortunately, that's what was going on in the church in Corinth.

Freedom for others, not from others. Another expression of the separation of the fruit from the exercise of the gifts arises when individuals insist on using the gift in their own way. Such a person may think, "I've got my freedom in Christ and that justifies my using this gift however I see fit!" This was going on in Corinth. Certain persons were attempting to use a gift of the Spirit without regard for others. They did so by claiming freedom in Christ. They took freedom to mean they didn't have to consider how the exercise of their gifts would affect others. But such an orientation is not going to come from the Spirit. The Spirit does not move persons to insist on their own way, even when it comes to serving others. Why not? Because, as Paul tells us in 1 Corinthians 13, insisting on your own way does not demonstrate Christ's love. The gifts are never to be used apart from the fruit. Paul tells us even he, the apostle, does not exercise all the freedoms he has. Why not? For the sake of the body, he tells us in 1 Corinthians 9:12.

Not seeking my own experience. There is another way in which we can take up an interest in the Spirit without much regard for others. This next point could be more controversial than the previous ones, but it needs to be brought up. Some turn to the Spirit primarily to have a strong, moving or powerful experience. The assumption seems to be that the ministry of the Spirit is primarily to give us an experience of the Spirit. The main result sought is being able to say, "I had an extraordinary experience of the Spirit." Some, by this means, are perhaps seeking greater assurance either of their salvation or perhaps of their spiritual growth or maturity.

But a survey of the New Testament doesn't support such an approach or view of the Holy Spirit. The ministry of the Spirit is not to give us special individual experiences, but to enable us to serve and to build up each other, to help and to assist each other and to deepen the quality of relationships within the church's in-reach and its ministry and outreach in service to others.

We will have experiences of the manifestation of the working of the Spirit. But the resulting benefit will not be saying, "Wow, I had an experience of the Spirit. Now if I could just have another one for myself." We all will have experiences of the Spirit, but they're going to be experiences of love, service, fellowship, joy and worship that look away from the experience itself. The experience is a byproduct of something else the Spirit is doing in us and for us.

Jesus wanted his disciples to learn this lesson when they returned from a short mission trip and had worked miracles. They came back elated that in Jesus' name they were given authority over demons. Jesus cautions them: "Nevertheless, do not rejoice at this, that the spirits submit to you, but rejoice that your names are written in heaven" (Luke 10:20).

Who we are worshiping and serving is more important than having some particular experience. The Spirit who is not preoccupied with himself is not likely to want to make us preoccupied with him or ourselves! A focus on seeking after or having individual experiences of the Spirit can disrupt the ministry of the Holy Spirit in the Body of Christ. The Spirit will not want to take us in a direction where everyone is saying: "I had an experience and then another! Let me tell you about them." Sharing in this way usually brings out responses such as, "How did you bring that about? Why did you have that experience and I didn't? God must not like me," or, "God must like me (because…well, I can't say this out loud, but I must somehow be more favored than others) since I was given such an awesome experience that others, too, should have." Spiritual pride of this sort can slip in when there is a focus on individual experiences of the Spirit.

Should we avoid talking about the Spirit and his fruits and gifts? No. But we can go about it in better or worse ways. In contrast, I suggest that the Spirit leads us to reflect more in this manner: "Wow! Someone noticed some fruit of the Spirit in my life. How did that happen? It must be the work of the Spirit!" Or, "Wow. I tried to serve somebody even though I wasn't sure how, and they benefited in a way that led them to love God more. How did that happen? It must have been by the Spirit! I hope by the grace of God I can live in the middle of that more often."

That response doesn't make the focus the Spirit himself or having some kind of spiritual experience. When I was part of the charismatic movement in the '70s, I interacted with many who became Christians but were primarily looking to get high on the Spirit (or Jesus) rather than something else. "I just want to get high on Jesus," some would say. There were plenty of ministries willing to feed that desire. It was a definite move in the right direction. But often, those whose Christian lives were not much more than going from one "spiritual" experience to another did not experience much of the fruit of the Spirit. The rest of their lives remained a wreck. There was little fruit and no service. Though they were having or seeking experiences with the Spirit, there was little sign of life transformation. Some moves on, grew and matured. But others didn't. They seemed stuck, getting "high on Jesus." Sometimes they'd go back to getting high on other things. Why not? One high is just as good as another, isn't it? Unfortunately, they were often looking for ways to escape their problems or gain affirmation or attention for themselves.

Admittedly, these are complicated situations. The point is that looking to the Spirit for personal experiences doesn't acknowledge the real, full ministry of the Holy Spirit, who enables us to respond more fully and freely to the truth and reality of God and the gospel.

Next, I'll make a few more comments about the shape of the ministry of the Spirit that might help us have a healthy approach.

A Theology of the Holy Spirit, Part 7

Our response to the Spirit

It's clear from the New Testament that the Holy Spirit works actively among us—both as a church and as individuals. A primary aspect of this ministry of the Spirit among us is to enable us to make a full and proper response to the truth and reality of who God is and what he has done, is doing and will do in our church, our world and within us. Enabling us to make that response is the key.

The Holy Spirit unbinds our wills and unscrambles our minds and refashions our affections so we can more fully respond with all that we are to all that God is. The Spirit frees us to be receptive at every level of who we are. Sometimes it seems we think the Holy Spirit only enables us to respond emotionally. We're human beings, and emotions are part of who we are, so the Spirit does enable us to respond emotionally to the truth and reality of who God is and who we are in him. That's part of it. In worship the Spirit moves us to thanksgiving, praise, adoration, joy and even sorrow and repentance.

But we are also thinking beings, so the Holy Spirit also enables us to respond with our minds. The Spirit is called the Spirit of truth (John 14:17; 15:26). He is involved with our hearts and minds, so (for example) he enables us to pray and praise not only with our spirits but also with our minds, with understanding or intelligence (1 Corinthians 14:15). As Paul indicates in Romans 6:17, our minds are set free to be obedient to the truth. Throughout the New Testament, the heart and mind are not split but coordinated together when healthy. The Holy Spirit enables us to respond with all of what we are. There is no reason to think the working of God in and among us is divided, as if Jesus addresses our minds and the Holy Spirit addresses our emotions. We're not compartmentalized like that. The whole of God interacts with the whole of our humanity.

Jesus assumed a whole human nature with all its aspects. Jesus is a full human being with body, mind and heart. In the Gospels we see him responding fully with all that he is to the truth and reality of his heavenly Father and his relationship to him and the Spirit. Jesus obeys in the Spirit and rejoices in the Spirit. He overcomes temptation by the Spirit. He overcomes evil by the Spirit and sets people free. He offers himself up on the cross to the Father through the Spirit (Hebrews 9:14). Jesus lives his fully human life in and by the Spirit.

So, when the Spirit of Jesus comes upon us, he enables us to respond fully to the truth and reality of who God is and who we are in relationship to him with all we are and have. If there's part of us not yet responding, whether the body, mind or heart, the Holy Spirit will work to bring us to the point that we do respond. The Holy Spirit doesn't divide us, but heals and makes us whole, giving us human integrity before our Lord and God.

The objective work of the Holy Spirit in us

We should not align the Holy Spirit exclusively with what is subjective, internal, or affective in human experience. The Holy Spirit cannot be identified with our subjectivity—our feelings, emotions or our consciences, as if they were identical. There is no denying that the Spirit works in our subjectivity, but he is not identical with our subjectivity (our subjective states). If he did not work in our subjectivity, we would remain in bondage to our fallen, rebellious wills, hard hearts, and our self-justifying and rationalizing minds. He works in our subjectivity, but does so objectively, so we can respond with our whole being to the truth and reality of who God is and who we are in relationship to God.

The Holy Spirit objects to our false, resistant, self-justifying subjective orientations. The Holy Spirit is not the subjective aspect of human beings that can be shaped and formed anyway we like, made to say what we want, made to reflect our own preferences, prejudices, biases and desires. The Holy Spirit has a particular character, mind, will, purpose, desire and heart, which is identical to that of Jesus Christ. We have no power over the Holy Spirit to recreate him in our own image. The Holy Spirit has his own objective reality, which works within our subjectivity to open our eyes, minds and hearts to God.

The Holy Spirit, then, is a healer who brings the whole of human being together from the inside out. He does not split us up. He does not say to us, "I'm just in charge of your emotions, your imagination and your desires. What you think and believe and come to know, the rational part, well, Jesus takes care of that. I don't know anything about that." The Holy Spirit does not divide up human being into compartments, but harmonizes the internal with the external, sharing with us the reestablished integrity of Jesus' sanctified humanity.

Humanizes us

A final aspect of the ministry of the Holy Spirit correlates with his ministry to make us whole in body, soul and spirit. The Holy Spirit's ministry is to make us more fully human, like Jesus, the one in whose image we were created and are being renewed or transformed (Colossians 3:10; 2 Corinthians 3:18). The Holy Spirit shares with us the sanctified humanity of Jesus, which makes us fully human, more completely human, more personal, filling us with the fruit of the Spirit. True spirituality is mature humanity in full and right relationship with God.

So we can say the Holy Spirit humanizes us by making us share in the glorified humanity of Christ. In the process, he brings us to have humility before God. The transformation he brings will involve our confession that God is God and we are not; that we are entirely dependent upon God; that we need the grace of God and that we must hand over to him all our sin in repentance and our whole selves in faith. But in doing so, the Spirit will not submit us to humiliation. He will not make us feel less than human or cause us to regret we were ever human or to think that God despises our humanity and creaturely limits.

There is a huge difference between humility and humiliation. This may be surprising, since some people teach that humility in the Spirit comes by way of our humiliation. Unfortunately, it's sometimes taught that the ministry of the Holy Spirit not only focuses exclusively on the subjective side of human being, but requires that we set aside our rationality or intelligence and act in less than human ways, perhaps like an animal or a person who has lost self-control (like a drunk person). It would be strange for the Spirit to lead persons to lose self-control and act in ways beneath human being, since part of the fruit of the Spirit is self-control (Galatians 5:23). The Holy Spirit is the Spirit of Jesus, who came to bring us into conformity with himself. He was humble before the Father and the Spirit, but he was never treated in a way that denigrated his humanity. Nor did he respond to God in ways that denied a healthy and whole humanity. Rather, Jesus' humanity came to be glorified. He fulfilled human nature and showed us what it really means to be a human being.

Given who the Spirit is and what we know of his ministry, we can affirm that the Spirit does not dehumanize or depersonalize us. Yes, we will be led into humility before God. But humility is a deeply personal and human thing. It's not alien to humanity, but a fruit of human maturity in relationship to God. In contrast, being humiliated involves being treated as less than a person, less than fully human, and that kind of relationship is the opposite of the kind of ministry Jesus performed in the power of the Spirit. Abject humiliation does not represent the kind of relationship Jesus had with his heavenly Father. Even though his enemies, especially at the end, attempted to humiliate him to the fullest extent they could, the end result was not his humiliation in the sense of him collapsing into a dehumanized heap of regret and shame for taking on humanity. Rather, Jesus was "the pioneer and perfecter of our faith, who for the sake of the joy that was set before him endured the cross, disregarding its shame, and has taken his seat at the right hand of the throne of God" (Hebrews 12:2). Jesus was exalted in his bodily (human) resurrection and ascension. He calls us his brothers and sisters and is not ashamed of us (Hebrews 2:11). Jesus shares with us his glorified and perfected humanity by the Spirit.

Rather than denigrating us, the Holy Spirit humanizes us. To be fully spiritual is not, on the one hand, to become non-human, or on the other, to become super-spiritual disembodied ghosts, vapors or ethereal gasses distributed throughout the universe. We should get our idea of spirituality in and through the life Jesus lived out in the Holy Spirit. True spirituality is a human being fully responding to the truth of who God is, firing on every cylinder, responding totally to who God is and who we are in relationship to him. True spirituality means responding in praise and prayer and in every other way of service and love. The Holy Spirit is the humanizing Spirit, sharing with us the perfect humanity of Jesus. His presence and working in our lives demonstrates that kind of spirituality and not another.

What about the Spirit in those not yet repenting and believing?

So far we've addressed the Spirit's ministry to people who are responsive to his work in their lives. But what about nonbelievers? Does the Spirit work with those who are not Christians? The answer must be yes. No one becomes a believing person except in response to the Spirit's ministry. Without contact with the Spirit, there is no conversion to Christ. If no one comes to the Father except by the Son who sends the Spirit, and it is the Spirit who opens eyes, convicts of the need for forgiveness and life in Christ, then no one becomes a conscious member of the Body of Christ except the Spirit draws them. The Spirit must work on those not yet believing and responding, or no one would ever become Christian, no one could enter into their salvation. The Spirit goes out after people to bring them to Christ and so to the Father. That is essential to the Spirit's mission in the world. We can see this in the conversion of Saul/Paul in the book of Acts in a dramatic way. The Spirit has a ministry to those not yet believing as well as a ministry to those who are believing.

A related issue is whether we can say that the Spirit is "in" everyone. While there is not a lot about this in Scripture, there is enough for us to address this issue. If by "in" everyone we mean in the deepest most personal and intensive way that the Spirit ministers, we have to say no. Jesus told some of those following him that the Spirit was "with" them, but soon would be "in" them (John 14:17). In the upper room, Jesus breathes on the disciples the Holy Spirit, leading to their having the Spirit in a way they didn't previously. But Jesus also tells them to wait for the coming of the Spirit in Jerusalem, indicating that there is more yet to come involving the Spirit. The Spirit became present at Pentecost in a new and different way. The Spirit can be present in a variety of ways, with a range of intensities, and at a number of different levels of depth.

Inhabiting, or dwelling in

In the New Testament, one way of speaking of the Spirit's presence is through the word that can be translated "dwelling in" or "inhabiting." This coming and indwelling of the Spirit in persons is viewed as the fulfillment of the promise God made through the prophets Joel (Joel 2:28) and Ezekiel (Ezekiel 18:31; 36:26) as indicated by Peter in Acts 2:17. The biblical notion of the Spirit's "dwelling in" or "inhabiting" is exclusively applied to those who are believing, receptive and responsive to the leading and working of the Spirit (Romans 8:9, 11; 1 Corinthians 3:16). The idea of this indwelling has to do with the most intense, personal and abiding presence of the Holy Spirit in persons individually and in the community of believers collectively.

But this special presence of the Spirit does not mean that the Spirit is absent from everyone else. The Spirit was with people in ancient Israel, and sometimes in special ways upon the prophets and some of the skilled craftsmen who worked on the Tabernacle and Temple. But that kind of presence of the Spirit did not represent God's ultimate promise of the Spirit's indwelling. That only occurred at Pentecost in the lives of those who were receptive to the gospel and the presence and working of the Spirit. Further, we can see that the dynamic nature of relationship to the Spirit continues even at the deepest level of indwelling. Those who are part of the believing body are not to quench or grieve the Spirit (1 Thessalonians 5:19; Ephesians 4:30) but rather are to be continually filled with the Spirit (Ephesians 5:18).

The Holy Spirit can be present to anyone and everyone. He is God's presence throughout the creation. The Spirit can work in anyone and everyone. His ministry is to open people's minds, soften their hearts, open their eyes to truth, unbind their resistant wills and convict them of the need for forgiveness and the life of salvation that only comes from God by grace. The Spirit delivers to unbelieving people the gift of repentance and faith, hope and love. Doing so requires working within them, within their persons, in their subjectivity. So the Spirit works in them and is present to them in that way. However, that kind of inner working does not represent the promised indwelling that comes only through receiving Christ in faith in response to the promptings of the Spirit.

In Christ, united to Christ by the Spirit

This seems to explain why in the New Testament only those who are receptive to the Spirit, not resistant, and those who respond with repentance, faith, hope and love to the gospel of Jesus Christ are said to be "in" Christ, or to dwell "in the Lord." They alone are said to be united to Christ (1 Corinthians 6:17). This relationship of Christ with his people is compared to marital unity (Ephesians 5:23; Revelation 19:7; 21:9; 22:17). The most intense, intimate, deep and personal unity described in the New Testament is reserved for those who as believers are said to be members of the Body of Christ, united to Jesus as the head, just as the body of a living being is united to its head.

So, by the use of certain words and images, the New Testament makes a distinction between the Spirit's relationship with those who are receptive and open to the ministry of the Spirit (believers) and those who are not yet responsive (non-believers). How the Spirit is present (whether or not he is indwelling or inhabiting a person) will involve whether or not that person is receptive to the gospel and the ministry of the Spirit to receive it and welcome it. How one responds to the ministry of the Holy Spirit makes a difference in the kind or quality of relationship they have with the Spirit, and thus with the Father and the Son.

But such a distinction should not be construed as meaning that the Holy Spirit is not for all persons, is not capable of ministering in and to all persons at the deepest level, speaking to their individual human spirits. The Holy Spirit is "for all" in the same way that Jesus Christ is for everyone who was created through him. The Father sends the Spirit for the same purpose as he sent the Son. But the Spirit is able to be present in a range of ways. This is represented in biblical understanding, so we have to account for it in our understanding as well.[1]

What about the Spirit in other religions?

What can we say about the Holy Spirit's ministry in other religions? As an extension of what we have just covered, we can say that no religion can keep the Holy Spirit out or away from people. The Holy Spirit is God's sovereign grace at work. He can be present to anyone, anywhere, without becoming polluted, just as we see take place in Jesus' presence among sinners. The Spirit is present to bring to bear all the fruits of reconciliation, accomplished for all humanity in Christ. So in those situations where the religion being practiced is hostile to the gospel and unreceptive to Christ, the Spirit will nevertheless be present and working within the people against those points of resistance. The non-Christian religion will not be responsible or earn any credit for the presence and working of the Spirit. If hostile, the religion is an impediment to the Spirit's working, an obstacle to receptivity to the ministry of the Spirit of Jesus. However, that does not stop the Holy Spirit. He will work to bring individuals and groups out of bondage to false ideas about God and false ideas about their relationship to God. The Spirit will work to open people's minds and hearts to be receptive to God's grace, love, faith and hope. He will work to draw people to a humble repentance and a dependence upon some kind of grace.

Individuals and groups can be drawn by the Spirit even while remaining outwardly a part of their non- or anti-Christian religious community. In that case, the Spirit will be making "heretics" within that religion. He will be leading individuals or sub-groups to take exception to at least some of what they have been taught by their religion. These persons may not know that they have become willing to follow the Spirit of Jesus. The Spirit may be anonymous to them, especially at first. But they, in their spirits, will have become responsive and receptive to the promptings of the Holy Spirit of Jesus.

People in this state can be said to have implicit faith, not explicit faith. There can be an analogy between these people and those of faith in the Old Testament, whose faith in Jesus was not explicit. Although they did not know Jesus by name, nor of the nature of his future work, they nevertheless lived by faith and repentance and trusted in the covenant love and free grace of God to renew it when they broke faith. They didn't know exactly how God's covenant was going to be fulfilled, but they knew and trusted and hoped it would somehow be fulfilled. That's how the New Testament depicts these Old Testament persons of faith. On the other side of their death, they will see how the promises they had hoped in were fulfilled. These persons are not excluded from God's salvation. So too, if through no fault of their own, persons responsive to an anonymous ministry of the Holy Spirit do not come to have explicit faith, there is no reason to believe that they will not be included in God's ultimate salvation. Such persons have not committed the absolute and complete repudiation (blasphemy) of the Spirit, but have been welcoming and receptive. Their implicit faith will become explicit as soon as it is made possible.[2]

It is normally God's will for all who have implicit faith to come to have explicit faith in this life. After all, everyone who comes to have explicit faith, first had, at least for a moment, implicit faith. But faith becomes explicit, it seems, only if and when there is a conscious and explicit proclamation of the gospel so that when it is heard, it is welcomed and received. Where there is implicit faith, the gospel is welcomed and received, since there has already been a responsiveness to the Spirit that is working even as these individuals hear an explicit announcement of the gospel. There are numerous missionary stories that corroborate this kind of scenario. People have somehow become ready to receive the proclamation of the gospel before any missionary arrived, so when the gospel is proclaimed, it is recognized as fulfilling what they have been waiting for. We know how this comes about—by the Spirit. That's how they were prepared.[3]

But it may be the case that in not every instance where there is implicit faith engendered by the Holy Spirit that God brings about an opportunity for that faith to become explicit in this life. It could be that this never comes about. It could be that in every case where there is genuine implicit faith, God may send dreams or angels or miraculously appearing evangelists, like Philip with the Ethiopian, so that their implicit faith can become explicit through a conscious testimony to Christ.[4] But we cannot know about all such situations. Knowing how God works in every case does not practically concern us. We do not need to know about situations in which we have no part to play. We do not need a final theory as to how things will necessarily play out in situations in which we have no part. Rather, our ministry is to serve in ways that count on the working of the Holy Spirit within people so that implicit faith can become joyfully explicit. In that way, our and their joy and thanksgiving will be increased. They will become members of the Body of Christ (Christians) and be able to join in explicit worship and consciously bear witness to God so that others can also come to have explicit faith as well. But in every case, we can rest assured that God will, one way or another, take care of all those situations where faith is implicit because he is merciful and faithful. He always acts on the basis of his sovereign grace, operating through the faithful working of the Holy Spirit.

We now come to the end of this series on the Holy Spirit. Not all questions have been answered. Not all the explanations have been complete. But hopefully, additional understanding has been gained of some of the fundamental concerns we have regarding the person and work of the Holy Spirit.

Endnotes

[1] Sometimes it is said that by virtue of the Incarnation, all humanity is "united" to (or "in union with") Christ. While true in one way, this can be misunderstood. The different kinds of relationships described in Scripture involve different kinds of unity/union that should not be confused. First, there is the unity between the eternal divine Persons, the Trinitarian unity. Second, there is the unity of the Son of God with all human nature forged by the grace of God in the Incarnation, called in formal theology the hypostatic union. This unity is a completed, once-and-for-all connection between Christ's human nature and the human nature of all persons. That is why Jesus is identified as the new Adam. Third, there is the unity of human persons with Christ brought about by the Spirit but fulfilled only as human persons are receptive to the ministry of the Holy Spirit and as they respond to the promptings of the Spirit to welcome his grace and repent and share in the faith, hope and love of Christ.

The incarnational union does not automatically or mechanically or causally guarantee everyone's personal and spiritual union with Christ by the Spirit. The incarnational union is the basis (or call it the platform), the foundational reality for the spiritual union that comes as people receive the gift of the Spirit and share in the glorified human nature of Christ and so become more and more like him. There could be no personal, spiritual union were there not the union of Christ with human nature forged in the Incarnation. But the one doesn't cause or absolutely guarantee the other—they are distinct kinds of union.

[2] On this topic there is controversy that can get heated. Some churches and teachers insist that faith must be explicit in this life for anyone to enter eternal life. But others affirm that there is no significance to the difference between implicit and explicit faith and that the Holy Spirit works positively in many religions with no interest in bringing persons to explicit faith in Jesus, either now or in eternity. This later view has little to no support in orthodox Christian teaching grounded in Scripture as held down through history. The view expressed in this article is different from both of these views.

[3] The position expounded here does not mean that every claim and practice in every non-Christian religion is evil or entirely wrong. There may be partial reflections of truth that coincide with the revelation in Jesus Christ according to Scripture. This coincidence may also be a product of the working of the Spirit. But it is on the basis of the biblical revelation that we can discern what will need to be set aside and what preserved and seen as fulfilled in Christ. Without that normative revelation, it is impossible for anyone to authoritatively discriminate between what is true and what is false and misleading. However, as

noted above, the Holy Spirit can lead persons to be discriminating anyway, although their sense of judgment will likely seem to them to be personal, esoteric and perhaps simply subjective since they won't have access, at that point, to the explicit, objective revelation in Christ according to Scripture to ground and validate their moral/spiritual discernment.

[4] If explicit faith in this life is a requirement for receiving salvation, as some believe, it would seem that creaturely limitations limit God's grace and mercy. God could not, then, be more faithful than we are! If that is the case, then there is no such thing as grace and God cannot exercise sovereign grace, cannot be faithful in every situation. In that view, God is dependent on and limited to creaturely limits and obstacles, since there would be people he would want to receive eternal life, but creaturely obstacles got in the way that he was unable to work around to bring them to explicit faith in this life and make their salvation possible. But since there are exceptions to the need for explicit faith recounted in Scripture, we do not have to affirm a theory that God always makes implicit faith explicit—nor do we need to deny it. One way or another, God will be faithful! That we can affirm with no reservation.

About the Authors

Gary W. Deddo received his PhD from the University of Aberdeen. He worked for many years as an editor for InterVarsity Press; he now works at Grace Communion International and is president of Grace Communion Seminary. He has written several books and e-books.

Neil Earle is a retired Grace Communion International pastor. He teaches church history courses at Grace Communion Seminary.

J. Michael Feazell served for many years as Vice-President of Grace Communion International, as Executive Editor of *Christian Odyssey* magazine, and host of the *You're Included* video series. He earned his Doctor of Ministry degree from Azusa Pacific Seminary and has written *Liberation of the Worldwide Church of God*.

Eugene Guzon is the National Director of GCI churches in the Philippines.

John Halford was a pastor, writer, and editor of *Christian Odyssey* magazine for Grace Communion International. He died in 2014.

Donald L. Jackson was an elder in the Worldwide Church of God when he wrote his article, which was originally published in a WCG pastoral journal.

Paul Kroll worked for Grace Communion International for many years, writing hundreds of articles for our magazines. He is now retired. He is the author of *Exploring the Word of God: The Book of Acts,* available in print or as a series of seven e-books.

C. Baxter Kruger received his PhD from the University of Aberdeen. He is the founder and president of Perichoresis, Inc., and author of several books.

Don Mears was an elder in the Worldwide Church of God when he wrote his article, which was originally published in a WCG magazine.

Michael D. Morrison received his PhD from Fuller Theological Seminary in 2006. After working for Grace Communion International in various writing and editorial capacities, he is an instructor and Dean of Faculty at Grace Communion Seminary. He is also an associate pastor of Grace Life in Glendora, California. He has written several books and e-books, and is the editor of this volume.

Joseph Tkach is president of Grace Communion International and presenter of the video series *Speaking of Life*. He received a Doctor of Ministry degree from Azusa Pacific Seminary. He has written *Transformed by Truth* and numerous articles and e-books.

Some articles are a corporate product.

About the Publisher

Grace Communion International is a Christian denomination with about 50,000 members, worshiping in about 900 congregations in almost 100 nations and territories. We began in 1934 and our main office is in North Carolina. In the United States, we are members of the National Association of Evangelicals and similar organizations in other nations. We welcome you to visit our website at www.gci.org.

If you want to know more about the gospel of Jesus Christ, we offer help. First, we offer weekly worship services in hundreds of congregations worldwide. Perhaps you'd like to visit us. A typical worship service includes songs of praise, a message based on the Bible, and opportunity to meet people who have found Jesus Christ to be the answer to their spiritual quest. We try to be friendly, but without putting you on the spot. Come and see why we believe the gospel is the best news there could be!

To find a congregation, phone us or visit our website. If we do not have a congregation near you, we encourage you to find another Christian church that teaches the gospel of grace.

We also offer personal counsel. If you have questions about the Bible, salvation or Christian living, we are happy to talk. If you want to discuss faith, baptism or other matters, a pastor near you can discuss these on the phone or set up an appointment for a longer discussion. We are convinced that Jesus offers what people need most, and we are happy to share the good news of what he has done for all humanity. We like to help people find new life in Christ, and to grow in that life.

Our work is funded by members of the church who donate part of their income to support the gospel. Jesus told his disciples to share the good news, and that is what we strive to do in our literature, in our worship services, and in our day-to-day lives.

If this book has helped you and you want to pay some expenses, all donations are gratefully welcomed, and in several nations, are tax-deductible. To make a donation online, go to www.gci.org/donate. Thank you for letting us share what we value most — Jesus Christ. The good news is too good to keep it to ourselves.

See our website for hundreds of articles, locations of our churches, addresses in various nations, audio and video messages, and much more.

www.gci.org
Grace Communion International
3120 Whitehall Park Dr.
Charlotte, NC 28273
800-423-4444

You're Included…

We talk with leading Trinitarian theologians about the good news that God loves you, wants you, and includes you in Jesus Christ. Most programs are about 28 minutes long. We've had more than 30 guests, including:

Douglas A. Campbell, Duke Divinity School
Elmer Colyer, Dubuque Theological Seminary
Cathy Deddo, Trinity Study Center
Gordon Fee, Regent College
Trevor Hart, University of St. Andrews
George Hunsinger, Princeton Seminary
C. Baxter Kruger, Perichoresis
Paul Louis Metzger, Multnomah University
Paul Molnar, St. John's University
Cherith Fee Nordling, Northern Seminary
Andrew Root, Luther Seminary
Alan Torrance, University of St. Andrews
Robert T. Walker, Edinburgh University
N.T. Wright, University of St. Andrews
William P. Young, author of *The Shack*

Programs are available free for viewing and downloading at www.youreincluded.org.

Grace Communion Seminary

Ministry based on the life and love of the Father, Son, and Spirit.

Grace Communion Seminary serves the needs of people engaged in Christian service who want to grow deeper in relationship with our Triune God and to be able to more effectively serve in the church.

Why study at Grace Communion Seminary?

- Worship: to love God with all your mind.
- Service: to help others apply truth to life.
- Practical: a balanced range of useful topics for ministry.
- Trinitarian theology: a survey of theology with the merits of a Trinitarian perspective. We begin with the question, "Who is God?" Then, "Who are we in relationship to God?" In this context, "How then do we serve?"
- Part-time study: designed to help people who are already serving in local congregations. There is no need to leave your current ministry. Full-time students are also welcome.
- Flexibility: your choice of master's level continuing education courses or pursuit of a degree: Master of Pastoral Studies or Master of Theological Studies.
- Affordable, accredited study: Everything can be done online.

For more information, go to www.gcs.edu. Grace Communion Seminary is accredited by the Distance Education Accrediting Commission, www.deac.org. The Accrediting Commission is listed by the U.S. Department of Education as a nationally recognized accrediting agency.

Ambassador College of Christian Ministry

Want to better understand God's Word? Want to know the Triune God more deeply? Want to share more joyously in the life of the Father, Son and Spirit? Want to be better equipped to serve others?

Among the many resources that Grace Communion International offers are the training and learning opportunities provided by ACCM. This quality, well-structured Christian Ministry curriculum has the advantage of being very practical and flexible. Students may study at their own pace, without having to leave home to undertake full-time study.

This denominationally recognized program is available for both credit and audit study. At minimum cost, this online Diploma program will help students gain important insights and training in effective ministry service. Students will also enjoy a rich resource for personal study that will enhance their understanding and relationship with the Triune God.

Diploma of Christian Ministry classes provide an excellent introductory course for new and lay pastors. Pastor General Dr. Joseph Tkach said, "We believe we have achieved the goal of designing Christian ministry training that is practical, accessible, interesting, and doctrinally and theologically mature and sound. This program provides an ideal foundation for effective Christian ministry."

For more information, go to www.ambascol.org

Printed in Poland
by Amazon Fulfillment
Poland Sp. z o.o., Wrocław